THE RESPONSIBLE PUBLIC SERVANT

KENNETH KERNAGHAN AND JOHN LANGFORD

SECOND EDITION

THE INSTITUTE OF PUBLIC ADMINISTRATION OF CANADA

IPAC IAPC

About the Authors

Kenneth Kernaghan is Professor Emeritus of Political Science and Management at Brock University. He served as President of the Institute of Public Administration of Canada and Editor of Canadian Public Administration and the International Review of Administrative Sciences. He is a Member of the Order of Canada, a Fellow of the Royal Society of Canada, and a recipient of the Vanier Medal for excellence in public administration. He received the Pierre de Celles/IPAC award for Excellence in the Teaching of Public Administration and the Brock University Award for Excellence in Teaching.

Dr. Kernaghan's many publications on public administration include several books, monographs, articles and reports on government ethics. He has advised international organizations and governments in Canada and elsewhere, and conducted many workshops on public service values and ethics. He served as Chair of the federal Task Force on the Disclosure of Wrongdoing.

John Langford is a professor in the School of Public Administration at the University of Victoria. Earlier in his career he worked for two years with the federal Royal Commission on Financial Management and Accountability. From 1993 to 2001, he was a chief federal negotiator in the BC treaty process. He was awarded the Pierre de Celles Award for teaching by the Institute of Public Administration of Canada in 2009.

Dr. Langford is the author or editor of several books, book chapters and articles on public sector ethics. He has provided advice on public sector ethical issues to governments in Australia and Canada as well as to the United Nations and the OECD. He has been actively involved in the design and implementation of standards of conduct, the transformation of ethical cultures in organizations, the development and delivery of ethics workshops and the mediation of public sector ethical disputes.

Dr. Langford received his B.A. from Carleton, M.A. from Oxford, and Ph.D. from McGill University.

Cover and book layout by: Jennifer Dany Aubé (www.JenniferDany.ca)

Printed in Canada

Canadian Cataloguing in Publication Data
Kernaghan, Kenneth, 1940—
Langford, John W., —

The responsible public servant

Published by the Institute of Public Administration of Caanda
1075 Bay Street, Suite 401, Toronto, ON M5S 4B2
(416) 924 8787 www.ipac.ca ntl@ipac.ca

Includes bibliographical references
ISBN 978-1-55061-000-0

1. Canada—Officials and employees—Professional ethics.
2. Civil service ethics—Canada.
3. Public Administration—Moral and ethical aspects.
4. Public administration—Canada

For Helgi and Kate again

Authors' Acknowledgments

This is the second edition of IPAC's best-selling book. The authors gratefully acknowledge the encouragement and financial support of the IPAC Research Committee and staff members at IPAC who helped take it from a proposal to a manuscript and finally to a hard copy volume and an e-book. They include Graham White, Robert Taylor, Wendy Feldman, Andrea Migone, Jennifer Dany Aubé and Suzanne Patterson. Others who helped in the production include Irene Huse, who sorted out the references, and Allison Gibson, who did the copy editing and indexing.

We also are very grateful for the assistance of our formal reviewers (eventually revealed to be Paul Thomas and Allan Tupper) and other individuals who provided research help or comments on individual chapters, including Irene Huse, Stuart Langford, Jim McDavid and Tim Scolnick. We also thank the participants at many ethics workshops over the years who focused us on important issues facing public servants across the country and provided the material for many of our case studies.

And, finally, a bow to each other. Our individual intellectual journeys since the publication of the first edition took us in different directions on some of the issues covered in the book. We discussed and even argued along the way but in the end found common ground.

Table of Contents

About the Authors   iii

Acknowledgements   vi

Foreword   viii

Avant Propos   ix

Introduction   1

Chapter 1 Taking Personal Responsibility   13

Chapter 2 Making Defensible Decisions   41

Chapter 3 Acting in the Public Interest   71

Chapter 4 The Politically Neutral Public Servant   101

Chapter 5 Conflict of Interest   131

Chapter 6 Confidentiality, Transparency and   163
          Privacy Protection

Chapter 7 The Accountable Public Servant   213

Chapter 8 Managing Ethical Behaviour   247

Index   279

FOREWORD

As governor general and patron of the Institute of Public Administration of Canada, I welcome the publication of this important volume. When I think of the elements that combine to make a smart and caring nation, effective public services and sound machinery of government rank prominently. They exist solely to serve the common good. Additionally, the public service values and standards of conduct of governments at all levels across the country are important statements to ourselves and to the world of that which we hold dear as Canadians.

There is a great reservoir of energy, talent and idealism among public servants. Each year at Rideau Hall I am privileged to present IPAC's Vanier Medal for distinctive leadership in public service, and I also know from my years as a university professor and administrator of the many students who desire to contribute to Canada as public servants. As a nation, one of our great challenges is to ensure our administrative machinery and governance systems are able to effectively harness the wealth of talent that exists in this country. This is no small task, but the strength of Canada is inseparable from the strength of its public institutions, and we therefore must succeed.

An effective public service requires careful study and a great deal of effort and imagination. I am confident that this volume will help to inform the dialogue relating to public service in Canada and to improve its practice.

His Excellency the Right Honourable David Johnston
Governor General of Canada

AVANT-PROPOS

En tant que gouverneur général et président d'honneur de l'Institut d'administration publique du Canada (IAPC), je salue la publication de cet important volume. Lorsque je songe aux composantes d'une nation avertie et bienveillante, je pense notamment à des services publics efficaces et à un appareil gouvernemental solide, qui ont comme seul but de servir le bien commun. En outre, les valeurs de la fonction publique et les normes de conduite des gouvernements à tous les niveaux dans l'ensemble du pays constituent d'importantes affirmations personnelles et publiques de ce qui nous tient à cœur en tant que Canadiens.

La fonction publique est un vaste réservoir d'énergie, de talent et d'idéalisme. Une fois l'an, à Rideau Hall, j'ai le privilège de remettre la Médaille Vanier de l'IAPC pour souligner le leadership hors pair en administration publique. De plus, durant mes nombreuses années comme professeur et administrateur d'université, j'ai rencontré bon nombre d'étudiants qui souhaitaient apporter une contribution au Canada en devenant fonctionnaires. En tant que nation, l'un de nos plus grands défis est de veiller à ce que notre appareil administratif et nos systèmes de gouvernance soient à même d'exploiter efficacement les talents dont regorge notre pays. Ce n'est pas tâche facile, mais la force du Canada est indissociable de celle de ses institutions publiques. Voilà pourquoi nous devons réussir.

Pour ériger une fonction publique solide, il faut des études rigoureuses, des efforts considérables et beaucoup d'imagination. Je suis certain que ce volume servira de fondement au dialogue sur la fonction publique du Canada et en améliorera le fonctionnement.

Son Excellence le très honorable David Johnston
Gouverneur général du Canada

Introduction

Should public servants be obliged to blow the whistle? Are public servants responsible for the outcomes of policies adopted on the strength of their advice? Should a public servant be able to moonlight? Should public servants be obligated to limit their rights to free political expression? To what levels of risk should public servants expose members of the public? Should public servants be proactive in providing relevant information to stakeholders and citizens? What is the nature of their obligation to protect the privacy of citizens and employees? To whom and for what are public servants accountable? This book does not provide definitive answers to questions such as these. In fact, we try hard not to be overly prescriptive about what responsible administrative behaviour is – except to defend the most basic proposition that a responsible public servant does not knowingly contribute to state actions or inactions that violate the law, misuse state resources or cause indefensible harm to those affected by them. What this book does provide is a practical examination of the arguments that are made on both – or many – sides of difficult questions about how public servants should conduct themselves. Thinking about these questions won't necessarily make decisions any easier, but it should cause public servants (or prospective public servants) to reflect on how they currently deal (or would deal) with difficult choices in their public lives, and it may even provoke them to approach some of these problems differently.

Our focus is the nature of responsible behaviour at all levels of government. So this is a book about professional or applied ethics – reflections on the guidance provided to public servants about how to behave in their relationships with their political masters, administrative superiors, colleagues, clients, the wider public and, lastly, with their own personal interests. This guidance can take the form of fundamental commandments (e.g., pursue the public interest, avoid conflicts of interest, be politically neutral, maintain confidentiality, protect privacy and be accountable), more specific rules found in legislation, standards of conduct, oaths of office and other policy directives (e.g., do not raise money for a political party, do not release information without authorization) and lessons learned from the on-the-job behaviour of superiors and colleagues (e.g., always give the minister what he or she wants, use information to secure advantage).

These formal and informal standards draw their legitimacy explicitly or implicitly from political and ethical theory. In the United Kingdom, Canada and Australia, for example, the interplay of ideas about how coercive state power should be distributed among and used by politicians, administrators and the judiciary has led over time to the development of the Westminster model of responsible cabinet government. This development, in turn, has spawned ideas about the proper role for public servants operating within that model and the principles of political neutrality, anonymity and accountability. Ideas about how public servants should act also emerge more directly from ethical theory, with its focus on the application of concepts such as responsibility, consequences, duty and virtue to the hard policy and administrative choices faced by public servants. For example, contending theoretical notions about the meaning and importance of privacy and the obligation to protect it have been drivers of contemporary efforts to establish fair information practices for public servants. In our view, arguments based on ethical theory ultimately trump the behavioural demands of particular governance arrangements, representing an important litmus test for questionable rules and practices (e.g., undiluted loyalty, high degrees of confidentiality) established by politicians and senior officials.

Public servants can confront the issue of responsible behaviour in a number of ways. First, they may simply encounter situations in which they don't recognize the contentious nature of a choice they face. Usually this means something like simple ignorance of a phenomenon such as conflict of interest. Here our task is largely to help the reader identify conflict of interest, explain why it is problematic and what forms it can take in contemporary public administration, clarify what it means to avoid conflict of interest and discuss the variety of methods governments have developed to combat this common phenomenon. In short, the book helps the reader to understand an easily defended – but still complex – obligation to keep considerations of private interest out of the administration of public responsibilities.

Second, public officials will encounter situations in which the standards of responsible behaviour are not so clearly articulated or are actually contested. A good example would be the often conflicting obligations a public servant experiences when deciding whether to keep information confidential or to share it more broadly with affected stakeholders and members of the public. Here our task is to reveal to the reader the contemporary debate about what a public official should do when the values of transparency and secrecy collide and the definition of what responsible behaviour looks like is in flux.

Third, and an extension of the second point, public servants may (only occasionally we hope) face situations in which there appears to be little prospect of finding a course of action that is not ethically wrong in some respect. This would involve making choices about what to do or recommend when all of the choices will harm some of those affected by the action or violate widely accepted ethical principles. Some commentators would refer to such situations as true moral dilemmas, "ethical conflicts in which, in order to do the right thing, one has to do the wrong thing; in which in order to do good, one must also be or do evil" (Parrish 2007, pp. 1-2). In a moral dilemma our task is to clarify the nature of the various harms that can emerge from the choice being confronted, explore the ethical principles at stake and provide tools for thinking about what an ethically defensible action would look like.

We will not be examining corruption and corrupt practices in public administration. There is obviously a very fine line between conflict of interest (where an official has a personal interest that could interfere with the performance of his or her public duty) and corruption (where personal gain is the key driver of a public servant's behaviour). We are fortunate to live in a society in which the latter is only occasionally found to be an institutionalized part of the administrative system. In any case, from a professional ethics perspective, activities such as extortion, embezzlement, solicitation of bribes and acceptance of kickbacks are not "interesting." No Canadian public servant has to be told that such activities are wrong. They are clearly prohibited by the *Criminal Code* and are ethically indefensible. For similar reasons, we also do not focus attention on workplace behaviours such as harassment or discrimination based on gender, race, ethnicity, religion, disability or sexual orientation, which are clearly condemned by law.

The ethical dimension of public sector employment is receiving much more attention than it did when we published the first edition of this book. Most schools of public administration and government training programs now offer courses, parts of courses or workshops on how public servants should behave on the job. Also, most governments have established standards of conduct and agencies and processes to encourage and enforce responsible administrative behaviour. Setting aside the effectiveness of such devices for the moment, this attention is a very positive development. In our view, nothing is more dangerous than a public servant who is technically fit but ethically flabby. Public servants and their political masters must recognize that much of the work they do involves difficult ethical choices. They must accept personal responsibility for the hard choices they make that negatively affect others and learn how to think ethically and justify their decisions. The most subversive purposes of this book are to speak up for the habit of ethical discourse in the conduct of public affairs and to make moral calculus as important as the quantitative analysis of policy options or the efficient management of financial resources.

Isn't Good Behaviour Obvious?

Why is there so little consensus today about what it means to be a responsible public servant? Why does the question of the morality of public officials remain such a contentious issue? An easy answer to these related questions is that the media are to blame. There is no doubt that traditional and social media are providing the public with much more coverage of cases involving questionable behaviour on the part of elected and appointed officials. Investigative reporting and more access to government information – through formal requests for information or through "leaks" – allow the media to present detailed stories about the means, ends and methods of modern governments and public servants. These stories make good copy and interact nicely with what many commentators argue is a burgeoning loss of public confidence in governmental institutions. Whatever their effect on public confidence, stories about such issues as abuse of authority, conflict of interest, partisanship of public servants and denials of responsibility for mistakes leave an impression that there is turmoil among both elected and appointed public officials about what responsible public behaviour looks like. A few commentators argue that there is no evidence that behaviour in the public sector has become worse. However, more suggest – on the strength of cases featuring involvement by public servants in partisan political activities or serious violations of the privacy of citizens, for instance – that traditional standards have weakened and that Canada's reputation for a professional, reliable and neutral public service is being eroded (Savoie 2008).

Media coverage of inquiries into such events as the sponsorship scandal and the Walkerton tragedy (Canada. Commission of Inquiry into the Sponsorship Program and Advertising Activities 2005; Ontario. Walkerton Commission of Inquiry 2002) may partly explain our continuing fixation with the integrity of government officials. However, such coverage does not in itself account for the widespread questioning about what it means to be a responsible public servant. For such an explanation we have to look at changes within government and the public service, and to the evolving relationship between public servants and politicians.

Two factors most commonly seized upon are the size and role of the public service. It is argued that the growth in the public service from the Second World War into the 1970s (and for some provincial and municipal governments into the 1980s and 1990s) was a deciding factor in the fragmentation of its organizational culture. What in virtually all jurisdictions in Canada had been tightly knit bands of career public servants, led often by "mandarins" with several years of military experience behind them, became big, anonymous bureaucratic units with large numbers of new, unsocialized recruits and a necessarily distant, inaccessible leadership group increasingly subject to rapid turnover. That leadership was incapable of commanding the deference toward its values and rules that had been accorded to those of the mythologized and long-serving mandarins. To complicate matters further, many of the new public servants came from the private sector and professional groups, bringing with them diverse and often very different values and standards of conduct. To this complex brew was added the factor of unionization and its potential for the introduction of competing values and loyalties.

Throughout this period the traditional organizational culture was further undermined by subtle but important changes in the role of public servants. The increased scope and complexity of government's intervention in the economy and society revealed more clearly that despite the mythology of a clear split between politics and administration, many decisions involving substantive policy were being made by public servants. This reality was reinforced by the impact of private sector "managerial" thinking on public sector organizations. The effect has been to encourage the devolution of discretionary decision-making power to lower and lower levels of management and supervision. As a result, public servants at all levels face new questions about the meaning of neutrality, how they go about deciding what policy, regulation or decision is in the public interest, and for what and to whom they should be accountable.

The explosion of public sector activity also brought new pressures on the public service culture from oversight organizations within government. Auditors general and comptrollers became powerful champions of the values of economy, efficiency and effectiveness. Similarly, the courts and provincial ombudspersons entered the arena on behalf of the values of fairness and procedural equity. Freedom of information and privacy commissioners fostered openness on the one hand, and privacy protection on the other. Conflict of interest commissioners, lobbying commissioners, equity and harassment officers, integrity officers, children's commissioners and commissions of inquiry have all added to the increasingly complex mix of agencies whose overlapping mandates were designed to clarify, communicate and enforce new standards of conduct for public officials (Langford and Tupper 2006). All of this has had the effect of disturbing the hierarchy of traditional standards and forcing the public servant to face hard choices between values such as privacy and efficiency, effectiveness and fairness, and openness and confidentiality. The reports of these oversight agencies on the shortcomings of public servants have also provided a regular flow of depressing tales of misbehaviour for the traditional media and the blogosphere.

But the suggested disintegration of the traditional principles of ethical behaviour does not end here. The public sector administrative culture has been more recently disturbed by the neo-conservative counter-revolution, which in many jurisdictions has taken the form of cutbacks and the privatization of public services. The high premium placed on mobility and term employment has had the inevitable effect of reducing the possibility of building strong organizational cultures based on the notion of a "career" public service. This disintegrative phenomenon is exacerbated in some jurisdictions by the politicization of the managerial ranks of the public service and the emphasis being placed on fairly simple-minded forms of loyalty to the "team." The traditional package of public service standards of conduct did not contemplate a situation in which public servants would become little more than agents of their political masters.

Every reader will undoubtedly be able to note other factors that have contributed to the contemporary questioning of the meaning and relevance of the traditional statements of public service standards of conduct. Such factors might be internal to the public service (e.g., downsizing, rapid staff turnover, diversification of work force) or shared with the wider societal culture (e.g., changes in information sharing and surveillance technologies, globalization). Some changes seem obviously contradictory in their impact. For instance, forces inclined to decentralize authority and increase the decision-making independence of public servants who deliver services would appear to be at odds with pressures designed to bind the public servant more tightly to the policy and communications leadership of his or her political master. The more important point for this study, however, is that both pressures tend to destabilize the classic relationship between politicians and public servants, leaving the latter uncertain both about their roles and what represents appropriate behaviour toward politicians, colleagues, clients and citizens more generally.

How Is the Book Organized?

What are the big ethical questions facing appointed officials? What issues do we focus on in this book? In general terms, we are concerned about how an individual public servant should act when he or she is involved in activities of government that affect members of the public, fellow employees, political and administrative superiors, and the society as a whole. We are interested in provoking thought and discussion about the nature of obligations and duties, the calculations of consequences, the balancing of conflicting values, and the goodness and badness of administrative practices and public policies. In our view, there is much more to being responsible than the mere avoidance of blatant corruption.

This study examines the traditional and current meanings of the primary principles to which the responsible public servant is widely expected to adhere. These commandments are: act in the public interest; be politically neutral; avoid conflicts of interest; do not disclose confidential information; protect the privacy of citizens and employees; and be accountable.

Before beginning our investigation of these commandments, or principles, we look at the more basic question of the personal moral responsibility of public servants. **Chapter 1** tackles a number of questions that are often used to deny the necessity for public servants to think ethically. It asks first if unethical behaviour is a pressing problem in the public sector? And, if it is a significant issue, is ethics really the concern of your average government employee? Aren't most public servants just bit players in a drama in which the hard moral choices are made by senior administrative and political superiors or, alternatively, by so many people that no one individual is responsible for them? Is moral responsibility also limited by the very nature of the role of a public servant, which, some argue, must allow for "dirty hands" (i.e., the violation in the public sphere of commonly accepted moral standards)?

If these arguments are insufficient to insulate the public servant from personal responsibility for his or her actions, we then face in **chapter 2** the question of how to make choices and justify our actions when confronting public sector moral dilemmas. We deal first with the contention that "it's all relative" – the argument that there are no universally accepted right actions. Why worry about justifying your behaviour if there is no possibility of determining what the right answer is? Rejecting the siren call of moral relativism, we move on to finding ways of establishing defensible answers to vexing moral dilemmas. This involves examining the key approaches to ethical dilemmas recommended by moral philosophers to see if any of these modes of ethical thinking help us cope with the kinds of choices we face in the public sector. The latter part of the chapter tries to provide the public servant with a practical ethical "tool kit," some techniques and theories for dealing with the hard questions.

Chapter 3 extends this discussion by examining the meaning, value and pervasive presence of the concept of the public interest. This is followed by a discussion of the relationship between public servants and politicians in the determination of the public interest. We explain the duty of public servants to "speak truth to power" while respecting the ultimate right of politicians to decide what is in the public interest. We give special attention to the critical role of public servants in providing analysis and advice to elected officials about the policy choices that best promote the public interest, and we emphasize the need for public officials to be sensitive not only to technical dimensions of public policy, but to ethical and value dimensions as well. This is especially important in regard to the application of cost-benefit analysis in general and risk-benefit analysis in particular, including respect for the "precautionary principle." These considerations lead to an examination of four major approaches to making the concept of the public interest operational. We conclude that while no single approach has been universally accepted as the best possible guide to decision making in the public interest, certain insights from each approach provide the responsible public servant with practical guidance.

Chapter 4 examines the duty of the public servant to adhere to the constitutional convention of political neutrality. Public servants are regularly advised that they have a duty to be politically neutral. But what does political neutrality mean? What are the laws and traditions that constitute the duty to be politically neutral? Is there general agreement on what these laws and traditions mean and on their current relevance? What are the links between merit, patronage and political neutrality? Where should the balance be struck between political rights and political neutrality? Where does one draw the line between political sensitivity and political partisanship? What does it mean to be loyal to the government of the day? Does political neutrality operate differently in municipal governments than in the federal and provincial governments?

Difficult issues of interpretation arise also in the examination of conflict of interest in **chapter 5**. The public servant's duty to avoid conflicts of interest is complicated by several factors. First, the definition of what constitutes a conflict has been significantly broadened in recent years. Public servants are enjoined to avoid not only real conflicts, but apparent and potential conflicts as well. Second, there are many variations of conflict of interest, including, for example, influence peddling, moonlighting and accepting benefits. Third, the nature, extent and application of conflict of interest rules vary from one government, even one department, to another. Fourth, the discretionary power of public servants, combined with the vast size and complexity of government, gives them many opportunities to use public office for private gain. Finally, the public and the media have become less tolerant of conflicts of interest involving public officials. Increasing attention needs to be directed to ensuring that rules designed to deter and punish conflicts of interest do not encroach unduly on the rights of responsible public servants.

Chapter 6 deals with the two interrelated issues of confidentiality and privacy. In respect of confidentiality, it is notable that the public servant's duty to keep certain information confidential clashes with a duty to satisfy the commitment of politicians to "open government" and to meet the disclosure requirements of freedom of information legislation. Despite the many rules providing direction as to what information public servants can or cannot disclose, there is considerable uncertainty as to how the responsible public servant should act in this sphere. This chapter reviews the arguments for and against secrecy and assesses the concepts of deception, disinformation, propaganda and censorship.

Protection of the privacy of individual and corporate citizens and of other governments is one of the primary justifications for confidentiality. But consideration of the public servant's duty of privacy requires an examination of what kinds of information governments should be collecting and what constraints should be placed on the means by which it is collected, the purposes for which it is used, and its manipulation and management. The tendency of many public servants to violate principles of fair information practice in the face of contending values is noted. The responsible public servant must design the protection of privacy into initiatives focused on enhancing security, public safety, and service delivery and taking advantage of new information technologies.

Chapter 7 explores the duty to be accountable. Our focus is on the personal accountability of middle- and lower-level public servants rather than the accountability of the most senior public servants, ministers and city councillors. We first examine the traditional messages that governments continue to send to public servants about the duty of accountability. We then look at the more recent efforts to tie performance reporting to traditional hierarchical accountability. We go on to examine the other forces that are challenging the traditional vision of accountability to a single supervisor, including the demands of courts, tribunals and more powerful monitoring agencies within government, obligations as professionals to external, self-regulating professional bodies, the emergence of accountability relationships between public servants and the wider universe of people and organizations with whom they work, and the impact of shared responsibility arrangements.

We ask how those challenges are reshaping the traditional duty of accountability. Finally, we look briefly at the notion that, ultimately, the public servant is accountable to his or her own conscience.

Chapter 8 focuses on how public sector organizations can build institutions and foster a culture in which public servants manifest a sense of personal moral responsibility. How can we create a hospitable climate for responsible behaviour within public sector organizations? How can we foster good behaviour, enforce rules and sanction offenders? In these tasks, we are faced with significant policy choices. Should we adopt a code of conduct? What form should this take? Should it, for instance, focus more strongly on values than rules? Is legislation necessary? How effective is ethics education and training? Do we need ethics counsellors and/or commissioners? Are criminal sanctions likely to be effective deterrents? What is the significance of role models and leadership and how can executives, managers, supervisors and ordinary employees exercise such leadership? In short, what regime should we construct to guide and regulate the behaviour of public servants and encourage responsible public service?

Within the commandments examined in chapters 3 through 7 are embedded most of the on-the-job ethical dilemmas that contemporary public servants confront. The problem is that these commandments – as interpreted within federal, provincial and municipal jurisdictions across the country – often do not provide public servants with uniform and clear messages about how they should handle such dilemmas. Or, where rules are stated relatively clearly, they are often seen to be inappropriate, anachronistic, contradictory or indefensible. There is no longer a widely shared consensus about what it means to be a responsible public servant. The orthodox religion of responsible behaviour is constantly under attack or simply declared to be irrelevant. In short, the traditional commandments governing the behaviour of public servants are suffering from a credibility gap.

As a result, public servants are confronted with a bewildering array of competing edicts, practices and pressures. Should I be loyal or politically neutral? Should I be open and accessible to the public, or should I maximize my efficiency? Is the effectiveness of the program more important than the privacy of its clients? Am I accountable only upward to the minister or horizontally to my colleagues and downward to my client groups? Can I help to build a new conservative social policy after a decade of involvement in the construction of the welfare state? Our concern, then, is to see what sense can be made of these commandments in the context of the often harsh contemporary world of choices that public servants face. We will be trying to strip away the rhetoric to examine the justification of positions for and against these rules and the actions they seem to dictate in specific situations.

Using this Book

The first edition of this book has been used successfully in both undergraduate and graduate courses devoted exclusively or in part to exploring ethical problems in public administration. It has also been employed equally successfully as background reading for management training seminars on public sector ethics. Each chapter contains cases that are for the most part based on real experiences and have been field-tested successfully in the classroom. Obviously, these cases do not begin to exhaust the variety of specific dilemmas that public servants confront as they go about their day-to-day work. Our experience suggests that students and management course participants are only too willing to provide case material from their own work world. While short, "snapshot" case scenarios can provoke the practical exchanges that make the discussion of difficult choices come to life, they usually suffer from one serious drawback. They rarely give the user an accurate feeling for the time frame over which public servants are pulled into more and more difficult dilemmas by the accretion of seemingly small and unimportant decisions or actions. Nevertheless, we are confident that this book and the cases included will make readers more alert to the ethical dimension of everyday life in the public service.

References

Canada. Commission of Inquiry into the Sponsorship Program and Advertising Activities (2005). *Who is responsible? Summary.* Ottawa: Public Works and Government Services Canada. Chaired by Justice J. H. Gomery.

Langford, J., & Tupper, A. (2006). How Ottawa does business: Ethics as a government program. In B. Doern (Ed.), *How Ottawa Spends: 2006-2007* (pp. 116-137). Montreal: McGill-Queen's University Press.

Ontario. Walkerton Commission of Inquiry (2002). *Part one: Report of the Walkerton inquiry.* Toronto: Queen's Printer for Ontario. Chaired by Justice Dennis R. O'Connor.

Parrish, J. (2007). *Paradoxes of political ethics: From dirty hands to the invisible hand.* Cambridge, UK: Cambridge University Press.

Savoie, D. (2008). *Court government and the collapse of accountability in Canada and the United Kingdom.* Toronto: University of Toronto Press.

Chapter 1

Taking Personal Responsibility

> Responsibility may well be the most important
> word in all the vocabulary of administration,
> public and private. (Mosher 1968, p. 8)

> It is not enough to ask, "Will my act harm other
> people?"...I should ask, "Will my act be one
> of a set of acts that will *together* harm other
> people."...If this is so I may be acting *very*
> wrongly. (Parfit 1986, p. 86)

> I did not think it was my role, as a simple
> bureaucrat, to call the police. (Testimony of an
> ex-engineer for the City of Montreal before the
> Charbonneau Corruption Commission). (*Globe
> and Mail* 2012, October 25)

Before beginning our examination of key commandments or principles
to which Canadian public servants are traditionally asked to adhere,
we have some underbrush to clear and foundations to lay. This chapter
tackles a number of questions which are often used to deny the
necessity for public servants to think ethically. Is unethical behaviour a
serious problem in the public sector? If so, is ethics really the concern of
the average government employee? Aren't most public servants just bit
players in a drama in which the hard ethical choices are made by senior
administrative and political superiors or, alternatively, by so many people
that no one individual is responsible for them? Is moral responsibility
also limited by the very nature of the role of a public servant, which,
some argue, must allow for "dirty hands" (i.e., the violation in the public
sphere of commonly accepted moral standards) and even outright
amorality?

If we find these latter arguments unconvincing, we are affirming
that public servants are morally responsible for their contributions
to government actions or inactions which benefit or cause harm to
stakeholders, citizens, colleagues or political masters. That is to say,
public servants are personally worthy of blame or praise for the way
in which they behave as officials because their behaviour is part of a
causal chain which has beneficial or harmful impacts, they are aware
of the actual or potential impacts, and they are not acting under
compulsion (Eshleman 2009).

If we are satisfied that a public servant is a moral agent, then how far does that personal moral responsibility go when he or she is faced with difficult choices which could result in harm to others? As we shall discuss in more detail later in this chapter, whistle-blowing legislation is increasingly putting pressure on public servants across the country to disclose situations in which colleagues or superiors are offending the public interest by violating the law, misusing resources or causing significant harm to people or the environment. It takes no leap of logic to insist that responsible public servants not engage in such activities themselves no matter what pressures are placed on them to do so. This means that public servants may face critical moments in their careers when expressing reservations is not enough, and they have to summon up the moral courage to make forceful arguments for more defensible courses of action, take a matter to a higher level, or just say no. As Sossin argues:

> While providing "loyal administration" to the government of the day, civil servants must, at the same time, always remain sufficiently independent of the political executive to exercise impartial judgment in the public interest. (Sossin 2005, p. 24)

Public Servants Exercise Considerable Power

Public servants often claim to be "powerless" (by which they mean "bound by the law," "lacking sufficient resources," "subject to political direction," etc.), but in fact many public servants have considerable decision-making discretion as well as policy-making capacity and therefore wield considerable power. By way of example, they have the power to allow a citizen to build a parking bay in front of his or her house, to shut down a nuclear reactor for safety violations, to pursue a minister's policy objectives aggressively, to include an advocacy organization in a policy consultation process and to do an accurate evaluation of a program's effectiveness. But, in all these examples, they also have the power to do just the opposite.

And They Don't Always Use That Power Well

If we start from the assumption that public servants are all basically decent folks going off to work in or around government to do good things for citizens in a professional manner, then it is easy to downplay the problem of public sector ethics. Governments are big, complex organizations trying to pursue the public interest, and public servants are using their power to help out in small or large ways. Occasional mistakes might be made by careless administrators (operator error, lax controls) and isolated instances of corruption, conflict of interest, inappropriate political activity, harassment of employees, etc. might rear their ugly heads, but there is no "big" problem about how public servants behave.

Many observers of public administration challenge this assumption. One scholar goes so far as to argue that a public service contains "knaves" as well as "knights," with the result that the public interest may on occasion be ignored by self-interested public servants (Le Grand 2010). One antidote to this perceived problem has been to increase centralized control of the public service and provide rewards and penalties to ensure that public servants do what they are told. But for other observers, the command and control model can create more ethical problems than it solves. They argue that destructive outcomes are frequently the predictable result in the public sector of the combination of coercive state power and strong hierarchical control over public service. Adams and Balfour, in their book, *Unmasking Administrative Evil*, explore "the social and organizational dynamics that lead individuals to comply with authority, even when the consequences of their actions are detrimental to other human beings" (Adams and Balfour 2004, p. XXX). They add that "[t]he common characteristic of administrative evil is that ordinary people within their normal professional and administrative roles can engage in acts of evil without being aware that they are doing anything wrong" (p. 4).

Many other authors have set out parallel lines of argument designed to alert us to the ethical dimension of public service and the ways in which public servants, for a variety of reasons, can engage – often enthusiastically – in activities that can do great harm to others. Consider – in the Canadian context – the record of bureaucratic involvement in the creation and perpetuation of residential schools for Aboriginal children (Milloy 1999), the successful efforts to block Jewish immigration to Canada during the era of Nazi persecution (Abella and Troper 1982) and the internment, dispersal and later deportation of Japanese Canadians in the 1940s (Roy et al. 1990). Consider also the activities during the Cold War of public servants on the federal government's Security Panel and their efforts to neutralize the perceived security threat of homosexuals and other individuals with "character weaknesses" in the public service (Kinsman and Gentile 2009). If you are tempted to believe that such things would never happen today because of the Charter of Rights and Freedoms, Supreme Court decisions and other institutional protections, you need only review more contemporary actions or inactions of public servants in organizations such as the Canadian Security Intelligence Service (Iacobucci 2008), the RCMP (British Columbia. Braidwood Commission 2010; Canada. Commission of Inquiry into the Actions of Canadian Officials in Relation to Maher Arar 2006), and the Walkerton Public Utilities Commission and the Ontario Ministry of the Environment (Ontario. Walkerton Inquiry 2002). Moreover, reports on the tainted blood scandal (Canada. Commission of Inquiry on the Blood System in Canada 1997), the federal sponsorship program (Canada. Commission of Inquiry into the Sponsorship Program and Advertising Activities 2005 and 2006), computer leasing by the City of Toronto (Bellamy 2005), the contracting practices at E-Health Ontario (Auditor General of Ontario 2009) and the regulatory practices of the Alberta Securities Commission (Mrozek 2005, December 12) also offer plenty of evidence of abuses of power by public officials which cause harm and erode public trust in the integrity of public administration in Canada.

Abuses of power can appear more pedestrian and procedural but still cause significant harm. The annual reports of ombudspersons, auditors-general, equity officers and other oversight agencies across the country feature many examples of public servants making tragic decisions with respect to children in care, denying income-assistance recipients their rights, treating candidates for employment or promotion unfairly, using sick leave to extend vacations, employing excessive force against prison inmates, illegally excluding citizens from planning meetings, failing to monitor long-term-care home standards, trying to reduce costs by refusing to fund expensive drug treatments or delaying follow-up health care, etc. Cases like these can often contribute more than scandals do to the erosion of public trust in the integrity of public servants.

But They All Too Often Reject Personal Responsibility for How They Have Used State Power

But here is the paradox. Despite the potential for public servants to misuse public resources, violate laws or established procedures and cause or contribute to substantial harm, there is an apparent reluctance on the part of some appointed officials to accept personal moral responsibility for the impacts of government policies and decisions that they have helped to create and implement. In fact, Canadian administrative history is replete with illustrations of a disconnect between public servants' power and their acceptance of personal moral responsibility for damaging outcomes to which they have contributed.

One alarming example is the interning of Japanese Canadians during the Second World War. Then Prime Minister Mackenzie King wanted a policy that would placate racist politicians, and some of his advisors responded with proposals for the relocation of all people of Japanese descent from coastal BC to internment and work camps in the BC interior and other provinces (Robertson 2000). Hugh Keenleyside and another advisor who showed less enthusiasm for the prime minister's approach were shunted to other positions (Keenleyside 1982; Sunahara 1981). Towards the end of the war, senior advisors to the prime minister in the Department of External Affairs dutifully set out options for dealing with more than 20,000 interned Japanese Canadians (75% of whom were British subjects[1]) when the war was over, including the development of proposals (Canadian Human Rights Museum, 2008), which led to individuals and families being pressured to accept deportation to an impoverished and destroyed postwar Japan (Robertson 2000; Roy et al. 1990; Sunahara 1981; Timmons 2004). In his memoir, Gordon Robertson is dismissive of Hugh Keenleyside's efforts to persuade the prime minister that internment was "unnecessary and unjust" (Robertson 2000, p. 42). When interviewed by the CBC many years later about his involvement in the development of the deportation scheme, Robertson refused to accept any personal responsibility for the fate of the almost 4000 Japanese Canadians – the majority of whom were British subjects (Miki 2004) – who were sent to Japan, arguing that the final decision on the deportation strategy was made by political superiors (CBC Fifth Estate 1995, October 24).

One doesn't have to go far back in history to find situations in which public servants appear to adopt an essentially amoral approach to their work, distancing themselves from any personal responsibility for the harm that their actions or inactions may cause. Among the possible examples to consider are Industry Canada advisors who put forward marketing and funding proposals in support of the federal government's policy of exporting asbestos to countries ill-equipped to ensure that these products will be handled safely by the end users (Rennie 2011, June 22). Or Health Canada officials who help to create and implement drug approval and surveillance processes that will be dominated by the pharmaceutical industry (Belluz 2012, November 20; Lexchin 2010). Or the federal Department of Fisheries and Oceans employees who develop a departmental reorganization proposal knowing it will gut the government's capacity to enforce the water quality sections of the *Fisheries Act* (Hume 2011, June 7). Or policy advisors from the

---

1. All Canadian citizens were legally known as British subjects until passage of the Canadian Citizenship Act in 1946.

Correctional Service of Canada and the Department of Justice who provide cover for more draconian approaches to criminal offenders despite the fact that many of these "tough on crime" measures have been demonstrated to be ineffective or harmful (Jackson and Stewart 2010, May).

In our experience, this ambivalence about moral engagement with outcomes can be found not only among senior public servants but also among junior and mid-level policy analysts, managers and service-delivery personnel as well as students who aspire to positions in the public service. Christopher Hood (2011) argues that far from taking responsibility for administrative actions and policy proposals, the focus of public officials – elected and appointed – is too often on "blame avoidance." In *The Blame Game*, Hood analyses a wide array of strategies that are used to ensure that negative risks associated with government actions or inactions are dissipated or deflected on to others. He argues further that common bureaucratic activities such as delegating responsibility, reorganization, partnering and outsourcing are often little more than "opportunities for blame-shifting, buck-passing, and risk transfer to others who can be placed in the front line of blame when things go wrong" (Hood 2011, p. 67). We will revisit this issue in chapter 7.

It is not our intention to suggest that all or even most public servants are amoral, self-interested and willing by nature to engage in harmful wrongdoing. There is no question that the evidence available from public inquiries and the reports of ombudspersons, auditors-general and others provides a one-sided and somewhat bleak picture of the sense of moral agency and courage of public servants. But in Canada, unlike the United States for instance (Cooper and Bryer 2007; Cooper and Wright 1992), we have little publicly available evidence of the willingness of public servants to recognize their personal moral responsibility and act on it. Such actions, except for the distressing accounts of whistle blowers who go public with their concerns, are usually hidden in unrecorded workplace exchanges among public servants and their administrative and political superiors.

However, it is our view that the pressures on public servants to deny moral agency and go along with or engage in behaviour that violates the public trust are substantial and growing. But is it defensible for public servants to reject a strong sense of personal moral responsibility for outcomes to which they contribute? To answer this question we have to explore contemporary pressures on public servants in the context of three closely intertwined arguments about moral *responsibility* and *role*, which are used to attempt to legitimize the denial of moral agency.

Responsibility Lies in a Superior's Hands

Public servants often begin arguing that they are not moral agents because their role is to support administrative superiors in the achievement of ends that they and their elected political masters have declared to be in the public interest (Amy 1984; Finer 1941; Thompson 1985). Higher-level officials – appointed and elected – are therefore the moral agents in these circumstances, and the policy advisor, manager and public service deliverer bear no personal moral responsibility for the efforts they make to help them reach the goals that have been endorsed by successful election, legislation or simply the positional authority of the senior administrator or politician. As Amy (1984) notes – referring specifically to policy analysts: "Value decisions, in this view, are best left up to policymakers, and need not or should not be the subject of policy analysis" (p. 576).

This general ethic of neutrality denies the legitimacy of a public servant bringing any moral considerations to bear on the development of policy or the implementation of programs with the exception of loyalty to the moral principles of his or her superiors. As Thompson (1985) puts it: "The ethic of neutrality portrays the ideal administrator as a completely reliable instrument of the goals of the organization, never injecting personal values into the process of furthering these goals" (p. 556). Contemporary attempts to model the policy-making process, for instance, still lean heavily on the notion that policy analysis is to be construed as an activity entirely in support of translating the vision of political masters into programs and actions to deliver outcomes (Parsons 2001). The moral responsibility of individual public servants is not a significant feature of the neutrality model. Responsible behaviour is that behaviour which is allowed by law, regulation, or policy manual, is responsive to hierarchical demands and is within the boundaries of the specific mandate of one's office. Within this model, public servants exhibit a wide zone of "indifference" or "acceptance," as Chester Barnard and his colleagues characterized it (Roe 1989), appearing willing to embrace without much deliberation any policy goal proposed by their superiors, put forward any and all policy options that would forward their superior's agenda and then oversee the implementation of whatever option was chosen regardless of the negative impacts which might flow from that policy (Savoie 2008, p. 142).

The acceptance of the notion that the primary obligation of a public servant is to provide support for any initiative that a superior wants to pursue means that there is no ethical dilemma even potentially inherent in the development, presentation and implementation of options and plans that the public servant knows from the outset would harm some or all of those who would be affected by them. This sense of indifference can extend beyond the presentation and implementation of potentially harmful options to include: the writing of policy briefs "to order"; the doctoring and suppression of data which would undermine the perceived effectiveness of a policy initiative or program; the contracting out of data collection and legal advice to firms "friendly" to the Government; the removal from policy or implementation teams of those participants deemed unfriendly by political masters; and willing participation in "spin" – the development of communications instruments designed to destroy the credibility of opponents of the policy proposal or program, mislead stakeholders and distract them from analytical or operational shortcomings of a government initiative. Contemporary illustrations of all of these activities are easily located throughout Westminster model jurisdictions including the United Kingdom, Australia and Canada (MacDermott 2008; Savoie 2008).

Thompson (1985) raises a potentially moderating feature of the neutrality model that calls for public servants to use their expertise to provide "frank and fearless" advice at least up to the point at which a decision has been made. But, particularly in a context in which political agendas are more polarized, this element of the neutrality package may have lost its salience. In contemporary governments, political and senior administrative leaders do everything they can to encourage loyalty as a key element of the ethic of neutrality. Public servants are often members of a ministry or even a cross-ministry team. Policy proposals or plans formed in response to direction from superiors are developed not in isolation from executive leadership, but in close collaboration with policy, political and communications operatives – at the federal or provincial level for instance – from the deputy minister's office, a minister's personal staff and even the premier or prime minister's office. At the municipal level, the mayor and council members can demand loyalty to the political vision from public servants throughout the wider bureaucracy. Anyone who challenges the team direction can be shunned, reassigned or fired; witness the fate of the general manager of the Toronto Transit Commission when he failed to enthusiastically support Mayor Rob Ford's subway expansion plan (*Toronto Star* 2012, February 21) and the president of the Canadian Nuclear Safety Commission when she opposed for safety reasons the Conservative Government's desire to reopen the Atomic Energy of Canada's medical isotope-producing nuclear reactor (CBC News 2008, January 16).

This team culture does not encourage individual public servants to provide "frank and fearless" advice at any point in the policy development or implementation process. Rather, a premium is placed on the provision of advice and other forms of assistance designed to forward the government's agenda. Advice is often proffered within the limits set down by the political and administrative executive's problem definition, standards of evidence, policy criteria, anticipated breadth of options and acceptable trade-offs (Bardach 2008). In more recent times, team loyalty seems to trump every other obligation, and the distance between the agenda and vision of the political and administrative executive and the work of the lower-level public servant has been significantly reduced (Mulgan 2007). As one of Jane Jacobs' (1992) characters in *Systems of Survival* puts it when explaining the ethical culture of the public sector: "If any single precept can be called key or central in guardian morality, it is *Be Loyal*" (p. 67).

In such circumstances, it is something of a shock when public servants "step up" and actually offer frank and fearless advice or refuse to do what they are ordered to do. Seymour Hersh (2011) recounts the story of the production of the U.S. Government's 2011 National Intelligence Estimate (NIE) on Iran's nuclear threat in which the analysts, humiliated by the way in which earlier NIEs on Iraq's and Iran's nuclear programs had been manipulated by pressure from political and administrative leaders, balked this time. He quotes a retired army intelligence officer, Patrick Lang, who said:

> "Analysts in the intelligence community are just refusing to sign up this time for a lot of baloney...These guys are not drinking the Kool-Aid" Lang said. "They stopped the NIE cold."
> (Hersh, 2011, June 6, p. 31)

In the Canadian context, going against the team can be a dispiriting and career-damaging move. Richard Colvin, a senior Foreign Affairs officer in Afghanistan during the war, was publicly rebuked by senior officials, military officers and the defence minister after he told his superiors and, subsequently, the Military Police Complaints Commission and a parliamentary committee that prisoners handed over to Afghan prison authorities by the Canadian military were at grave risk of being tortured (FAIR 2009). Munir Sheikh, the head of Statistics Canada, felt obliged to resign when the Industry Minister suggested publicly that Sheikh supported the Government's view that a voluntary survey could become an adequate substitute for the mandatory long-form census (Chase and Grant 2010, July 21). And Edgar Schmidt, a senior federal Department of Justice lawyer, was "isolated and warned that rocking the boat would make him ineligible for promotion" when he protested to his superiors that the department was "short-circuiting a legal requirement that new laws be vetted to see whether they comply with guarantees in the Charter of Rights and Freedoms" (Makin 2013, February 23, n.p.).

The *ethic of neutrality* argument denies the moral responsibility of public servants by focusing on the notion that to "step up" is to illegitimately force one's personal views of the public interest on political and administrative leaders. But taking moral responsibility has nothing to do with forcing personal views on superiors and everything to do with the positive professional obligation as a public servant to clearly signal to and, if necessary, resist superiors when a proposed action or specific approach to achieving a policy objective would cause indefensible harm – an obligation supported by long-standing convention (see chapter 4), codes of conduct and by the more recent creation of whistle blower protection regimes. These laws or policies clearly define for public servants the circumstances in which they have the duty or the right to report actions or omissions that they observe or in which they are asked to participate. For instance, the federal government's overview of the *Public Servants Disclosure Protection Act* (2005) specifies the right to report:

> ...serious violations that go against the public interest such as:
>
> - violating any Act of Parliament or any Act of the legislatures of the provinces;
>
> - misusing public funds or public assets;
>
> - gross mismanagement;
>
> - doing something – or failing to do something – that creates a substantial and specific danger to the health, safety or life of persons or to the environment;
>
> - seriously breaching the Treasury Board or your organization's code of conduct; or
>
> - directing or counseling a person to commit a wrongdoing.
>
> (Treasury Board of Canada Secretariat 2012, n.p.; see also *Public Servants Disclosure Protection Act*, 2005)

Other Canadian governments, including Alberta, British Columbia, Manitoba, Ontario, Nova Scotia and Saskatchewan, use identical or very similar language. In some jurisdictions, whistle blower protection provisions indicate that a matter may not be considered a wrongdoing if it "results from a balanced and informed decision-making process on a public policy or operational issue" (e.g., Saskatchewan's *Public Interest Disclosure Act*, 2011). It is uncertain what meaning will be attached to such language over time, but it seems unlikely that "balanced and informed" decision making would mitigate the violation of a law, regulation or code of conduct, but as we shall see shortly, it could possibly be used to legitimize some forms of apparent wrongdoing in the wider public interest.

It is perhaps self-evident that if governments state a public servant has a right or an obligation to report certain actions or omissions as wrongdoings, then no responsible public servants should by action or omission contribute to such wrongdoings, regardless of who orders them to do so. Governments are providing a clear message to public servants that their role does not obligate them to follow orders blindly if the resulting actions or omissions would cause indefensible harm to the public interest. In short, where public servants have a choice and are or should be aware of the harm they can contribute to, they are clearly morally responsible for any contribution they make to a wrongdoing.

The *ethic of neutrality* argument for avoiding personal responsibility also masks the degree of discretion available to public servants in vaguely defined policy analysis or implementation circumstances. On the policy analysis side, it underplays the opportunity they have to identify potential harm associated with certain options, make that harm known to decision makers and provide less harmful alternative options. In addition, on the implementation side, the ethic of neutrality understates the enormous discretion often available to public servants to make regulations and policy in the context of very general direction provided by legislation. It is in such circumstances that service recipients and individuals or groups subject to regulation are most affronted by public servants who deny responsibility and attempt to shift the blame for inadequate service or harmful regulation on to superiors and political leaders (Friedrich 1940; Schafer 1999).

Public servants often argue that the wrongdoing only revealed itself in later stages of the policy or program development process after the advisor had already made initial recommendations and initial actions had been taken. In such circumstances, it is contended, the public servant has already helped to move the proposal forward, and it is now too late to object to the course on which the government has embarked. An argument like this looks self-serving to the public and to inquiry commissioners who rightly insist that late is better than never when it comes to identifying and resisting illegal or harmful actions or omissions. Politicians or administrative superiors do ultimately make many of the tough choices, but they would do a better job of it if public servants' sense of personal responsibility obligated them to clearly communicate the ethical dimension of these choices as they reveal themselves, to make it clear when an option may not be legally or morally defensible, whatever calculus one uses, and to react more strongly if pressed by superiors to cooperate in initiatives that would constitute wrongdoing.

The "Many Hands" Excuse

The team culture provides the lead-in to another common objection to the notion that a public servant is a moral agent. This is often referred to as the "ethic of structure," and it rationalizes the refusal of public servants to accept individual responsibility for outcomes of government actions or inactions in which they have been involved by stressing the fact that "many hands" are at work. As Thompson (1985) again puts it:

> The ethic of structure asserts that, even if administrators may have some scope for independent moral judgment, they cannot be held morally responsible for most of the decisions and policies of government. Their personal moral responsibility extends only to the specific duties of their own office for which they are legally liable. (p. 559)

Let's examine this "ethic" from a policy-making perspective. Policy advising within government has moved a long way from the mythical model of a small group of officials packaging the results of internally generated research and monopolizing the attention of their administrative and political masters. Contemporary policy proposals are developed through complex webs of interaction involving relations with many units within a department and with other departments, as well as with affected interest groups, industry associations, think tanks, other knowledge generators and possibly other levels of government. Policy analysis is increasingly portrayed as a network management function, encouraging, clarifying and brokering the views of many players, and, thus, about as far as you can get from a simple one-to-one service encounter between a service deliverer and a client in which the former can see what his or her decision will do to the latter (McArthur 2007; Savoie 2008, p. 292). Hood (2011) argues that other ways to diffuse responsibility include:

> partnership working, multi-agency arrangements, or institutional machinery so complex that blame can be shuffled about or made to disappear...[O]rganizations

> also engage in processes of defensive
> reorganization and revolving-door movement of
> officeholders so that by the time blame comes
> home to roost, the organizational structure
> that produced the perceived harm has long
> been superceded and the relevant individuals
> have all moved out or on... (p. 19)

Public servants involved in service delivery have experienced all of these phenomena, and many inhabit a world in which service delivery is devolved into the hands of for-profit information technology vendors and community-based not-for-profit organizations. In such circumstances it is easy to plead the narrowness of one's individual role and succumb to the temptation to push responsibility for outcomes on to superiors who designed the system and the independent agencies actually providing the service.

In these cluttered and rapidly changing organizational circumstances, the argument runs, it makes no sense to insist that any one of the players (except ultimately the minister, town council, deputy minister or city manager) holds enough power or influence to be praised or blamed for the outcome and thus establish a significant degree of moral responsibility. It is noteworthy that in virtually all of the public inquiries held in recent years to examine government scandals, we can recall only one public official – Monique Begin, federal health minister during the tainted blood affair – who considered it her duty to take her share of the responsibility (Picard 1996, August 21). But Ms. Begin's acceptance of responsibility was tempered by her assertion that the health department in general was "blameless," therefore she was blameless (Schafer 1999, p. 7). Eventually, Health Canada public servants and officials in the Canadian Red Cross Society and a pharmaceutical company involved in managing the safety of the blood supply were charged with criminal negligence causing bodily harm under the *Criminal Code*. In the end, however, none of them was held to be legally responsible for the outcome – an excellent illustration of the potential gulf between legal and moral responsibility.

But the *ethic of structure* or "many hands" argument is hardly compelling. It contends that being one of a number of participants in a team, network or partnership context makes it unreasonable for any one individual to assume any significant degree of personal responsibility for wrongdoing. But we don't accord great significance to the fact of group action when ascribing personal responsibility in other contexts. Thompson (1985) uses the example of the gang of thugs beating an old man to death to argue that we don't allow the existence of a group of assailants or our inability to determine which one made the fatal kick to stop us from attributing responsibility and blame to all members of the gang (pp. 559-560). Being part of the gang and contributing to the death of the old man by striking him or failing to try to stop other gang members from doing so is enough to establish personal responsibility.

If in a governmental context as part of a team you make a significant contribution to an action or omission, are aware of possible consequences and are not acting under compulsion beyond the demand of a superior that you participate, then there is little to excuse you from personal responsibility for the outcome. In fact, little sense can be made of the alternative approach, which is to hold the group collectively responsible. "How, critics ask, can groups, as distinct from their individual members, be understood to have bad intentions? To be morally faulty? To have a moral character, faulty or not? How, in other words, can they be understood as appropriate bearers of moral blameworthiness, guilt, or shame?" (Smiley 2011, n.p.). Groups may provide the vehicle for individuals to do harm, but the group cannot replace the individual members of it as a moral agent.

In cases of shared responsibility, omissions are often as important as commissions. Commenting on what might appear a troubling notion of "negative responsibility," Thompson (1985) contends that "in the context of organizations we can more often point to specific omissions that made a significant difference in the outcome and are ascribable to specific persons" (p. 560).

The "Dirty Hands" Excuse

"Well, I have dirty hands. Right up to the elbows, I've plunged them in filth and blood. But what do you hope? Do you think you can govern innocently?" (Sartre 1955, p. 224). There is a centuries-long thread of argument about the moral status of public officials focusing on the thesis raised so graphically by Jean-Paul Sartre in his play, *Les Mains Sales*. Put most bluntly, the argument is that this world is so dangerous, corrupt and power-focused that politicians and public servants inevitably are forced to do bad things to make good things happen or to avoid even worse things. Thus – paradoxically – the concept of "dirty hands" has emerged to denote the public official's obligation to do things in public life that are demonstrably wrong to both protect the public interest and create public good. For example, it may be deemed necessary to torture a suspected terrorist to discover the hidden bomb that could devastate a city; or it might be necessary to mislead citizens about the efficacy of an available medical treatment to avoid panic about the outbreak of a disease. These acts and more can be portrayed by supporters of the dirty hands concept as obligatory in the blighted and hard landscape of public life.

But does acceptance of the concept of dirty hands force us to absolve public servants of moral responsibility? The argument in favour of absolution would focus on the fact that since public officials may be obligated to do harm if necessary to secure the public interest, then it is illogical to hold them blameworthy for causing harm – no matter how great – if it is done in the public interest. They are effectively beyond morality. One finds support for this idea in Machiavelli's (1513) advice to the prince to learn how not to be good, and, more than a century later, in Hobbes' (1651) argument that state power had to be exercised ruthlessly in order to keep enemies at bay and avoid society slipping into anarchy. These thoughts are echoed in the more contemporary works of *realpolitik* authors such as Hans Morgenthau (2006), who argues for creating distance between public life and morality. Rigid – and somewhat simplistic – consequentialists (see chapter 2) have also been accused of advocating an approach to public sector morality that can border on outright amorality, pushing public servants to do whatever they have to do to get a demonstrably better outcome or avoid a greater evil (Nielsen 2000). Thus, calculations of costs and benefits may at any time support the taking of an action that would harm some in the name of enhancing the position of others. Such "realist" logic gives considerable comfort to public servants who want to reject moral agency without shame or guilt in favour of an undiluted focus on achieving good, or at least less bad, ends.

But most contemporary "dirty hands" advocates don't buy this argument, putting forward a more nuanced conception of the prerogative of officials to ignore traditional moral responsibility. In this view, the public world is not universally nasty, but both politicians and public servants may encounter extreme circumstances in which it will be necessary to "dirty" their hands. For example, Jane Jacobs' (1992) "guardian moral syndrome" establishes a distinctive set of professional standards for public officials (e.g., be obedient and disciplined, respect hierarchy, be loyal, deceive for the sake of the task, be fatalistic) which, in its inclusion of deception, could be seen to embrace the necessity for the suspension of normal morality in some circumstances. However, Jacobs insists that standards of behaviour for most public officials involved in domestic policy making would be more restrictive than the standards for those engaged in police, military or foreign policy fields. Referring, for example, to the prerogative of public officials to "deceive for the sake of the task," one of her characters argues that "[m]ost guardian tasks in modern democratic societies carry no legitimate reasons for deception...The job of most bureaucrats is to serve the public openly and aboveboard. Deceiving it is thus disloyal" (Jacobs 1992, p. 76). Similarly, Applbaum (1999), at the end of his lengthy analysis of the power of role to excuse "the violations of persons in ways that would otherwise be wrong," concludes, "This argument, despite its appearance of sophistication and its pose of knowing worldliness, is much weaker than supposed. The truth is more simple: institutions and the roles they create ordinarily cannot mint moral permissions to do what would otherwise be prohibited" (p. 257). Michael Walzer, probably the most famous contemporary apologist for "dirty hands", argued in 1973 for fairly expansive circumstances in which public officials should be able to do whatever is required to forward or preserve the public interest. But by 2004 he had limited those circumstances to situations he describes as "supreme emergencies" (Coady 2011). By tightening up his own sense of the circumstances justifying dirty hands, Walzer implicitly cautions us not to allow too much elasticity in the definition of the moments in which a public official can legitimately feel free of the tug of traditional moral reasoning.

In addition, most contemporary supporters of the "dirty hands" thesis want public officials to accept personal moral responsibility for the use of ruthless means. Thomas Nagel, for instance, agrees with the notion that public morality is more impersonal than private morality, focusing more attention on reaching the government's goals and allowing the public servant more latitude with respect to the options recommended and the actions eventually taken to achieve those ends. Restrictions on means will be weaker, "permitting the employment of coercive, manipulative or obstructive methods that would not be allowable for individuals" (Nagel 1978, p. 84). But in Nagel's view, decisions about using such methods would all be made within the bounds of moral reasoning, and there would be no hiding the fact that one was advocating an evil action to avoid an even more evil outcome. Thus, public servants may be able to justify adopting a different moral calculus than a private citizen in some circumstances, but they are still personally responsible and blameworthy for their contribution to actions or omissions that would qualify as wrongdoing.

The precise latitude to be allowed to public servants to recommend or implement plans for actions or inactions that would harm some in order to reduce the harm to or improve the lot of others remains a contestable issue, depending on the circumstances in each individual case. What is significant from the perspective of this discussion is the demand of the more compelling of these "dirty hands" discussants that public officials acknowledge the ethical dimension of such situations, accept personal responsibility for their choices, and concede the need to be able to justify their hard choices to those affected by their advice or actions in ethical terms that the affected can understand. Public administration may require a modification in the normal moral calculus in some situations, but it does not provide an unrestricted ticket to ignore personal moral responsibility, more widely recognized standards of behaviour or the obligation to defend harmful actions or omissions in which one is involved as an advisor, decision maker or implementer.

Accepting Responsibility Raises Some Big Questions

To many observers, these three arguments – designed to deny the existence of moral agency, to severely limit the personal moral responsibility of public servants or to provide cover for engaging in "realist" moral calculus that might shock the public – are bogus and self-serving. The arguments obscure the fact that the individual actions or inactions of public servants – however dictated by role, subsumed in the powers and influences of other actors or influenced by an overwhelming danger to the community – easily meet widely accepted *causal* and *volitional* criteria for personal moral responsibility (Thompson 1987, pp. 40-41, 47-48). These criteria would hold public servants morally responsible for a wrongdoing by government insofar as their actions or omissions make an identifiable contribution to the wrongdoing, they are or should be aware of the potential outcomes and they do not act or fail to act under compulsion; or as Thompson puts it, they "could have done otherwise" (1987, p. 48).

The obligations of public servants as professionals run beyond avoiding procedural faults such as conflict of interest and political favouritism. They are moral agents, often with considerable power, who must take personal responsibility for the impact of their activities on those affected by them. In the end, it is really a matter of personal honour. This is not a call for moral perfection, but rather a plea for moral courage – an acceptance of the need to sort out in difficult situations what personal behaviour will nourish your self-respect as a professional and avoid regret and even shame in the future if your actions or inactions are held up to public appraisal or personal reflection. You don't want to have to look back later in your life on moments when you worked on difficult issues such as aboriginal rights, regulation of financial institutions, water quality, work safety or trade policy and regret your self-interested, cowardly or lazy indifference to the harmful impact of actions or inactions in which you were involved on clients, citizens, foreign nationals or the environment.

But there is no denying that embracing personal moral responsibility for one's actions or inactions may create a conflict between loyalty to superiors, team members and organizational confidentiality rules, on the one hand, and obligations to serve the wider public interest on the other. If a public servant feels morally obliged to "step up" when involved in a policy-making, management or service-delivery initiative which risks violating the law, misusing resources or visiting significant and possibly indefensible harm on some of those affected, he or she confronts a cascading set of questions about what level of dissent is acceptable. Do the public servant's obligations extend beyond clarifying to immediate superiors one's concerns about potential or actual harm, exercising the "art of voice," as Hirschman (1970, p. 43) put it? Or should the public servant refuse to explore and set out certain harmful options in policy memoranda? Would cooperating on the policy development side and attempting to mitigate the harm levels during the implementation phase be an appropriate compromise? Should a public servant seek the support of other members of the unit's staff or his or her wider professional community? Is it appropriate or even obligatory to open up lines of communication on certain proposed initiatives with stakeholders likely to be affected by them? Is it sufficient, for instance, to find ways to avoid personal involvement in activities that run the risk of doing indefensible harm to others, or does the public servant have an obligation to try to stop colleagues from doing such harm? Should a public servant resort, if pushed, to more formal avenues of internal and even external disclosure available under most whistle blower protection legislation? In what circumstances is resignation or changing jobs – Hirschman's "exit" option – the only defensible choice (Hirschman 1970)? These provide just a suggestion of the difficult questions about appropriate behaviour that would arise in a world in which public servants take personal moral ownership of their actions on the job.

Questions like these will be front and centre as we look in subsequent chapters at the types of ethical dilemmas that public servants experience. These questions will also play an important role in thinking through the steps governments are taking to try to define, sustain and enhance public sector ethical standards and the personal accountability of public servants.

Testing the Personal Responsibility Thesis

The following cases provide readers with the opportunity to test their own views on whether or not public servants in a variety of circumstances bear moral responsibility for decisions, actions or inactions in which they are involved. The first case focuses on the personal responsibility of a policy analyst and advisor.

CASE 1.1: I JUST GIVE ADVICE

A federal policy advisor (now long retired) was recently confronted by an investigative reporter with a copy of a recently released memorandum, which the advisor had written several years ago. In the memo, responding to a request from his minister, he had put forward a number of different plans for relocating a First Nations community from its traditional territory to an area with which it was completely unfamiliar. This area was close to a non-native community and would not support the traditional life style of this First Nation. None of the alternate resettlement plans put forward by the advisor appeared to address this reality satisfactorily. After considering the advice, the minister and cabinet agreed on one of the proposed plans and relocated the community. Its members led miserable lives in the new area for several years after.

In the interview with the reporter, the policy advisor accepted no responsibility for the actions of the government and scoffed at the idea that he should in any way be held accountable for the fate of the community. He argued that he had done his job by putting forward various relocation plans in the context of the Government's resolve to proceed with the move for strategic reasons. What the government eventually did with his memo and the impact of the plan adopted by the politicians on the people affected was not his concern as he had had no further role in the decision-making process or the implementation of the relocation. He appeared to be unmoved by the accounts of the impact that the relocation had had on the individuals and families affected.

Can this policy advisor legitimately deny any responsibility for the impact on this community of a plan he put forward?

The second case deals with the problem of establishing personal responsibility in an important regulatory agency going through a significant change in its business model.

CASE 1.2: PUSHED TO APPROVE

You and your colleagues in the Food, Drug and Pesticide Approval Branch are becoming increasingly dispirited. Food inspection staff has been reduced by half, and further cuts are promised. The drug research group has been largely dismantled. The result is that the regulation of pharmaceutical, food and pesticide corporations has been transformed into a "client-focused" activity in which public servants are directed to "help those seeking approvals to comply with regulations as easily as possible, promote voluntary compliance and earn good will from the regulated community." The regulated companies are also being required to pay for the branch's oversight of this new self-regulation regime through a "cost recovery" initiative. This has made the companies even more aggressive in seeking quick approvals of new drugs and processes. In certain cases, such as the testing of an experimental drug that might cure an intractable disease, the companies have been able to enlist public support for speedy approval.

Despite the changes in the regulatory process, the branch's obligations under the *Food and Drugs Act* have not yet been reduced. There are consultations going on with the three industries to develop new legislation that "modernizes" health protection, but at this point, the branch is still completely responsible for ensuring the effectiveness and safety of new drugs, food preparations and pesticides.

You and your colleagues know that you have been rushed into approving a number of drugs for which the industry-based testing has been much less stringent than the testing you used to do in-house. Three scientists in the branch who complained publicly about the speedy approval of potentially dangerous new veterinary drugs were recently fired, so there is little appetite for whistle blowing. But you are wondering how you should go about doing your work in circumstances in which you may be cooperating in placing the health of citizens and animals at risk.

When the Government makes the decision to change the way it regulates, are the public servants who implement that decision responsible for the outcomes? What should they do in such circumstances?

The third case raises the question of personal responsibility in circumstances in which many hands are at work.

CASE 1.3: THE CONSOLATION PRIZE

You lead a small financial analysis group providing advice to a multi-ministry team of public servants negotiating the sale of a large Crown transportation corporation, which the Government has committed to privatizing. As such, you are also a member of that larger, multi-ministry negotiating team. At a meeting involving the negotiation team and senior officials and ministerial staffers from the three ministries involved, concern is expressed about one of the two interested bidders dropping out, thus providing the remaining bidder with the leverage to drive down the eventual purchase price of the Crown corporation being privatized. One ministerial staffer recommends that the negotiating team persuade the reluctant bidder to stay in the game by offering the company a "consolation prize" – another public transportation asset soon to be put up for sale. The team agrees to consider the idea.

At the follow-up negotiating team meeting, some members express real enthusiasm for the strategy, arguing that it could realize a net gain of more than $300 million for the province. No team member reacts negatively to the strategy despite the fact that they all know that it would involve deceiving the major bidder in this competition as well as seriously bending the rules of the next competition to ensure that the reluctant bidder actually gets the "consolation prize." You don't say anything. The team leader asks your financial analysis group to help develop a plan for putting the strategy into action.

When you meet with your group the next morning, you can see that some of them are reluctant to support this strategy. You argue that the other negotiating team members seem to be onside and that the financial analysis group's role in implementing the strategy would be a minor one. "We are one of many players on this file. We didn't recommend the strategy and we won't be directly responsible for implementing it, but the team is counting on us doing any analysis required to refine the strategy."

Is it reasonable to argue that you and your team members bear no personal responsibility for the implementation of this strategy and should provide advice as requested?

The final case, explores the "dirty hands" thesis that the role of public officials and the environment in which they work allows public servants in some circumstances to escape responsibility for recommendations, decisions or actions which cause harm in the cause of avoiding a greater harm. The case was adapted from a dilemma described by Harold Gortner (1991, pp. 2-4).

CASE 1.4: DIRTY HANDS

Ed, the senior contract administrator in the Department of Energy, discovers that someone in the Premier's Office has given a "friendly" consultant access codes to a data bank containing secret information on proven energy resources and production in the province. This data was made available to the government by individual energy companies on the absolute condition that it would not be shared with third parties.

Ed approached his supervisor about this issue and was told to leave it alone. The supervisor didn't want to touch it. Ed was worried that if he brought the security breach to the attention of any member of the department's executive team, the story would get back to the Premier's Office and he would suffer retaliation from those responsible for the security breach. When Ed raised the issue informally with the consultant, he threatened retaliation from the political level if Ed pursued the matter. The confrontation confirmed for Ed that the consultant had access to the secret database.

Ed then noticed that the consultant had put in a bid on a large job posted by the Department of Energy. His bid was higher in price and less credible than the five competitors' bids. Ed immediately awarded the contract to the consultant anyway. In short order he got the consultant to sign the standard non-disclosure clause, allowing the government to press charges against him if he misused or revealed any confidential government information during the course of the contract. This would buy Ed time to work out a longer-term solution.

Does Ed work in such a hostile environment that he need not concern himself with the moral dimension of his actions? Can he do whatever is required to keep this data bank secret?

References

Abella, I., & Troper, H. (1982). *None is too many: Canada and the Jews of Europe 1933-1948*. Toronto: Lester and Orpen Dennys.

Adams, G., & Balfour, D. (2004). *Unmasking administrative evil* (2nd ed.). Armonk, NY: M. E. Sharpe.

Amy, D. J. (1984). Why policy analysis and ethics are incompatible. *Journal of Policy Analysis and Management, 3*(4), 573-591.

Applbaum, A. (1999). *Ethics for adversaries: The morality of role in public and professional life*. Princeton: Princeton University Press.

Auditor General of Ontario. (2009). *Ontario electronic health records initiative* Toronto: Queen's Printer for Ontario.

Bardach, E. (2008). *A practical guide for policy analysis: The eightfold path to more effective problem solving* (3rd ed.). Washington, DC: CQ Press.

Bellamy, D. (2005). *Toronto computer leasing inquiry,* Vol. 1-4. Toronto: City of Toronto.

Belluz, J. (2012, November 20). Canada's drug problems. *MacLeans.* Retrieved from http://www2.macleans.ca/2012/11/20/canadas-drug-problems

British Columbia. Braidwood Commission on the death of Robert Dziekanski (2010). *Why? The Robert Dziekanski tragedy.* Retrieved from http://www.braidwoodinquiry.ca/report/P2Report.php

Canada. Commission of Inquiry into the Actions of Canadian Officials in Relation to Maher Arar. (2006). *Report of the events relating to Maher Arar: Analysis and recommendations.* Ottawa: Minister of Public Works and Government Services. Retrieved from http://www.pch.gc.ca/cs-kc/arar/Arar_e.pdf

Canada. Commission of Inquiry into the Sponsorship Program and Advertising Activities. (2005). *Who is responsible? Phase I report.* Ottawa: Minister of Public Works and Government Services. Chaired by Justice J. H. Gomery.

Canada. Commission of Inquiry into the Sponsorship Program and Advertising Activities. (2006). *Restoring accountability – Recommendations: Phase II report.* Ottawa: Minister of Public Works and Government Services. Chaired by Justice J. H. Gomery.

Canada. Commission of Inquiry on the Blood System in Canada. (1997). *Final report.* Ottawa: Public Works and Government Services Canada. Chaired by Justice H. Krever. Retrieved from http://www.hc-sc.gc.ca/ahc-asc/activit/krever-eng.php

Canadian Human Rights Museum (2008). Memorandum from Gordon Robertson (Department of External Affairs) to Norman Robertson (Under Secretary of State for External Affairs, no relation), 20 March 1944. [cited source is: Library and Archives Canada-RG 25, Volume 5761, File 104(s)-1-1940, 20 March 1944. e010692346]. Retrieved from http://humanrightsmuseum.ca/media/imagegallery/detail/579

CBC Fifth Estate. (1995, October 24). Throwaway Citizens: Deportation.

CBC News. (2008, January 16). Nuclear safety watchdog head fired for 'lack of leadership': minister. Retrieved from http://www.cbc.ca/news/canada/story/2008/01/16/keen-firing.html

Chase, S., & Grant, T. (2010, July 21). Statistics Canada chief falls on sword over census. *Globe and Mail*. Retrieved from http://www.theglobeandmail.com/news/politics/statistics-canada-chief-falls-on-sword-over-census/article1320915

Coady, C. (2011). The problem of dirty hands. In E. Zalta (Ed.), *The Stanford encyclopedia of philosophy*. Retrieved from http://plato.stanford.edu/archives/sum2011/entries/dirty-hands/

Cooper, T., & Bryer, T. (2007). William Robertson: Exemplar of politics and public management rightly understood. *Public Administration Review, 67*(5), 816-823.

Cooper, T., & Wright, D. (1992). *Exemplary public administrators: Character and leadership in government*. Hoboken, NJ: Jossey-Bass.

Eshleman, A. (2009). Moral responsibility. In E. N. Zalta (Ed.), *The Stanford encyclopedia of philosophy*. Retrieved from http://plato.stanford.edu/archives/win2009/entries/moral-responsibility

FAIR. (2009). The Richard Colvin case. Retrieved from http://fairwhistleblower.ca/cases/richard_colvin

Finer, H. (1941). Administrative responsibility and democratic government. *Public Administration Review, 1*(4), 335-350.

Friedrich, C. J. (1940). Public policy and the nature of administrative responsibility. In C. J. Friedrich & E. S. Mason (Eds.), *Public policy* (pp. 3-24). Cambridge, MA: Harvard University Press.

Globe and Mail. (2012, October 25). *Poor Mr. TPS, whose name was synonymous with corruption*. Guest editorial. Retrieved from http://www.theglobeandmail.com/commentary/editorials/poor-mr-tps-whose-name-was-synonymous-with-corruption/article4667204

Gortner, H. (1991). *Ethics for public managers*. Westport: Praeger Publishing.

Hersh, S. (2011, June 6). Iran and the bomb. *New Yorker*, pp. 30-35.

Hirschman, A. (1970). *Exit, voice and loyalty*. Cambridge, MA: Harvard University Press.

Hobbes, T. (1651). *Leviathan*. London: Printed for Andrew Crooke, at the Green Dragon in St. Pauls Churchyard. Retrieved from http://socserv.mcmaster.ca/econ/ugcm/3ll3/hobbes/Leviathan.pdf

Hood, C. (2011). *The blame game*. Princeton: Princeton University Press.

Hume, M. (2011, June 7). DFO restructuring caused confusion, hampered fish habitat protection. *Globe and Mail*. Retrieved from http://www.theglobeandmail.com/news/british-columbia/dfo-restructuring-caused-confusion-hampered-fish-habitat-protection/article4260891

Iacobucci, F. (2008). *Public report of the internal inquiry into the actions of Canadian officials in relation to Abdullah Almaki, Ahmad Abou-Elmaati and Muayyed Nureddin*. Ottawa: Minister of Public Works and Government Services.

Jackson, M., & Stewart, G. (2010, May). Fear-driven policy: Ottawa's harsh new penal proposals won't make us safer, just poorer and less humane. (Cover story). *Literary Review of Canada, 18*(4), 3.

Jacobs, J. (1992). *Systems of survival: A dialogue on the moral foundations of commerce and politics*. New York: Random House.

Keenleyside, H. L. (1982). *Memoirs of Hugh L. Keenleyside: On the bridge of time*, Vol. 2. Toronto: McClelland and Stewart.

Kinsman, G., & Gentile, P. (2009). *The Canadian war on queers: National security as sexual regulation*. Vancouver: UBC Press.

Le Grand, J. (2010). Knights and knaves return: Public service motivation and the delivery of public services. *International Public Management Journal, 13(*1), 56-71.

Lexchin, J. (2010). Drug safety and health Canada. *International Journal of Health Services*, 22(1), 41-53.

MacDermott, K. (2008). *Whatever happened to frank and fearless? The impact of new public management on the Australian public service*. Canberra: ANU Press.

Machiavelli, N. (1513). *The prince*, translated by W. Marriott. Retrieved from http://www.gutenberg.org/files/1232/1232-h/1232-h.htm

Makin, K. (2013, February 23). Justice department whistleblower on a crusade to sustain the rule of law. *Globe and Mail*. Retrieved from http://www.theglobeandmail.com/news/national/justice-department-whistleblower-on-a-crusade-to-sustain-the-rule-of-law/article9001991

McArthur, D. (2007). Policy analysis in provincial governments in Canada: from PPBS to network management. In L. M. Dobuzinski, M. Howlett & D. Laycock (Eds.), *Policy analysis in Canada: The state of the art* (pp. 238-264). Toronto: University of Toronto Press.

Miki, R. (2004). *Redress: Inside the Japanese Canadian call for justice.* Vancouver: Raincoast Press.

Milloy, J. (1999). *A national crime: The Canadian government and the residential school system*, 1879-1986. Winnipeg: University of Manitoba Press.

Morgenthau, H. J. (2006). *Politics among nations: The struggle for power and peace* (7th ed.). Boston: McGraw-Hill Higher Education.

Mosher, F. (1968). *Democracy and the public service.* New York: Oxford University Press.

Mrozek, A. (2005, December 12). The right connections. *Western Standard.* Retrieved from http://www.westernstandard.ca/website/article.php?id=1282

Mulgan, R. (2007). Truth in government and the politicisation of public service advice. *Public Administration*, 85(3), 570-586.

Nagel, T. (1978). Ruthlessness in public life. In S. Hampshire (Ed.), *Public and private morality* (pp. 78-79). Cambridge, UK: Cambridge University Press.

Nielsen, K. (2000). There is no dilemma of dirty hands. In P. Rynard & D. P. Shugarman (Eds.), *Cruelty & deception: The controversy over dirty hands in politics* (pp. 139-155). Peterborough, ON: Broadview Press.

Ontario. (2002). Walkerton Inquiry. *Part one: Report of the Walkerton Inquiry: The events of May 2000 and related issues.* Toronto, ON: Ministry of the Attorney General. Chaired by Justice D. R. O'Connor. Retrieved from http://www.walkertoninquiry.com

Parfit, D. (1986). *Reasons and persons.* Oxford: Oxford University Press.

Parsons, W. (2001). Modernising policy-making for the twenty first century: The professional model. *Public Policy and Administration,* 16(3), 93-110.

Picard, A. (1996, August 21). Blame me for blood scandal, Begin says. Globe and Mail, pp. A1, A7.

Public Interest Disclosure Act. (2011). In Statutes of Saskatchewan, c. P-38.1. Retrieved from http://www.qp.gov.sk.ca/documents/English/Statutes/Statutes/P38-1.pdf

Public Servants Disclosure Protection Act. (2005). In Statutes of Canada, c. 46, s. 8. Retrieved from http://laws-lois.justice.gc.ca/PDF/P-31.9.pdf

Rennie, S. (2011, June 22). Canada blocks asbestos from hazardous chemicals list at UN summit. The *Toronto Star.* Retrieved from http://www.thestar.com/news/canada/2011/06/22/canada_ blocks_asbestos_from_hazardous_chemicals_list_at_un_summit. html

Robertson, R. G. (2000). *Memoirs of a very civil servant: Mackenzie King to Pierre Trudeau.* Toronto: University of Toronto Press.

Roe, E. M. (1989). The zone of acceptance in organization theory: An explanation of the Challenger disaster. *Administration and Society, 21*(2), 234-264.

Roy, P., Granatstein, J., Iino, M., & Takamura, H. (1990). *Mutual hostages: Canadians and Japanese during the Second World War.* Toronto: University of Toronto Press.

Sartre, J-P. (1955). *No exit and three other plays*, translated by L. Abel. New York: Vintage.

Savoie, D. (2008). *Court government and the collapse of accountability.* Toronto: University of Toronto Press.

Schafer, A. (1999). A wink and a nod: A conceptual map of responsibility and accountability in bureaucratic organizations. *Canadian Public Administration, 42*(1), 5-25.

Smiley, M. (2011). Collective responsibility. In E. Zalta (Ed.), *The Stanford encyclopedia of philosophy.* Retrieved from http://plato.stanford. edu/archives/fall2011/entries/collective-responsibility/

Sossin, L. (2005). Speaking truth to power? The search for bureaucratic independence in Canada. *University of Toronto Law Journal, 55*(1), 1-59.

Sunahara, A. G. (1981). *The politics of racism: The uprooting of Japanese Canadians during the Second World War.* Toronto: Lorimer and Company. Updated 2000 and retrieved from http://www. japanesecanadianhistory.ca/Politics_of_Racism.pdf

Thompson, D. F. (1985). The possibility of administrative ethics. *Public Administration Review*, 45(5), 555-561.

Thompson, D. F. (1987). *Political ethics and public office.* Cambridge, MA: Harvard University Press.

Timmons, D. J. (2004). '*Evangelines of 1946': The exile of Nikkei from Canada to Occupied Japan.* Victoria: Department of History, University of Victoria, MA Thesis.

Toronto Star. (2012, February 21). *Mayor Rob Ford hurts the TTC by unjustly firing Gary Webster as general manager.* Editorial. Retrieved from http://www.thestar.com/opinion/ editorials/2012/02/21/mayor_rob_ford_hurts_the_ttc_by_ unjustly_firing_gary_webster_as_general_manager.html

Treasury Board of Canada Secretariat. (2012). *Overview of the Public Servants Disclosure Protection Act.* Retrieved from http://www.tbs-sct.gc.ca/ve/oaal-eng.asp

Walzer, M. (1973). Political action: the problem of dirty hands. *Philosophy and Public Affairs, 2*(2), 160-180.

Walzer, M. (2004). "Emergency ethics" in *Arguing about war.* New Haven: Yale University Press.

Chapter 2

Making Defensible Decisions

> (O)ne such inescapable obligation is this: when
> you do something that harms someone else, you
> must be able to justify it." (Appiah 2006, p. 151)

If the ethics of neutrality and structure and the "special" role of public servants in a "dirty" environment are insufficient to insulate the public servant from personal responsibility for his or her actions, we then face the question of how to make choices and justify our actions when confronting public sector moral dilemmas. Before we tackle the question of ethical justification, however, we should deal with the contention that "it's all relative" – the argument that there are no universally accepted right actions. Why worry about justifying your behaviour if there is no possibility of determining what the right answer is? So our first task in this chapter is to look at the issue of moral relativism and to see if we feel comfortable moving beyond it to find ways of establishing defensible answers to vexing moral dilemmas. If we do, then our next step is to look at the various approaches to ethical dilemmas recommended by moral philosophers to see if any of these modes of ethical thinking help us cope with the kinds of choices we face in the public sector. At the end of the chapter we provide public servants with an ethical "tool kit" – some techniques and theories for dealing with hard ethical questions – and work through a difficult case to illustrate how these tools can be put to use.

Ethical Relativism: Is There No Right Answer?

People often disagree about what is morally defensible behaviour. Some ethical relativists argue that such disagreements reflect the facts that there are no objective ethical standards and that, therefore, we must respect and tolerate different perceptions of what is right and wrong. If these claims are correct, they can be damaging to efforts to develop widely accepted normative standards for the community of nations, individual societies, and governments and their public officials.

Ethical relativism surfaces most starkly when two different cultures are involved. Where two individuals come from different societies with distinctly different value structures they may disagree about the ethical defensibility of a host of practices such as nepotism, bribery, euthanasia, or honour killing. But such disagreements can also emerge in the context of a single society and even a single organization. Moreover, it is argued by some relativists that such disagreements are not only possible but inevitable because there is no universally accepted approach to ethical reasoning that allows us to deal in a totally convincing way with situations in which the moral judgments of one person conflict with the moral judgments of another. Morality, for the relativist, is subjective, "something like a set of social customs or traditions" (Bennett 2010, p. XV). Paraphrasing Brandt (1967), the ultimate and extreme expressions of ethical relativism are the linked propositions that if a person *believes* that an action is right for him then he ought to do it, and if a society or group endorses a certain action in certain circumstances, then that action is right. This claim is part of a more widespread questioning of objectivism and universalism inherent in the enlightenment view of the world around us. As Crotty (1998) notes of relativism:

> Once this standpoint is embraced, we will
> obviously hold our understandings much more
> lightly and tentatively and far less dogmatically,
> seeing them as historically and culturally
> effected interpretations rather than eternal
> truths of some kind. (p. 64)

To truly appreciate how ethical relativism might work, try to imagine a discussion about the practice of genital mutilation of pre-pubescent girls among visiting Health Canada officials and local political leaders in a regional health district of one of several African countries in which such mutilations are practiced. To local supporters of the practice, it is a normal and essential part of becoming a mature and respected female member of society and a repository of a family's good reputation. It is a practice with complex and deep cultural roots. To critics, including our Health Canada officials, it is simply a barbaric and medically dangerous set of procedures visited on girls without their consent – procedures, by the way, which were employed in some Western societies during the 19th century but later shunned as morally indefensible. But the moral relativist would argue that the practice is grounded in the local culture and is morally right for members of that society who believe in it. In this view, attempts to criticize or suppress the practice in a previously colonized society represent a form of neo-colonialism. If practitioners believe it is right then it is right for them and we should not judge or interfere. Intense tolerance is the watchword of relativists who see moral positions as no more than reflections of beliefs or strongly held feelings.

A less alarming example of ethical relativism can be seen in the effort to extend conflict of interest rules for local government officials that seem completely appropriate in large Canadian urban communities to officials in smaller rural communities. In the former, it is widely accepted that city officials should not have any personal business interests that might subvert the performance of their public duties. In a small town, the community may accept the fact that officials can have private business interests that intersect with their public duties. The community may, for instance, prefer to have the municipal government purchase supplies from the only local hardware store, which happens to be owned by the mayor, rather than see that business go to a hardware store in another community. Two different communities with two different attitudes towards potential conflict of interest.

Moral relativism can create troubling forms of "double standards." *Cultural moral relativism*, in particular, allows us to accept double standards by permitting the argument that we wouldn't allow such behaviour in our society or community, but we have to put up with it in another society or community because it is a legitimate reflection of a local culture. This argument may be used by government officials supporting the building of trade relations, for instance, with countries that condone violations of what we define as basic human rights. It could also be used, as in our example above, by Canadian health officials attempting to build public health partnerships in rural areas of Sudan. Moral relativism also provides ethical ammunition to supporters of practices such as the export of pesticides, pharmaceuticals or materials such as asbestos, which are banned in our country, to countries with inadequate safety standards governing their use. Some observers distinguish such forms of double standard from more common, garden-variety forms of state moral hypocrisy, such as supporting a ban on the spread of nuclear weapons while retaining them for your own nation or advocating free trade in agricultural products while subsidizing your own farmers or otherwise protecting them from competition.

The overall thrust of the relativist argument is to undermine the possibility of meaningful dialogue about right and wrong, and the necessity of justifying one's actions to others. We have all experienced in class or in the workplace the caution with which individuals approach the discussion of actions or practices that might have significant cultural roots for other participants in the discussion. We are also aware of cases in which the Charter of Rights and Freedoms is being invoked to both attack and defend practices such as polygamy, the suppression of the political and economic rights of Aboriginal women in some Aboriginal communities, the refusal of medical treatment, and the wearing of religious clothing or symbols (e.g., the ceremonial kirpan or the niqab). Such cases reinforce the public sense that culturally based practices might have more moral and legal standing than the majority of Canadians would have intuitively thought. By extension, they also tend to reinforce the notion that there is no right answer to moral dilemmas – that both sides of an argument can simultaneously be right.

However, a number of counter-arguments have been made which tend to cast doubt on some aspects of the relativist position. First, it has been argued that the anthropological evidence supporting descriptive ethical relativism is often misleading. It is not as easy as was once thought to demonstrate that individuals from different societies or cultures are in conflict on what is the right course of action when faced with a common set of facts. As observation and testing become more sophisticated, accepted practices are reinterpreted and much more uniformity of approach to ethical problems is observed. In addition, the widespread acceptance of statements of fundamental human rights suggests a higher degree of moral congruence across societies than cultural relativists posit (Gowans 2012).

Second, the notion that an action is right merely because I believe or feel it is right or the group or society of which I am a member endorses it does not stand up to close scrutiny. While my belief that a course of action is right may go some way toward absolving me of blame for any harm I might cause if I pursue that course of action, it is not an adequate basis for determining right or wrong. If it were, beliefs and feelings would become an impenetrable substitute for justification, thereby offending our most basic sense about moral judgments: *that they must be defensible in forms that other people can understand and debate*. The validity of moral judgments implies more than that they are believed or felt to be right by the individual or group making the judgments.

Hardly more acceptable is the related thesis that an action that a group or a society endorses as right is right for an individual member of that group or society. Again, the major problem with this argument is that it makes disagreements meaningless by setting up the views of the community as the final arbiter of right and wrong. It means that two people can make contradictory judgments ("bribery is right" and "bribery is wrong") and as long as they have the support of two different groups or communities, both statements are ethically defensible. "It follows too that however ignorant or mistaken a given community may be concerning the nature of the action being morally assessed, the statement by a member of a community that the action is right will be true as long as his community does approve of it" (Harrison 1967, p. 80). Even more damaging to this facet of ethical relativism is the implication that "no member of the society can disagree with his society about the morality of an action...Yet it is a fact of moral life that people do sometimes disagree in some instances with what the other members of the society believe regarding moral matters" (De George 1982, p. 32).

Clearly, this relativist position, which attaches such significance to individual or community belief as a basis for moral judgments, offends our common-sense approach to moral validity. When we make moral judgments (e.g., "bribery is wrong") we mean more than just "bribery is wrong for me or my community." We mean to say that bribery is wrong for everyone or, at the very least, that we have found no circumstances so far in which bribery is ethically defensible.

The third and final point about ethical relativism centres on this issue of universal validity. The relativists force us to confront one important reality: there is, as yet, no form of ethical reasoning which can resolve *all* disputes between conflicting ethical positions. This is so even when all the facts and circumstances are agreed upon and both parties to the dispute share a common culture and are impartial, their views untainted by positions derived from class, ethnic, sexual, or ideological considerations. Ethical conflicts between individuals remain.

Because in a multicultural society we do not all share common cultural traditions, we can learn from the diversity of ethical views that we encounter. But we don't want to let diversity divert us from working towards ethical standards for public service that make sense to everyone (politicians, public servants, citizens and foreign nationals) affected by them. While ethical argument on some public policy or administration issues (e.g., regulation of immigration, confidentiality) seem interminable, it is not uncommon for two people arguing about commonly agreed upon facts and circumstances from the perspective of different cultural perspectives and employing different ethical theories to see eye to eye on how they should act. Our ethical conflicts and arguments about the methods to be used to settle them are embedded in a considerable degree of consensus about what is right and what is wrong in most circumstances.

The following case provides an opportunity to test your support for the idea of moral relativism and, by extension, your tolerance of culturally bound ethical behaviour.

CASE 2.1: WHEN IN ROME

Mary is a new junior trade official in the Canadian High Commission in a South Asian country. When she arrived in the capital, she became the liaison officer to a Canadian-funded development project designed to help local jute producers find new foreign markets for their products. As she becomes more familiar with the file, she is sent on a tour of jute mills outside of the capital. In most of the plants, she is surprised to find young boys and girls involved in dirty and often dangerous parts of the production process. She asks a few questions and determines that child labour is a continuing fact of life in many of these plants. The children get the equivalent of 80 cents a day, sometimes working 11 to 12 hours a day, six days a week, and have no regular access to schooling. Injuries are a fairly regular occurrence, and there are no medical benefits. Most of the children involved have been effectively "sold" to the mill owners for periods up to five years by their parents, who get a cash payment in exchange.

When she raises her concerns about this at a meeting with the development project manager (a Canadian-educated national) and her boss at the High Commission, they indicate that they have brought up the issue with the plant owners a number of times but that nothing has happened. In fact, during an earlier field trip, a delegation of leaders from a village next to one of the plants met with them to ask them not to interfere with the child labour practices. Her boss expresses the hope that if the project is successful, the plants will earn more money and the owners of the plants will improve the working conditions for the children. He tells Mary to just forget about it. "It's a different world over here," he says. "When in Rome, do as the Romans do."

Should Mary and her superiors ignore the gross differences in the approach to child labour between Canada and some developing countries?

By contrast with relativism, *ethical pluralism* accepts the existence of different moral standards but focuses more on emphasizing the underlying common ground among cultures and ethical standards, thereby narrowing the range of apparent differences between cultures and communities and building ethical convergence around shared ideals. More *moderate relativists* inhabit some of the same ground, respecting differences while placing limits on tolerance for the application of certain standards, especially where significant abuses of rights or interests are evident. This opens the way to ethical argument and the demand that proponents of particular standards be prepared to defend and justify those standards in ways that people from other communities or cultural traditions can engage. This is quite a jump from the more common ethical relativism, which downplays ethical justification in favour of tolerance of multiple standards.

This book is an attempt to explore the pluralism of our views about how public servants should act and to point out areas of agreement and disagreement. But the fact of ethical pluralism and society's tolerance for different ethical views should not be seen to lend strength to the advocates of ethical relativism. The fact that we have not yet reached a consensus on whether a practice is right or wrong does not mean that we won't eventually or that we shouldn't try to do so.

Justifying Moral Choices

Assuming that public servants must justify their ethical choices and that this effort is not doomed by relativism, how should this be done? Some public officials take a rather rough-and-tumble approach to deciding whether a particular action is right or wrong. Their simple operating rule is: "Don't do anything you wouldn't want to read about in your local newspaper in the morning." This maxim is a variation on advice that President Harry Truman gave to a Senate committee witness during the Second World War: "Generals should never do anything that needs to be explained to a Senate committee" (Drucker 1981, p. 28). The "ethics of prudence," as Peter Drucker refers to it, directs public officials to "shun actions that cannot easily be understood, explained or justified" (p. 28).

While this approach to ethical decision making may have a certain populist charm, its democratic base is also its undoing. As Drucker (1981) points out:

> Concern with what one can justify becomes, only too easily, concern with appearances — Machiavelli was by no means the first to point out that in a "Prince," that is, in someone in authority and high visibility, appearances may matter more than substance. The ethics of prudence thus easily decay into the hypocrisy of "public relations." (p. 28)

Unfortunately, a negative reaction by the public to the media's portrayal of your decision does not make it the wrong ethical choice. The obverse is equally true. Right and wrong cannot necessarily be determined or justified by votes or opinion polls.

As noted, we also start from the premise that when we make a moral argument in favour of a particular action we are doing more than reflecting a personal belief or stating a command. We are saying that there are good reasons to take this action and that these reasons should make this action (at least in these particular circumstances) morally obligatory for everyone. Let's also start from the premise that an ethical justification has to be comprehensible and accessible to those who hear it. It is for this reason that divine revelation is not an acceptable form of ethical justification – at least for public servants in their professional lives. When you are working with colleagues and affected stakeholders in or around the public sector, you need robust arguments to back up your position on what could conceivably be life-and-death situations. This means, then, that we may ultimately need to engage one or more normative ethical theories to justify the rule that we are establishing or following, to support the actions that we recommend or to criticize the actions, recommendations or decisions of other public officials.

Different ethical theories provide different perspectives on the ethical defensibility of an action, and we see reflections of various theories in the different approaches to ethical problem solving visible to us in the public service. Deontologists, or *duty theorists*, look outside nature for support for ethical assertions, finding it in *a priori* laws and reason, divine law and intuition. For duty theorists, the nature of the act itself (e.g., lying) is far more relevant to its justification or condemnation than the consequences which flow from it. *Duty ethics* finds its public service resonance in the standards of behaviour laid down for public servants in the Constitution, law and policy (Rohr 1999). Here the emphasis is on following rules that have been established through reason, revelation or intuition, without making calculations of consequences.

Consequentialists, on the other hand, defend an action as right by relating it to observable phenomena such as the hedonistic satisfaction of desire, the production of pleasure for the greatest number or the fostering of historical progress. The consequential approach grounds ethical action in human nature and the fulfilment of biological and social needs: an action or rule is right because of its propensity to produce good outcomes. *Consequentialism* encourages public servants to base their ethical choices on outcomes rather than trusting to the duty to observe established rules. As an approach to ethical decision making, consequentialism relates closely to the professional capacity of public servants to analyse and discuss the impacts of proposed actions on those who will be affected by them.

Virtue ethics focus on the development within the individual of morally desirable characteristics, or virtues, which will strengthen their capacity to make virtuous choices when confronted by ethical dilemmas. It is not so much a way of justifying choices as an attempt to assure that individuals develop the character traits required to make good ones. One sees reflections of virtue theory in the public service in the increasing reliance on value statements (rather than rules) emphasizing values or virtues that should guide the actions of public servants.

While these three theoretical perspectives are the most commonly employed in justifying hard choices made by professionals such as doctors, lawyers and public servants, there are other relevant ethical theories which have emerged or re-emerged in recent years (as did virtue ethics) to complement consequential and duty ethics or deal with their perceived shortcomings. These include *feminist ethics* and, in the context of public service, the closely related *ethics of care*. As variations on virtue ethics, both of these approaches feature virtues or values (e.g., nurturing, cooperation, sharing, peace) that are more communal (as opposed to individualistic) in character and more attuned to the concept of care and the building and sustaining of relationships (Held 1987; Held 2006). The ethics of care is particularly relevant to the approach public servants might take to social policy issues such as poverty and homelessness as well as the structuring and management of work relationships in a bureaucratic setting (Noddings 2002; Robinson 1999). *Contractarianism*, another prominent stream of moral theory, complements both duty ethics and consequentialism by proposing circumstances and ways in which individuals and groups might rationally cooperate to seek and maintain moral agreements on principles or actions that enhance human dignity or maximize benefits for all stakeholders with the least disruption to their individual or group interests (Gauthier 1986; Rawls 1971).

Duty Ethics

"Why shouldn't you do that? Because it's against the rules!" One simple response to a request for justification is to indicate that the action you are recommending or taking does or does not violate the rules or principles of right behaviour established in your public sector workplace. "Since the focus of our inquiry is the ethics of one very specific role, it seems that the moral foundation we are looking for must be tailored to the demands of that limited role" (Rohr 1976, p. 400). From this premise, John Rohr goes on to argue that public servants should base their justification of right and wrong behaviour on the rules of the regime within which they work. In Canada, the most basic rules for a public servant would be found in the Constitution, the Charter of Rights and Freedoms, the law, regulations, Supreme Court decisions, an oath of office, policy directives and written standards of ethical conduct for his or her particular public service. Thus principles such as "avoid conflict of interest," "be politically neutral" and government-endorsed statements of rights such as freedom of expression for all citizens create obligatory restraints on the behaviour of public servants or positive obligations to act (unless trumped by another more significant duty).

Advocates of duty ethics would be sympathetic to this approach – even if they were not persuaded that all of the rules that public servants are asked to embrace are morally defensible. This important theory of ethical justification focuses on the nature of the action itself – on what is *right*, as distinct from and more important than what is *good*. Actions are right because they are intrinsically or inherently right (or not wrong), not because of the social good they produce. Two important features of contemporary duty ethics are its reliance on overriding moral rules and its respect for human dignity, characterized by the autonomy, independence and rights of each individual. For duty theorists, the dignity of individuals as individuals is more important than the maximization of the overall good of the society.

The duty school of ethical justification covers a wide spectrum of approaches. *Natural law* theorists (e.g., Thomas Aquinas, John Locke) see basic moral rules as reflecting the inclinations that have been instilled in each human being by God or nature. We discover the obligations to be honest, tell the truth, preserve human life, act fairly and keep promises through revelation, reason, or empirical observation; we follow such precepts regardless of their consequences because they represent a divine or natural standard of right human behaviour.

Another variation on this theme is *intuitionism*. W.D. Ross (1930) and others argue that a number of key ethical rules or constraints are self-evident; that is to say, they are plainly true to a rational, mature person. These include utilitarian principles, such as promoting the happiness of oneself and others and refraining from harm to other people, as well as more traditional standards, such as telling the truth, keeping promises, and showing gratitude. Jane Jacobs' (1992) commandments for public officials, including "be obedient and disciplined," "respect hierarchy," "be loyal" and "deceive for the sake of the task" are based on intuition and history (p. Appendix). Intuition, tradition and constitutional convention are also the source of most of the codes of conduct that have been developed for specific public services. For example, the obligation to be politically neutral is supported by the constitutional ideal of a professional, career public service disengaged from the struggles between political parties or particular politicians vying to form the Government.

As the previous paragraph betrays, intuitionists do not always agree on which rules are self-evident. But they do come together around the notion that such rules represent *prima facie* duties; in other words, they are duties that must be carried out unless more compelling moral obligations intervene. They argue that this approach is more defensible than consequentialism (which we will examine shortly) because it recognizes the fact that principles other than those relating to consequences are important to people when they confront moral choices.

Immanuel Kant developed the most widely known version of the argument that right and wrong can (and must) be determined without reference to the consequences of particular actions. According to Kant, moral law is to be found not in intuition, but in human reason. To be moral is to act rationally. Since reason is common to all human beings, moral duty would be the same for each individual, and each individual has within himself or herself the capacity to discover morality. Therefore ethics articulates rationally based moral principles, which all rational individuals would be bound to follow. Kant would not feel bound by moral rules gaining legitimacy simply by being dictated by intuition or an external authority such as a church or government.

Then how do we discover whether a specific action or rule is morally defensible? Kant's rational tool or test for determining morality is the categorical imperative. An action or rule is right (and becomes a duty) if it meets the criteria set down for a *categorical imperative*. These criteria are reflected in three complementary but distinct formulations.

A rule is right if it can be made universal. Conversely, an action or rule would be morally wrong if you could not accept the notion of everyone following it. Kant did not want a person to act in ways that would make that person an exception. He famously applied this formulation of the categorical imperative test to the question: is it permissible to lie? He argues that it is not permissible because, as a public servant, if I intentionally mislead a supervisor, colleague or stakeholder, then I must be willing to have everyone lie in similar circumstances. But widespread lying would erode trust and put me in the position of endorsing a practice that would undermine the effectiveness or credibility of the lie I wanted to tell. This would be self-contradictory and irrational and therefore not morally defensible (Ellis 1998, pp. 99-100). Imagine applying this test to difficult choices you might face. Suppose you use your discretion to provide emergency shelter funds to a social assistance client. Would that be defensible if funds were limited and therefore you could not provide similar funding to every client in similar circumstances? How would a rule forbidding or allowing such behaviour be framed? The universalization test is particularly critical when applied to actions a public servant might be considering when that public servant has a personal interest that might influence his or her decision. As we shall see when we examine the problem of conflict of interest more closely, this disability is best dealt with by disclosing the possible conflict and thus opening up your choice to a more disinterested and rational consideration involving colleagues and superiors.

An action or rule is right if it treats individuals as ends in themselves. This formulation focuses our attention on the idea that all persons are rational beings and cannot, therefore, be used by us – in our private or official capacities – as means to an end. The emphasis here is on equality and the irrationality of our being allowed to create rules or act in ways that deprive others of their rights. These rights include, for many commentators, not only the basic rights to life, freedom and property, but the wider spectrum of political, legal, economic and social rights fostered by contemporary liberal democracies. We are regularly confronted with cases in which the potentially positive and widespread societal consequences of actions are juxtaposed against claims that the action will have corrosive effects on "the integrity of the person as a freely choosing entity" (Fried 1978, p. 109). Kant and others want to draw our attention to the significance of the dignity of the individual. Duty theorists are not impressed by rules or actions that may create good outcomes for some stakeholders but offend the dignity of others. Thus, state policies or rules allowing for activities as diverse as assisted suicide, fracking to release natural gas, unrestrained business monopolies, insider trading, tax reductions for the wealthy and widespread monitoring of Internet use may not pass muster with a duty ethicist if they offend the dignity and limit the freedom of some of those affected by them. We can see strong echoes of this formulation of the categorical imperative test in many codes of conduct for public servants. The federal *Values and Ethics Code for the Public Sector,* for instance, states that "Treating all people with respect, dignity and fairness is fundamental to our relationship with the Canadian public" (Treasury Board of Canada Secretariat 2012, n.p.). The Alberta public service code makes respect one of its core values, indicating an intention to "foster an environment in which each individual is valued and heard" (Alberta 2012, p. 3).

A final variation on this theme is that a rule is right if you would be prepared to have that rule directed at yourself. Put another way, you should have a duty to act as if you were a member of a wider community and might become the subject of the action you are proposing. If you are contemplating setting a new rule to reduce welfare payments to single parents, would you still be prepared to recommend that rule if you might wake up in the morning as a welfare recipient trying to raise two children alone on the reduced payment levels? Similarly, would you approve of intrusive violations of personal privacy to fight terrorism or radical political action if you would be the subject of such intrusions? And finally, would you, as an executive of Canada Post, approve a policy of wage differentials for male and female employees doing the same work if you might find yourself a female employee working alongside male colleagues in one of the corporation's sorting operations? This formulation of the categorical imperative test places a high priority on the concepts of fairness and reciprocity and, to borrow a now famous phrase from John Rawls, insists that we make decisions about public policy and administrative practice from behind a "veil of ignorance" concerning our own place in society (Rawls 1971, p. 22).

The parallels between the categorical imperative – or ultimate moral principle – and the golden rule (do unto others as they should do unto you), the Confucian rule of reciprocity, and Rabbi Hillel's saying (what is hateful to you do not do to your neighbour) seem obvious and significant to some (but not to all) observers. They see contemporary duty ethics as a reason and individual centred restatement (or "ghost") of the traditional Judeo-Christian morality founded on the divinely revealed commandments (MacIntyre 1981, p. 105).

How useful is duty ethics to public servants looking to justify the rules they observe or the actions they choose? While it is "intuitively" attractive to think that we could establish principles of professional conduct which were so solid that we had a duty to observe them without reference to consequences, that may not be an easy end to achieve.

The first problem is one that is foundational. If a fundamental principle (e.g., treat people as ends) is not indubitably proved, then why should it be viewed as the ultimate arbiter of right and wrong? The fact that duty theorists do not agree on the tests for the establishment of "categorical" rules suggests that none of the various sources of duties – revelation, reason, intuition, common sense, hypothetical social contracts, constitutional convention, tradition, etc. – provides adequate guides to ultimate moral criteria.

The second problem is the capacity of duty ethics advocates to deal with clashes of duties. Duty ethics provides little assistance when you are faced with the situation where rules are in conflict or the dignity and rights of two different groups or individuals cannot *all* be protected by rules applicable to the situation. If all such rules are categorical, how can we say that one rule is more significant than another? For instance, increasing the right of some citizens to have access to information held by government may decrease the right to privacy of other individuals, groups and corporations. Both rights may be legitimate according to a duty theory litmus test, but the test doesn't help us much with the issue of settling conflicts between rules designed to protect those rights.

Third, and related to the previous point, following categorical rules can lead to patently bad outcomes. The classic examples of telling a murderer the truth about the location of his intended victim, or protecting the rights of a single terrorist thus endangering the lives of many citizens seem ethically perverse to both potential victims and neutral observers. The duty ethics focus on the protection of individual rights can also significantly narrow the potential scope of state action, limiting it to initiatives that do not offend the basic rights of anyone (Nozick 1974). This limitation can also contribute to perverse outcomes like the denial, for instance, of the capacity of the state to raise taxes. Such examples suggest a serious deficiency in this rules-based approach to ethical justification.

Finally, there is a concern about process and mechanics. The establishment of rules, especially using the rigorous standards laid down by Kant, is a demanding business. Would the attempt to create universal rules of behaviour in the complex world of public service not end up in almost endless debate about the precise circumstances in which the rules would be defensible?

Focusing on Consequences

Consequentialism takes the polar opposite approach to ethical justification, arguing that we should focus our attention not on the rightness of actions themselves, but on their outcomes – the creation of public good or the reduction of harm. This is a pragmatic approach to making tough ethical choices which focuses on the particulars of the situation, generally rejects making absolutist statements about how to behave, attaches no special significance to the protection of individual rights, usually ignores a moral agent's intentions and focuses instead on impartial calculation of the effect of proposed actions on all affected stakeholders. In the public service context, that calculation should be "agent-neutral," that is, the weighting of the benefits or costs of consequences should not be affected by the interests of the evaluator. This opens up the possibility of productive debate among interested parties about the potential impacts of an action (who benefits, who is wronged and how?) and about why, on balance, those impacts make the action right or wrong. Consequentialism accepts the fact that in the public sector, the solution of true ethical dilemmas can represent a compromise and feature winners and losers, with the former outnumbering the latter in good decisions.

Public servants, with their analytical skills and their obligation to foster the public interest, have a natural affinity for this approach to ethical decision making. Environmental, health, security and social policy are dedicated to enhancing the quality of life and minimizing harm to citizens. Evaluations of government programs focus on the analysis of benefits and costs. Welfare economics draws heavily on utilitarian ethics. We increasingly see our courts speaking in the language of consequences, demanding that lawyers in rights cases (including those focused on the political rights of public servants) demonstrate the harm or good that a law or regulation does. Consequentialists are active participants in debates about criminal laws establishing stronger punishments for criminal offenders, questioning the efficacy of such laws and, therefore, the moral basis for a retributive approach to sentencing. Kymlicka (2002) notes that consequentialism "seems to provide a straightforward method for resolving moral questions. Finding the morally right answer becomes a matter of measuring changes in human welfare, not of consulting spiritual leaders or relying on obscure traditions" (p. 12).

Classical 19th century utilitarianism as initially formulated by Jeremy Bentham is the most well-known form of consequentialist ethical theory. The basic thesis driving classical utilitarianism is: what is right is the rule or action that produces – or tends to produce – the greatest amount of good, utility or usefulness for the greatest number of people in particular circumstances. Utility originally was defined in terms of happiness as a balance of pleasure over pain. Thus, the essence of moral calculus is to determine which course of action creates the most happiness for the greatest number of stakeholders – that is, *everyone* who is significantly affected by that action now and in the future. Equality is a key component of the utilitarian calculus. The focus is on maximizing the happiness of all. No particular person's or group's happiness is any more important than the good of any other person or group. As Bentham is said to have put it, "everybody to count for one, nobody for more than one."

Most proponents of this approach want to calculate the consequences of individual actions or decisions (act utilitarians), while others (rule utilitarians) are content to endorse rules that have tended consistently in the past to produce the greatest good. The latter approach removes the need to apply a detailed analysis to each action contemplated but also opens up the need to consider exceptions when following a rule in certain circumstances would lead to perverse results, thus lapsing into act utilitarianism. Regardless of the variation adopted, the common thread is the identification of the right action – one's duty – with that alternative which creates the greatest good or the least harm for the greatest number of people.

Contemporary consequentialism has moved away from some aspects of classical utilitarianism but still retains the strong focus on the basic notion that the morality of an act should be determined by its impact on human well-being. There has been considerable debate about how to define utility, driven by the criticism that the maximization of happiness can lead to the adoption of seemingly perverse policies (e.g., providing drugs that produce pleasure rather than providing opportunities to lead a more productive life). Defining utility in terms of stakeholders' *expressed interests or preferences* potentially gets round this problem but also raises questions for some about the connection between expressed preferences and what people ultimately view as worthwhile. These questions might be dealt with by defining utility in terms of *informed or rational preferences*, "those preferences which are based on full information and correct judgements, while filtering out those which are mistaken and irrational" (Kymlicka 2002, p. 16). This approach places a strong obligation on public officials to share information with affected stakeholders whose interests or preferences they are trying to establish, to counter misinformation and propaganda, and to engage in dialogue as part of the effort to maximize the informed preference satisfaction of all affected stakeholders. It may also be possible for a government (and public servants) to partially get round the challenge of identifying the optimal interest maximizing strategy by providing options within a specific policy initiative so that individuals affected by a new program or set of regulations are presented with a variety of ways to maximize their satisfaction. Pragmatism, experiment, public engagement and reliance on evidence are hallmarks of the application of contemporary consequential ethics in the public sector.

Other related problems with the consequentialist approach are well known. Anyone familiar with the complexities of cost-benefit or risk-benefit analysis applied to even an apparently simple problem will appreciate the mechanical difficulties confronting calculations of probable long-term outcomes in the context of a complicated moral dilemma. Identifying everyone who is likely to be significantly affected either directly or indirectly by a decision, clarifying, aggregating and weighting their various interests or preferences, establishing all the likely consequences of the various alternative strategies designed to meet these interests, and calculating net benefits and costs in the context of interests expressed are not likely to be simple tasks in most instances. They are also tasks that can be compromised by previous commitments and loyalties of the responsible public official to one or more stakeholders (e.g., one's supervisor, a specific community or group).

Mechanical difficulties associated with implementation are not enough to sink any ethical theory. As noted, rule utilitarians would argue that it isn't necessary to do detailed analysis in most cases because past experience often suggests a rule of behaviour which, if followed, generally produces good outcomes in the circumstances presently being confronted. But consequentialism faces other more substantive challenges. It is argued by some that consequentialism does not clarify whether very positive outcomes for a small number of stakeholders should outweigh exposure to a degree of risk for many. Put another way, consequentialism, in its fixation with maximizing public good, seems to some critics to be overly preoccupied with efficiency and indifferent to distributional considerations involving merit and need. This concern is related to the charge that consequentialism may occasionally favour actions that violate our basic sense of justice. The classic example is the sheriff who chooses to turn a suspected criminal over to a lynch mob because to do otherwise would precipitate a riot and lead to the loss of several lives. This consequentially based decision, it is argued, flies in the face of the widely accepted notion that it is the sheriff's duty to protect prisoners in his custody. It raises the wider criticism that consequentialism focuses too much on the outcomes or ends (it is called "end-point ethics" by some) and ignores the means by which these ends are achieved – which can include in some circumstances the oppression of minorities.

Consequentialists counter arguments such as these by pointing out that simple examples often misrepresent the consequential calculus. A consequentialist would argue, for instance, that if the goal of maintaining and increasing respect for the law or a right was seen as an important consideration by the stakeholders, then that interest would become a major factor in the sheriff's decision. Some consequentialists temper their analysis of the wider good by a commitment to the protection of widely agreed upon rights. However, others would insist that no right or duty is sacred; you can justify the violation of a widely respected duty (e.g., the protection of prisoners) if the benefits of doing so clearly outweigh the costs of adhering to that practice in particular circumstances.

Similarly, it would be noted that a sophisticated consequentialist is not blind to distributional considerations. Given the diminishing marginal utility of any good, the consequential calculus is bound to discount the illegitimate preferences of the minority to have all the resources for themselves in favour of a more equal distribution of goods to the majority. Because of the significance attached to individual self-esteem by consequentialists, there is a strong presumption in favour of equal treatment.

Consequentialism remains a defensible approach to ethical decision making, and it is particularly suited to circumstances in which public officials are faced with the responsibility of helping to determine what action is right for a large group of employees, a whole community or even the whole country. Thomas Nagel (1978) famously argued that the demand that public officials be impartial and treat the interests of all relevant stakeholders equally justifies according a greater weight to the consideration of outcomes in public morality than would be the case in private morality. Peter Singer (1979), looking at a series of difficult social policy issues, echoes this point, arguing that the imperative attached to treating the interests of every affected citizen equally "requires me to weigh up all these interests and adopt the course of action most likely to maximize the interests of those affected. Thus I must choose the course of action which has the best consequences, on balance, for all affected" (p. 12).

Virtually all public servants intuitively resonate to the premium attached in democratic societies to being able to defend actions or rules in terms of their impacts on all affected stakeholders in specific situations. The consequential approach to establishing the public good and testing specific rules of conduct fits nicely with the roles of public servants as impartial advisors to political superiors, providers of services to the public, enforcers of laws and evaluators of state action. Brady (2003) argues that a public servant "may like to act on principle, but her experience tells her the situations she has encountered are so rich with relevant detail that acting on principle just feels too stubborn" (p. 531). Robert Goodin (1995) supports this argument and has harsh words for those who would ignore this reality:

> It would be simply irresponsible of public officials (in any broadly secular society, at least) to adhere mindlessly to moral precepts read off some sacred list, literally "whatever the consequences." Doing right though the heavens may fall is not (nowadays, anyway) a particularly attractive posture for public officials to adopt. (p. 10)

Virtue Ethics

Virtue ethics has emerged in recent years as an antidote to the apparent standoff between duty and consequential ethics. The biggest impact of virtue ethics in most public services has been the contemporary trend to place less emphasis on enunciating detailed rules of behaviour in codes of conduct, and more emphasis on statements of values or virtues that should imbue an "excellent" public servant. For instance, the federal government's *Values and Ethics Code for the Public Sector* "outlines the values and expected behaviours that guide public servants in all activities...These values are a compass to guide public servants in everything they do" (Treasury Board of Canada Secretariat 2012, n.p.). *The Alberta Public Service Vision and Values Handbook* states: "Our four core values of Respect, Accountability, Integrity and Excellence guide our decisions and actions in achieving our vision" (Alberta 2012, n.p.).

Virtues have been defined as "character traits or dispositions in a person that embody and express values that are judged desirable or admirable. A person's virtues define the *ethical character* of a person" (Lombardo 2008, p. 5, emphasis in original). Public sector ethics scholars (e.g., Cooper 2006, Garofalo and Geuras 1999, Hart 1994, Lynch 2004, Preston 1998) have recognized the importance of virtue ethics to public service. Thomas Lynch (2004) notes that virtue ethics is relevant for the field of public administration "because its professional purpose is the benevolent pursuit of the public interest. Those in public administration can and should use and develop virtues such as justice, courage, and truthfulness to help them counter the common institutional temptations that drive lesser ethical people to seek wealth, fame, and power instead of advancing the public interest" (p. 32). Other public ethics scholars have specified the core virtues of public service as honour, justice and benevolence (Denhardt 1991), or prudence, justice, fortitude and temperance (Hart 1994). Preston et al. (2002) view integrity as the main core virtue "because it requires a commitment to something beyond oneself; in the case of public administration, this commitment is to the public interest in the context of democratic governance and the fundamental principles of the good society" (p. 30). Similarly, using the language of values rather than virtues, the 1996 federal Task Force on Values and Ethics describes integrity as one of the most fundamental public service values in that it involves holding "a public trust and putting the common good before private interest or advantage" (Canadian Centre for Management Development 1996, p. 56).

How does virtue ethics help the public servant decide what to do when faced with an ethical dilemma? Most simply put, correct behaviour would be defined in terms of adherence to the bundle of interconnected ideal traits, values or virtues that define the character of an "excellent" public servant and that have been adopted and internalized over time. So right action is character-driven and determined by the set of prescribed virtues that the individual public servant facing the dilemma has embraced. Adherents of virtue ethics ask what would constitute good behaviour for the virtuous public servant. "An action is right if and only if it is what an agent with a virtuous character would do in the circumstances" (Oakley and Cocking 2001, p. 31).

While virtue theorists make no reference to consequences or to universalizable rules or principles when deciding what good behaviour is in a specific situation, Hursthouse (1999) reminds us that the specification of what virtuous action is can look very much like the statement of a rule: "Each virtue generates an instruction – 'Do what is honest', 'do what is charitable'; and each vice a prohibition – 'Do not act, do what is dishonest, uncharitable'" (p. 17). Most statements of public service values do expand on the meaning of a particular value by setting out rules of behaviour that a person imbued with a specific value would follow. Connecting values and rules in this way suggests that virtue and duty approaches to solving ethical dilemmas may face similar challenges.

The first of these challenges – clearly mirroring a problem faced by duty theorists – is sorting out precisely what makes up the bundle of admirable character traits that a good public servant should embrace. Oakley and Cocking (2001) provide a strong defence of the application of virtue ethics in professional settings, but they note that virtue may not be "clear or detailed enough to serve as the basis of a criterion of rightness." They ask:

> How do we determine what the basic virtues are, and so, what a virtuous agent would be like? What would a virtuous agent do in the great variety of situations in which people find themselves? Further, there is a plurality of virtuous character-traits, and not all virtuous people seem to have these traits to the same degree, so virtuous people might not always respond to a particular situation in the same way. (p. 31)

Oakley and Cocking note that for virtue ethicists, "which character-traits count as virtuous is determined by their involvement in human flourishing or their admirability" (p. 32). In the public sector, to sort out a defensible set of character traits you would need to clarify your views of the proper role of government in society, the role and goals of a public servant in that conception of government and the interrelated set of character traits or virtues required to optimize the performance of that professional role. A number of public sector organizations in Canada have put considerable effort into establishing the "value" combination that should define the exemplary public servant. For example, the federal Task Force on Public Service Values and Ethics developed an eloquent analysis of the changing nature of the roles and responsibilities of federal public servants and on that basis set out an extensive list of core public service democratic, professional, ethical and people values (Canadian Centre for Management Development 1996). The recommendations of the Task Force resulted in the adoption in 2003 of a *Values and Ethics Code for the Public Service*, which was subsequently updated as a *Values and Ethics Code for the Public Sector* (Treasury Board of Canada Secretariat 2012). The Alberta public service went through a similar exercise in 2005-6, resulting in the establishment of a public service vision and values statement (Alberta Public Service 2012).

Obviously, attempts to specify the collection of values that should define the admirable public servant are not without controversy, especially in a period in which the nature of public service is argued to be changing rapidly (Aucoin 1997; Langford 2004). One of the most pressing issues in this context is the establishment of the legitimacy of those virtues or values which are chosen. As Pettit (1991) notes in reference to virtue ethics more generally, "[i]t is one thing to make a list of values which allegedly require honouring...It is another to say why these values are so very different from the ordinary run of desirable properties" (p. 38).

Another challenge confronting virtue ethics as a guide to ethical behaviour for public servants is the interaction among the bundle of virtues that in their totality define the character of the exemplary public servant. In circumstances in which different values counsel acting in different ways, how is a virtuous public servant to choose which voice to follow? Terry Cooper (1982) approvingly quotes Rowland Egger on this important question: "An administrator needs 'some bench marks for relating the various and frequently conflicting claims of competing values which enter into his official actions'" (p. 54). Ralph Heintzman (2007) acknowledges that "there are no short cuts or handy tools for consistently prioritizing values, or deciding whether a rule or action is defensible" (p. 587), but he observes that the Task Force on Public

Service Values and Ethics "clearly thought the democratic values and the notion of the public interest could help to sort out the priority of values in specific circumstances" (p. 588). Similarly, Cooper (2006) suggests that at the level of ethical analysis a public servant should consider "all other commitments and values" in relation to the basic principle of the public interest. "Ultimately the principle of democracy and the integrity of democratic government are also at stake" (p. 25).

When a public servant faces a dilemma involving competing values, John Rohr (1976) argues that "he will have to choose the position he finds most appealing and persuasive...Just how those values are interpreted is a decision only the bureaucrat himself can make" (pp. 404-405). For the cynical public servant, a collection of core values affords an opportunity to "value shop" (Langford 2004, p. 439). It is argued that the longer the list, the more likely it is that a public servant, facing a hard choice or questions from superiors about an action taken, could rationalize his or her position by adhering to one core value rather than another. Even among responsible public servants, one might advance the value of service in a particular situation, another might see the value of accountability as dominant, and still another might feel compelled by the demands of fairness. On the other hand, "renewed attention to public service values" makes "us more aware... of the conflicts and tensions that already exist in the concrete world in which we have to act. Public servants who do not realize they function in a world in which, say, democratic values may be in tension with, say, professional values are stumbling in the dark" (Heintzman 2007, p. 585).

Virtue ethics is appealing because it appears to offer the opportunity to forego complex calculations of consequences and the legitimization of rules and focus instead on building character through such means as ethics education, practical public service experience and statements of values. As explained above, the virtue ethics approach, like the duty and consequential ones, has weaknesses as an approach to ethical justification. Indeed, none of these approaches is entirely satisfactory, but they are also not entirely at war with each other. In many cases, applying any of the three approaches would bring you to the same conclusion (Garofalo and Geuras 2006, p. 112), and efforts have been made to integrate apparently conflicting ethical theories (Ellis 1998). The key feature of these ethical frameworks is that they force public servants to rise above laziness, bias, and the routine of following orders or rules without thought when faced with difficult ethical dilemmas. The most basic duty of a responsible public servant is to pay attention to such dilemmas and be ready to think ethically.

Looking Ahead to Problem-Solving

This chapter has attempted to establish the necessity of ethical choice and to assess various theoretical ways of analysing and defending the kinds of ethical choices that public servants confront. It started with the observations that public servants in most jurisdictions have a wide variety of directions provided to them by their employers about what good and bad behaviour look like. In many instances they can simply follow those rules. But sometimes the rules don't cover the problem, provide contradictory guidance or would appear to counsel action which would cause significant harm. In such circumstances public servants need to be able to draw on ethical decision-making frameworks to help them sort out what an ethically defensible response looks like. The thumbnail sketches of three important ethical theories do not presume to provide public servants with the equipment they need to become sophisticated ethical analysts. But these sketches should make public servants sensitive to what is at stake and how they might begin thinking when confronted with a genuine moral dilemma.

First, how do we know if we are confronting a serious moral dilemma? The primary requirement is that the issue be *controversial*. In other words, there has to be evidence that there is a lack of agreement about what right behaviour looks like. The moral agent, the individual faced with deciding what to do, can see moral reasons for taking more than one action but is forced to choose only one. The second requirement is that the resolution of the issue has the potential of *significantly harming stakeholders* by affecting their health or safety, diminishing a significant right or claim, misusing resources, etc. Thus, whether or not to mislead the public about the health risks of a vaccination in order to ensure that as many people as possible are vaccinated represents an important moral dilemma. On the other hand, whether or not to force cyclists to wear a helmet may not qualify. The former raises significant questions about benefits vs. harm, personal freedom, honesty and informed consent, whereas the loss of freedom involved for the unwilling helmet-wearer may be seen by most people as little more than an inconvenience in the face of the obvious benefits that the regulation would create for all stakeholders.

Once a potential ethical dilemma is recognized, what steps should the responsible public servant take? An orderly approach to reaching a "reflective equilibrium" – inspired by a process set out by Peter Brown (1981) – might include the following:

- *Clarifying the facts of the situation.* Many apparent ethical dilemmas disappear when the facts are made clear. For example, establishing that a public servant's second job does not interfere with the performance of his or her public duties makes it clear that there is no potential for harm and no dilemma to be concerned about.

- *After establishing that there is an ethical dilemma, coming up with an initial view on how to act.* As a professional you should be able to use your "moral imagination" (Werhane 1999) to establish what is at stake in the problem you confront, different ways in which you might respond and an option that you find defensible. For example, being asked by your superior to misrepresent some data in a presentation to the public may immediately provoke a sense of revulsion against lying which overwhelms a competing sense of loyalty to the employer and obligation to follow orders.

- *Checking your initial reaction against existing rules that seem to apply to the situation.* To do this successfully you need to be familiar with your oath of office, codes of conduct and value statements established by the government and any professional group to which you belong, as well as any relevant guidance set out in the Constitution, legislation, regulations and policy directives. This process works within the confines of existing rules and practices and does not question their appropriateness.

- *Bringing ethical theory to bear.* In some cases it will be difficult to establish a fit between an initial view about how to act and relevant rules. Perhaps no rules or a number of conflicting rules or values may appear to apply, or following a particular rule would in your view lead to indefensible harm. In such circumstances, the individual is forced to move to the level of fundamental ethical theory and seek guidance by asking some basic theory-driven questions about the alternative courses of action being considered and the relevant rules.

A brief example of an attempt to establish reflective equilibrium may help to bring this important process to life. Suppose an air safety analyst is faced with a situation in which his superiors in the transportation regulatory agency have reduced funding for aircraft safety inspection and refuse his request to release new data he has developed indicating that the risk of being involved in an accident is now much higher on certain small commuter airlines than on other carriers. The facts suggest that the analyst faces a serious ethical dilemma: travellers on these smaller airlines are making potentially dangerous travel plans because they do not have the access to relevant information which has been declared confidential and the agency is not able in the short run to increase levels of inspection required to lower the risk levels. The initial, intuitive view of the analyst is that a way must be found to provide that information to the travelling public. However, an important operative rule within the organization is to keep confidential information confidential. Moreover, this rule is endorsed by the analyst's oath of office and code of conduct. The code also stresses the public servant's duty of loyalty to the government. But the duties of confidentiality and loyalty to the employer may be contradicted by a duty under whistle blower protection legislation to report an action or omission that creates a substantial danger to public safety. The public servant reviews the facts, his initial view, and the applicable professional "commandments," but can find no way to bring them into harmony. He believes that his intuitive reaction is well grounded in a general moral obligation not to expose people to risk without their consent when there is an opportunity to reduce that risk, in this case through transparency or enhanced levels of inspection.

At this point he turns to his ethical tool kit for assistance. Looking at the problem from a consequentialist perspective, he sees that the risk to travellers is real but still statistically small. On the other hand, the release of the information might have a negative impact on the credibility and effectiveness of the agency, the profitability and viability of an important segment of the air transport industry and the businesses in the rural communities that depend on it. The expressed preference of these stakeholders (as well as his superiors) would be to keep silent and take steps over time to enhance safety. He has little hard data at this point on the informed preferences of affected travellers but suspects that few would support an outcome that increased their risks. From a duty perspective, however, he is impressed by the compelling power of the *prima facie* obligation not to expose people to risk without their informed consent. Moreover, he recognizes that he would see it as a fundamental violation of his rights to be placed in the situation of the average citizen making travel plans without access to the information in question. If inclined to think "virtuously," it would be surprising if the analyst didn't feel the tug of the values of transparency and honesty. He may even be a member of a self-regulating profession with a code of conduct espousing such values. Which way should he go to achieve "reflective equilibrium"? What should he do if he concludes that the information must be made available to the public, but his superiors do not agree?

As this example suggests, the interplay of facts, initial views, existing rules or accepted practices and ethical theories can be difficult to follow and may not lead to unequivocal answers. On the theory side, it is unusual in a controversial case for a particular consequential, virtue or categorical duty argument to decisively "trump" another. This is especially true in the team or committee context in which so many government decisions are made and so many perspectives may be represented. On the other side, however, for a public servant to ignore the obligation to confront difficult ethical dilemmas and simply subscribe to questionable directions or rules with the attendant risk of significant harm is to ignore the essence of responsible public service.

The first two chapters of this book have focused on, first, establishing the degree of personal moral responsibility a public servant bears for government decisions and actions to which he or she contributes and second, on reviewing fundamental ethical theories underpinning efforts to justify the choices he or she faces when confronting difficult choices. We dig deeper into both of these topics in chapter 3, where we discuss the public servant's obligation to pursue the public interest.

References

Alberta. (2012). *Alberta public service vision and values handbook.* Retrieved from http://chr.alberta.ca/apsvisionandvalues/ documents/manager-supervisor-handbook.pdf

Appiah, K. A. (2006). *Cosmopolitanism: Ethics in a world of strangers.* New York: W. W. Norton and Company.

Aucoin, P. (1997). A profession of public administration? A commentary on "A Strong Foundation." *Canadian Public Administration, 40*(1), 23-39.

Bennett, C. (2010). *What is this thing called ethics?* New York: Routledge.

Brady, F. N. (2003). "Publics" administration and the ethics of particularity. *Public Administration Review, 63*(5), 525-534.

Brandt, B. (1967). Ethical relativism. In P. Edwards (Ed.), *The encyclopedia of philosophy,* Vol. 3 (pp. 75-78). New York: Macmillan.

Brown, P. (1981). Assessing officials. In J. Fleishman et al. (Eds.), *Public duties: The moral obligations of government officials* (pp. 289-305). Cambridge, MA: Harvard University Press.

Canadian Centre for Management Development. (1996). *A strong foundation: Report of the task force on public service values and ethics*. Ottawa: CCMD. Retrieved from http://publications.gc.ca/collections/Collection/SC94-72-1996E.pdf

Cooper, T. L. (1982). *The responsible administrator*. Port Washington, NY: Kennikat Press.

Cooper, T. L. (2006). *The responsible administrator: An approach to ethics for the administrative role* (5th ed.). San Francisco: Jossey-Bass.

Crotty, M. (1998). *The foundations of social research: Meaning and perspective in the research process*. London: Sage.

De George, R. (1982). *Business ethics* (2nd ed.). New York: Macmillan Publishing.

Denhardt, K. (1991). Unearthing the moral foundations of public administration: Honor, benevolence and justice. In J. S. Bowman (Ed.), *Ethical frontiers in public management* (pp. 91-113). San Francisco: Jossey-Bass.

Drucker, P. (1981). What is "business ethics"? *Across the Board*, 18, 22-32.

Ellis, R. (1998). *Just results: Ethical foundations for policy analysis*. Washington: Georgetown University Press.

Fried, C. (1978). R*ight and wrong*. Cambridge, MA: Harvard University Press.

Garofalo, C., & Geuras, D. (1999). *Ethics in the public service: The moral mind at work*. Washington, DC: Georgetown University Press.

Garofalo, C., & Geuras, D. (2006). *Common ground, common future: Moral agency in public administration, professions and citizenship*. Boca Raton, FL: Taylor & Francis.

Gauthier, D. (1986). *Morals by agreement*. Oxford: Oxford University Press.

Goodin, R. E. (1995). *Utilitarianism as a public philosophy*. Cambridge, UK: Cambridge University Press.

Gowans, C. (2012). "Moral relativism" in The Stanford Encyclopedia of Philosophy. Retrieved from http://plato.stanford.edu/cgi-bin/encyclopedia/archinfo.cgi?entry=moral-relativism

Harrison, J. (1967). Ethical subjectivism. In P. Edwards (Ed.), *The encyclopedia of philosophy*, Vol. 3 (pp. 78-81). New York: Macmillan.

Hart, D. L. (1994). Administration and the ethics of virtue. In T. Cooper, (Ed.), *Handbook of Administrative Ethics*. New York: Marcel Dekker.

Heintzman, R. (2007). Public-service values and ethics: Dead end or strong foundation? *Canadian Public Administration, 50*(4), 573-602.

Held, V. (1987). Feminism and moral theory. In E. Kittay & D. Meyers (Eds.), *Women and moral theory* (pp. 111-128). Totowan, NJ: Rowman and Littlefield.

Held, V. (2006). *The ethics of care: Personal, political and global*. Oxford: Oxford University Press.

Hursthouse, R. (1999). *On virtue ethics*. Oxford: Oxford University Press.

Jacobs, J. (1992). *Systems of survival: A dialogue on the moral foundations of commerce and politics*. New York: Random House.

Kymlicka, W. (2002). *Contemporary political philosophy: An introduction* (2nd ed.). Oxford: Oxford University Press.

Langford, J. W. (2004). Acting on values: An ethical dead end for public servants. *Canadian Public Administration 47*(4), 429-450.

Lombardo, T. (2008). *Ethical character development and personal and academic excellence*. [Online workshop]. Retrieved from http://www.centerforfutureconsciousness.com/pdf_files/Readings/EthicalCharDevWrkshp.pdf

Lynch, T. D. (2004). Virtue ethics, public administration, and telos. *Global Virtue Ethics Review 5*(4), 32-49.

MacIntyre, A. (1981). *After virtue*. Notre Dame: University of Notre Dame Press.

Nagel, T. (1978). Ruthlessness in public life. In S. Hampshire (Ed.), *Public and private morality* (pp. 78-79). Cambridge, UK: Cambridge University Press.

Noddings, N. (2002). *Starting at home: Caring and social policy*. Berkeley, CA: University of California Press.

Nozick, R. (1974). *Anarchy, state and utopia*. New York: Basic Books.

Oakley, J., & Cocking, D. (2001). *Virtue ethics and professional roles*. New York: Cambridge University Press.

Pettit, P. (1991). Consequentialism. In P. Singer (Ed.), *A companion to ethics* (pp. 230-240). Oxford: Basil Blackwell.

Preston, N. (1998). Virtue and ethics for the public sector. *Professional Ethics 6(*3-4), 69-80.

Preston, N., & Sampford, C. with Connors, C. (2002). *Encouraging ethics and challenging corruption*. Sydney: The Federation Press.

Rawls, J. (1971). *A theory of justice*. Cambridge, MA: Harvard University Press.

Robinson, F. (1999). *Globalizing care: Towards a politics of peace*. Boston: Beacon Press.

Rohr, J. (1976). The study of ethics in the P.A. curriculum. *Public Administration Review, 36*(4), 398-406.

Rohr, J. (1999). *Public service ethics and constitutional practice*. Lawrence, KS: University Press of Kansas.

Ross, W. D. (1930). *The right and the good*. Oxford: Oxford University Press.

Singer, P. (1979). *Practical ethics*. Cambridge, UK: Cambridge University Press.

Treasury Board of Canada Secretariat. (2012). *Values and ethics code for the public sector*. Retrieved from http://www.tbs-sct.gc.ca/pol/doc-eng.aspx?id=25049&section=text#cha5

Werhane, P. (1999). *Moral imagination and management decision making*. New York: Oxford University Press.

Chapter 3

Acting in the Public Interest

> The notion of the public interest...is for the public
> service what justice and liberty are for the legal
> profession, or what healing and mercy are for
> the medical profession. (Canadian Centre for
> Management Development 1996, p. 37)

Public servants are frequently exhorted to "act in the public interest."
Yet there is substantial debate about what the public interest means and
whether it is a helpful guide to appropriate conduct for public servants.
Is the pursuit or the determination of the public interest really any of the
public servant's business? Do public servants have a duty to "speak
truth to power" when assisting politicians to decide what policy choices
are in the public interest? Do policy analysts and advisors pay enough
attention to the ethical dimension of public policy? In seeking the public
interest, how much risk should public officials take with the public?
Does the notion of the public interest offer practical guidance for public
servants who provide policy advice, assess risk and implement policy?
This chapter considers each of these questions.

The chapter expands on the discussion in chapter 1 of the
obligation of public servants to take responsibility for their actions and
inactions. It asks whether the public servant's moral responsibility to
act in the public interest extends beyond a duty not to contribute to
indefensible harm or wrongdoing to include a more positive obligation to
improve the lot of those affected by their actions. It also continues the
discussion of the ethical defensibility of recommendations and decisions
begun in chapter 2, showing how combining different approaches to the
public interest will allow a public servant to provide better advice and
make more defensible decisions.

The Utility of the Public Interest

Public servants receive conflicting messages regarding their duty to
act in the public interest. Frequently, they are advised or required
to establish what the public interest is and to safeguard it. On other
occasions, they are told that determining the public interest is the job of
elected politicians, not of public servants.

The message that public servants should seek out and protect the public interest is often set down in government statutes, regulations, guidelines and other documents. The term "public interest" is used 224 times in 84 federal statutes alone (MacNair 2006). For example, the federal *Consumer Packaging and Labelling Act* authorizes inspectors to refrain from seizing a product where, in their opinion, such seizure is not necessary in the public interest. The *Ontario Statutory Powers Procedure Act* (1990) allows closed hearings when the tribunal decides that the desirability of avoiding disclosures of certain information "in the public interest outweighs the desirability of adhering to the principle that hearings be open to the public" (s. 22).

Values statements and ethics codes often affirm the public servant's obligation to act in the public interest. The 2012 federal *Values and Ethics Code for the Public Sector* states that "[f]ederal public servants have a fundamental role to play in serving Canadians, their communities and the public interest" (Treasury Board of Canada Secretariat 2012, n.p.). The New Brunswick *Public Service Values and Conduct Guide* (2009) declares that "New Brunswick's public servants act in the public interest." A model code of conduct for municipal staff in Canada asserts that one of the Code's purposes is to "promote and protect the public interest" (Levine 2009, p. 92).

A different message to public servants is that the determination of the public interest is not their concern, but rather the concern of the elected officials to whom they report. According to the ethic of neutrality (Thompson 1985) explained in chapter 1, public servants do not have to exercise independent judgment as to the content of the public interest because they are expected to perform their duties in a neutral, objective and impartial manner. It is argued that they should simply implement policies decided upon by elected officials; and where public servants have authority to make decisions on their own, they should do so within a framework of values provided by these officials.

However, as we argued in chapter 1, the ethic of neutrality does not deal adequately with the contemporary role of public servants. It is widely recognized that public servants exercise significant power in the political system, both in developing public policies and in implementing them. As a result, public servants, especially those at the middle to upper levels of the administrative hierarchy, have many opportunities to make recommendations and decisions as to how the public interest can best be served (Denhardt and Denhardt 2003, ch. 4; Hamilton 2007, p. 11). Public servants exercise their substantial discretionary powers in several ways. They influence the content of legislation by initiating policy proposals and by preparing policy options at the request of political or administrative superiors; they pass regulations under authority delegated to them by ministers and legislators and they interpret, apply, clarify, amend, and enforce these regulations; they consult and negotiate with individuals and groups seeking to influence government decisions and expenditures; they mobilize support for their policies and programs; and they frequently question or resist courses of actions favoured by their political superiors. The power and influence wielded by public servants mean that the values and ethical standards they bring to their decisions and recommendations are extremely important to the determination of the public interest.

For some commentators, the degree to which public servants are exhorted to protect the public interest does little to mitigate a more fundamental problem – the elusiveness of the concept. Some theorists, who can be described as "abolitionists" (Cochran 1974), contend that the concept is so elusive as to be meaningless and irrelevant. Glendon Schubert (1960) argues that there is no "statement of public-interest theory that offers much promise either as a guide to public officials who are supposed to make decisions in the public interest, or to research scholars who might wish to investigate the extent to which governmental decisions are empirically made in the public interest" (p. 220). Arthur F. Bentley refers to the public interest and the general welfare as "mindstuff, appropriately discussed by writers of fiction who spun fantasies, but with no place in the reality which it was the business of the social scientist to explore" (quoted in Schubert 1957, p. 357).

The abolitionists emphasize the central importance of interest groups in politics. In their view, government decisions result from competition among the interests of individuals and groups seeking to maximize their self-interest. They claim that there is no such thing as the public interest or the common good; rather there are only the various interests of many publics. Moreover, they interpret interests as preferences or wants; thus, selfish interests cannot be distinguished from altruistic interests. Public choice theorists belong to the abolitionist school of thought. A central element of public choice theory is that all political actors, including public servants, act in a rational, self-interested manner. Thus, it is argued, bureaucratic behaviour can best be explained in terms of public servants seeking such selfish objectives as power, income and prestige. Such concepts as the public interest and the general will are viewed as "mystical notions" (Buchanan and Tullock 1962, p. 11). Even altruism is explained in terms of a self-interested search for personal satisfaction.

A different school of thought, whose proponents are described here as "preservationists," views the public interest as a viable and valuable concept. Most preservationists view people "as social beings who form associations, including political associations, for a better common life and not simply for private benefits" (Cochran 1974, p. 330). They do not just form interest groups seeking private interest; rather they form communities seeking a common good (the public interest). The preservationists believe that the concept of the public interest has important effects on the operation of political systems and on the content and implementation of public policies. They define the public interest in such terms as a "spur to conscience and to deliberation" (Pennock 1962, p. 182) and as "the highest ethical standard applicable to political affairs" (Cassinelli 1962, p. 46).

The public interest has been described as "a touchstone of motivation for public servants" (Canadian Centre for Management Development 1996, p. 37). Denhardt and Denhardt (2003) argue that "it is impossible to understand the depth and breadth of public service without a recognition of the role of the public interest" (pp. 67-68). Donald Warwick (1981), after examining five ethical principles providing guidance on public servants' exercise of administrative discretion, concludes that "[t]he first and most general principle is that the exercise of discretion should, on balance, serve the public interest" (p. 115). Moreover, among four kinds of "goods" commonly sought by public servants – public interest, constituency interests, bureaucratic interest, and personal interest – "the public interest must be paramount for the responsible administrator...In the end, the common good must stand above the other three goods and act as the arbiter of ethical ambiguities in the use of discretion" (p. 116).

CASE 3.1: PUBLIC INTEREST AND MOTIVATION

This discussion takes place between two federal public servants.

Dave: Morning, Bashir. Did you go skiing this weekend?

Bashir: No, I drove down to Toronto for the inaugural meeting of this new public sector service-delivery group.

Dave: Well, we had perfect powder for skiing. Why are you spending your free time doing government work? What's in it for you?

Bashir: There aren't any extrinsic rewards, but it's great to be surrounded by public servants dedicated to improving service delivery. We agreed to turn our community of practice into a formal organization to conduct research and share good practices.

Dave: But what's your motivation? Do you think that you have to work harder because you're now at a more senior level?

Bashir: Being more senior doesn't have much to do with it. The touchstone of my motivation as a public servant has always been the public interest. It's devotion to the public interest that motivates public servants to work beyond their formal job requirements.

Dave: I beg to differ. There are lots of motivations other than the public interest for working hard and doing a good job. Moreover, many public servants are motivated largely by self-interest. In my view, the public interest is a nebulous, touchy-feely notion that provides little incentive or guidance.

To what extent is the public interest a touchstone of motivation for public servants? Do most public servants act largely on the basis of self-interest most of the time?

The description of the public interest as a touchstone of motivation (featured in case 3.1) is in keeping with the construct of public service motivation (PSM) that has become an important theme in scholarly writings about human resource management (Perry and Hondeghem 2008). Public service motivation is often described as a public service ethic. It has been defined as "an individual's predisposition to respond to motives grounded primarily or uniquely in public institutions and organizations" (Perry and Wise 1990, p. 368). Commitment to the public interest is a central component of PSM (Perry 1996, p. 20). Research findings indicate that the higher a person's PSM level, the more likely that person is to be attracted to public sector employment (Alonso and Lewis 2001; Brewer et al. 2000; Crewson 1997; Hondeghem and Perry 2009; Perry 1997). After reviewing a large volume of empirical research on PSM, Vandenabeele (2009) asserted that "[t]he presence of PSM leads to higher levels of commitment and satisfaction for employees working in a public sector environment, thus rendering higher levels of performance" (p. 15). PSM is viewed as an alternative to the public choice approach to motivation – an approach that does not show why public sector employees "strive...support...and sacrifice on the job" (Dilulio 1994, p. 281).

Politicians, Public Servants and Public Interest

Public servants, in assisting elected officials to decide policy issues in the public interest and in making discretionary decisions of their own, should keep in mind that:

It is both inevitable and desirable for public
servants to make their own judgments about
the public interest. It is inevitable, because
the hundreds of operational, policy and
management decisions they make every day
necessarily involve some implicit or explicit
notion of what the public interest requires:
without such a notion the decisions would
not be good ones, or would be so only
accidentally. Public service judgment about
the public interest is also desirable, because,
without their own ideas about what the public
interest requires in specific circumstances,
public servants would not be able to provide
useful advice to ministers, nor would they
be able to identify the very few cases where
the divergence between political and public
service definitions of the public interest is
sufficiently grave to create a problem that must
be resolved in some way, depending on the
available tools. The only precondition for public
service judgments about the public interest
is a deep conviction that, when political and
public service ideas do not coincide, democratic
political judgment trumps public service
judgment. (Heintzman 2010, p. 52)

Thus, excluding situations in which indefensible harm would result, the
determination of the public interest should be left to elected officials.
The "faithful execution of democratic decisions is what a public service
is for, not to substitute for them some other definitions of the public
good...Public servants must remember what they are - delegates of
their minister. And what system they serve - a democratic one where
elected officials have legitimacy to define the public interest" (Canadian
Centre for Management Development 1996, pp. 16-17). In exercising
their discretion to make decisions, public servants should strive to
reflect or anticipate the wishes of political superiors. Moreover, in
making recommendations, public servants should set forth a range of
alternatives rather than a single or favoured option. A secretary to the
cabinet in a provincial government wrote to deputy ministers as follows:

The Premier and other members of Cabinet
are concerned that some recent Cabinet
submissions have presented only one option,

or the analysis of alternatives has been heavily
slanted towards one particular course of
action...The Premier feels...the need for every
Minister and Deputy to ensure that Cabinet is
presented with a set of realistic options when
being asked to make a decision. Single option
proposals do not assist the government in
making policy choices. (Ontario, Secretary of
the Cabinet, typescript, 1989)

Like their federal and provincial counterparts, municipal employees
are frequently urged to act in the public interest. Among the many
occupational groups in the municipal sphere, the municipal Chief
Administrative Officer (CAO) and professional planners play particularly
significant roles in influencing or determining the public interest.

The CAO occupies a critical position – "at the pinchpoint in the
hourglass between the council that makes policies and the public
servant who delivers them" (Siegel, forthcoming). Siegel's case studies
of five Canadian CAOs show the different ways in which municipal
leaders of high integrity can serve the public interest and in which they
deal with the admonition that they should not get too far out in front of
council. Judy Rogers, Vancouver's city manager, is described as treating
"both council and individual councillors with a great deal of respect, and
there was no question that she was loyal in implementing the wishes of
council. However, there was also a sense that she saw herself working
for the community and in that role wanted to ensure that council was
aware of community issues and needs" (Siegel, forthcoming, p. 137 of ms).

Compared to many other municipal employees, community
planners are conditioned by their training and professional affiliations
to be especially sensitive to public-interest considerations. "A dominant
view of the planning profession is that the planner's primary obligation is
to serve the public interest" (Hodge 1991, p. 354). Defining the public
interest is often challenging because "[p]oliticians will argue that voters
have sanctioned their views; citizen groups will argue that their 'grass
roots' views truly reflect the public interest; and planners may argue
that their comprehensive view of the community provides the best basis
for such a definition" (Hodge 1991, p. 355). Clashes often occur when
politicians believe that planners are placing undue emphasis on such
factors as public participation or environmental sustainability.

Speaking Truth to Power in the Public Interest

While public servants must in most circumstances respect the ultimate right of politicians to determine the public interest, they are expected to assist that determination by "speaking truth to power." This duty is captured by the political neutrality tenet set out in chapter 4 requiring public servants to provide forthright and objective advice to their political superiors in private and in confidence. The ability and willingness of public servants to fulfill this duty depend substantially on several other components of the political neutrality model. For example, ministers will be more inclined to seek, accept and trust the advice of public servants (other than their own political appointees) who have been selected on the basis of merit, who refrain from active involvement in partisan politics and critical public comment, and who strive to retain their anonymity.

Several former senior public servants have provided helpful insights on the duty to speak truth to power. James Mitchell (2007) argues that public servants fail to speak truth to power when they tell their hierarchical superiors what they want to hear rather than what they need to hear; when they hide the facts rather than bring them forward, even if the facts "run counter to received wisdom, or someone's preferred course of action"; and "when they try to make their superiors feel comfortable rather than helping them to do the right thing" (p. 3). It is especially important for public servants to speak frankly to a minister who is contemplating a course of action that is illegal or unethical.

Ralph Heintzman (2008, December 2) identifies the negative consequences of failure to speak truth to power as a reduction in honest dialogue, lower public service morale and consideration of fewer perspectives and insights on particular issues, especially about the competing public goods involved in government decision making. If public servants are not fully aware of the tensions between public goods they can't make wise decisions, and they "can't give good policy advice, advice which makes a genuine effort to understand and to capture the public interest" (p. xx).

The duty to speak truth to power can be interpreted in various ways. Ruth Hubbard (with academic scholar Gilles Paquet) (2009) found that some public servants view the duty purely as a matter of information – "making the politician aware of what the bureaucrat feels to be in the public interest" (p.15). Other public servants see it as a duty to persuade the politician to accept their preferred course of action. But still others believe that their duty to speak truth to power requires that they use ethical creativity to develop options that effectively blend their own view of the public interest with that of the politician. This latter group believes that the duty can often be better fulfilled by collaborating with ministers than by confronting them. Creativity can be as important as courage (Heintzman 2008, December 2; Hubbard 2009; Mitchell 2007, p. 4). Hubbard suggests that public servants should seek ways "to enable the public interest to be served by effectively marrying the public trust invested in ministers with that invested in public servants" (p. 11).

Ministers, in turn, have a duty to encourage and enable public servants to speak truth to power. Public servants need to know that speaking truth to power will not threaten their career prospects or, indeed, their security of tenure. The 2012 federal *Values and Ethics Code for the Public Sector* notes that ministers "are responsible... for upholding the tradition and practice of a professional non-partisan public sector" and "ministers play a critical role in supporting public servants' responsibility to provide professional and frank advice" (Treasury Board of Canada Secretariat, 2012, n.p.).

Discussion of the duty to speak truth to power arises most frequently in the context of ministerial-public service relations, but the duty also applies to superior-subordinate relations in the public service. Public servants at all levels should encourage their subordinates to provide the kind of milieu for frank advice that they would like ministers to provide for them (Heintzman 2008, December 2). "Speaking truth to power — as long as it is accompanied by a duty of faithful execution once decisions have been taken — is not something important for deputies and ministers alone. It is just as relevant or precious between employees and supervisors, at the level of middle managers, directors, directors general, and ADMs" (Canadian Centre for Management Development 1996, p. 48).

Municipal employees are also encouraged to speak truth to power so as to promote the public interest. Local government administrators, especially CAOs, are required to make recommendations on a wide variety of matters directly and openly to council and to outline the positive and negative implications of these recommendations. They also have a responsibility to speak truth to council in a frank and scrupulously non-political manner when council is contemplating an ill-advised course of action. "No one, least of all councillors, is well served by a situation where staff attempt to provide council with the advice it wants to hear rather than the advice it should hear" (Siegel 1994, p. 28).

Ethics, Public Policy and the Public Interest

Public servants, including policy analysts, often pay more attention to technical and other dimensions of policy choices than to their ethical dimension. However, as we noted in the introduction to this book, "nothing is more dangerous than a public servant who is technically fit but ethically flabby."

A full discussion of the large and complex subject of ethics and public policy cannot be provided here, but it is essential to recognize that the ethical element of public policy is often a key one. An examination of policy issues with sensitivity to their ethical implications will reveal that this ethical element is more pervasive and vital than is generally realized. For example, a single page of a single issue of the *Globe and Mail* newspaper contained the following three stories:

- A federal Member of Parliament introduced a motion asking the House of Commons to condemn discrimination against females resulting from sex-selective pregnancy termination (also called gendercide or female feticide). Margaret Somerville, a leading Canadian ethicist, pointed to the fact that criminal law prohibits "female mutilation but not the killing of an unborn girl just because she's a girl" (Somerville 2012, September 29, p. F9).

- Professor Andy Sumner, a leading scholar on poverty, noted the traditional "moral and ethical argument for global redistribution – essentially taxing citizens in the rich countries to pay for poverty reduction" (Saunders 2012, September 29, p. F9). He observed, however, that some formerly poor countries could now tax the "middle class" (many of whom make only a few dollars a day) to help the poor. These countries still need international aid, but will Canadian taxpayers want to send anti-poverty money to countries that have advanced economically, and will these countries accept being told how to handle their poverty problems?

- The Canadian government was reviewing whether the proposal of the Chinese National Offshore Oil Corporation (a state company) to take over Nexen Inc., a Calgary-based energy company, constituted a net benefit for Canada. However, commentators noted that no Canadian corporation would be permitted to take over an equivalent Chinese company. Should Canada insist that state-controlled corporations that want to buy Canadian assets "play by a fair set of rules" by granting reciprocal access to their markets (Cousineau 2012, September 29, p. F9)?

It is understandable in such cases that elected officials should look to public servants for assistance in determining what policy choices best promote the public interest – assistance that includes consideration of the ethical implications of these choices. Note, in addition, that not only professional policy analysts but also public servants in general, including those at the middle levels of the public service, make important contributions to public policy.

Boston, Bradstock and Eng (2010) identify several ethical issues that arise in the policy-making process:

> [W]hat norms and values should guide the behaviour of those involved in the policy process? What procedures should be adopted in the event of conflicts of interest? How should the need for secrecy...be balanced against the desirability of openness and public participation? Further, for departmental officials working for a democratically elected government, there are a variety of quite specific ethical issues. For example, to what extent is it legitimate for officials to challenge the priorities and policies of the government? What are the boundaries of free and frank advice or loyal and obedient service? Is it appropriate for officials to advocate for particular social, cultural, economic, or environmental outcomes within the performance of their public duties? (n.p.)

Each of these issues was discussed earlier in this chapter or will be discussed in subsequent chapters. It is essential also, however, to examine ethical considerations that arise in respect of policy and risk analysis because "policy analysis has tended to overlook, neglect or dismiss questions of values and ethics" (Dunn 1983, p. 2).

Among the commonly cited reasons why policy analysts often give short shrift to value and ethical considerations are these:

- while policy analysts can legitimately analyze factual questions, such as the probable impact of a certain policy, values questions concerning whether a policy is good or just or equitable are beyond the bounds of rational analysis...

- value decisions...are best left up to policymakers, and need not or should not be the subject of policy analysis...

- the [policy analysis] profession already has an adequate technique for evaluating normative questions – cost-benefit analysis...

- policy analysts fear injecting their own biases into the inquiry...

- ethical analysis is too abstract and philosophical to provide practical guidance for specific policy choices...[and] analysts rarely have time to complete an adequate cost-benefit analysis, let alone embark on an analysis which incorporates other forms of ethical evaluation... (Amy 1984, pp. 575-579)

Amy describes these arguments as weak and inadequate and responds to each of them by noting that:

- moral philosophers...now widely agree that moral and value claims can be subject to some degree of rational analysis...

- all policy questions are eventually resolved politically, but... ethical analysis can help make those decisions better ones...

- cost-benefit analysis is not equipped to handle the multiplicity of value concerns that are present in policy choices unless [as we discuss in chapter 2] it is informed by the preferences of stakeholders likely to be affected by actions or decisions...

- many ethicists believe that it is clearly possible to investigate the subject of ethics while at the same time maintaining one's objectivity...

- moral philosophers have turned increasingly to the practical, real-life implications of their work...[and] there is little reason to believe that ethical analysis is inherently more complex or impractical than other techniques used by policy analysts... (Amy 1984, pp. 575-579)

Donahue (2008) captures succinctly the essence of the contending positions:

> Inevitably, disagreements about values arise in the policy process. Some argue that because value claims cannot be demonstrated empirically..., they cannot enter rational debate. Others, however, hold that policy debates and analysis should be founded on explicit statements about ethical rules and ethical principles, although debates about the legitimacy of value choices can only be resolved politically. (p. 697)

Analyzing Risk in the Public Interest

Public servants regularly provide advice and make judgments as to the degree of risk they should take with the public. Many decisions involving risk are relatively easy to make, but others are complex and have significant consequences. "Usually understood to embody an element of possible danger, hazard or threat, risk in the broadest sense is associated with a willingness to take a chance on uncertainty in order to achieve some potential gain" (Treasury Board of Canada Secretariat 2006, n.p.). Risk to the public is involved in such decisions as whether a prisoner should be paroled, what trade-off should be made between expenditures on prison guards and police officers, how stringent regulations on the transport of hazardous products should be, and how vigorously regulations on the use of pesticides should be enforced.

Risk-benefit analysis is a component of the broader concept of cost-benefit analysis in that it involves the determination of possible costs in the form of harm to the public as opposed, for example, to an increase in expenditures. It is, however, difficult to quantify the costs of harm to health or the environment, especially long-term costs. Faced with this uncertainty, government decision makers may be tempted to take undue risks with new products or technologies. *Risk assessment* is used to determine whether a product or a practice is potentially harmful. The limitations of this approach include the considerations that the full range of risks involved may not be examined (e.g., cancer but not lesser threats), and those who are subject to the risk (e.g., toxic fumes) may not be consulted. Some of the risk issues with which public servants must deal are raised in case 3.2.

This discussion of risk is related to questions examined in chapters 1 and 2, including methods of ethical analysis, the acceptability of "dirty hands" and public servants' personal responsibility for the activities of the governments they serve. In regard to the methods question, consider that when public servants take part in a decision to license a drug, they increasingly use quantitative scientific data produced by the pharmaceutical companies to establish the benefits and risk level. They will also have to consider the argument that any risk is too much and that it is unjust to permit or force people to take a drug (e.g., health workers required to take flu vaccine) that might have even a remote chance of injuring them. Ralph D. Ellis (1998) notes that "[o]ne of the most distressing problems facing policy analysts and planners is the apparent incommensurability between the quantitative methods used to calculate beneficial outcomes...and the reasoning of opponents who charge that the resulting policies are 'unfair'" (p. 1).

On the matter of "dirty hands," should public servants support a military intervention in Afghanistan that helps a corrupt Afghan government ward off Taliban insurgents but results in the death of many innocent civilians? The personal responsibility debate warns public servants against taking part in activities that are indefensibly harmful (e.g., exposing citizens to a drug that is known to have significant injurious side effects), but it doesn't say much about how to proceed when the risk of harm may be small, unknown or focused on a minority of the affected citizens.

When recommending or making decisions involving an appreciable measure of risk, public servants should take account of the "precautionary principle," that is, "when an activity raises threats of harm to human health or the environment, precautionary measures should be taken even if some cause and effect relationships are not fully established scientifically" (Wingspread Statement 1998, January). The principle can be succinctly expressed in such colloquial terms as "better safe than sorry," "be careful" and "do no harm." The main components of the principle are (1) taking precautions in the face of scientific uncertainty; (2) placing the burden of proof on proponents of an activity rather than on victims or potential victims of the activity; (3) exploring alternatives to possibly harmful actions; and (4) using democratic processes to carry out and enforce the principle, including the public's right to informed consent (Science and Environmental Health Network 2000, January).

CASE 3.2: THE RISK OF EXPOSURE

The following conversation takes place between Morena, the senior site engineer employed by EXPO (a Crown corporation), and Alan, an EXPO VP for Operations, two days before the official opening of the fair. Please note that for purposes of this case we are accepting that dioxins in high concentrations in asphalt can be dangerous to the health of someone who comes into direct contact with them.

Morena: A week ago, we saw signs of a strange oily residue in the asphalt being used to pave the EXPO site. I thought that I had better check it out. I sent some samples from different parts of the site to the lab for investigation. The results came back today. Of the twelve samples I sent, six were positive. Three of the six positive samples showed high levels of dioxin contamination. There is a real chance that people using the site could come in contact with dioxins.

Alan: I can't believe it...You said your results indicate only a "chance" of a threat to public health?

Morena: Well, yes, but dioxins in high doses are toxic. Do we want to risk it? I want to recommend to the board that we postpone the opening and run more tests. I can't get more tests done in two days.

Alan: I don't agree. If we delay the opening, the problem will be blown way out of proportion by the local and international media and EXPO could be a failure. The media will be all over Prince Charles stuck on the royal yacht in False Creek unable to visit the site for fear of being poisoned. The whole province is counting on the economic impact of EXPO to kick-start the depressed economy. I am going to recommend that we go ahead and open, despite the risk. We can work on the problem quietly while the fair is on.

Is Alan justified in recommending to the President and the board that EXPO open on schedule?

In seeking the public interest, public servants are widely urged or required to heed this principle. For example, the federal government, in the Risk Communication section of its Communications Policy, provides that "[i]nstitutions must anticipate and assess potential risks to public health and safety, to the environment, and to policy and program administration" (Treasury Board of Canada Secretariat 2006, n.p.) and that federal institutions are required to:

a. foster open dialogue with the public on issues involving risk and build a climate of trust, credibility and understanding by being forthcoming about facts, evidence and information concerning risk assessments and decisions taken;

b. facilitate the interactive exchange of information on risk and risk-related factors among interested parties inside and outside of their institution;

c. respond to public perceptions and provide factual information to address misconceptions or misunderstandings about risk;

d. integrate environment analysis and communication planning and strategy into risk assessment and decision-making processes; and

e. follow Treasury Board policy direction on risk management in the delivery of programs and services, and consult Treasury Board guidance on the subject...

Consider the appropriate course of action in a hypothetical case involving a single confirmed case of "mad cow" disease on a Canadian farm, coupled with widespread recognition that public knowledge of such cases can have a disastrous effect on a country's beef industry. The farmer removes all of the other cattle from the barn and Health Canada's Chief Veterinarian visits the farm, arranges for the dead cow to be incinerated, and orders the farmer to disinfect the stalls. When the farmer reports the next day that all of the other cattle are healthy, the Chief Veterinarian tells the farmer that everything is now under control and the incident receives no public or media attention. What are the questions that the Chief Veterinarian should ask in dealing with this situation? Should more have been done?

It is obvious that public servants involved in regulatory activities must be especially sensitive to the precautionary principle's importance and requirements, but its relevance is pervasive in government, and it is frequently an important consideration in determining the public interest. Consider, for example, British Columbia's *Freedom of Information and Protection of Privacy Act* (1996), which stipulates that:

> [W]hether or not a request for access is made, the head of a public body must, without delay, disclose to the public, to an affected group of people or to an applicant, information (a) about a risk of significant harm to the environment or to the health or safety of the public or a group of people; or (b) the disclosure of which is, for any other reason, clearly in the public interest. (s. 25)

The Public Interest as an Operational Guide

Public servants can employ several tests to figure out whether their policy advice and decisions are in the public interest. These "are tests we should be applying to ourselves, and to all of our actions, every day" (Heintzman 2004, September 25). The four tests examined here are the *dominant principle, cost-benefit, procedural, and consensualist* tests. These tests, or approaches, are derived from the extensive scholarly literature on the concept of the public interest and echo the more general approaches to moral justification set out in the discussion of duty and consequential ethics in chapter 2. The following argument proceeds on the premise that the preservationists are correct in their contention that the public interest is a credible concept, one worth retaining.

The Dominant Principle Approach

According to this approach, a specific precept focusing on a core concept such as justice, freedom or equality should be viewed as the ultimate criterion, or at least as a centrally important one, for deciding what actions are in the public interest. For example, the criterion of *justice-as-fairness* has been presented as the overriding principle by which the public interest should be determined. Justice-as-fairness is the central concept in the work of the contractarian philosopher John Rawls, who argues that two principles of justice should be applied to determine the public interest. The first principle is that "each person is to have an equal right to the most extensive total system of equal basic liberties compatible with a similar system of liberty for all." The second principle is that "social and economic inequalities are to be arranged so that they are both: a) to the greatest benefit of the least advantaged... and b) attached to offices and positions open to all under conditions of fair equality of opportunity" (Rawls 1971, p. 302).

In the event that these principles clash with one another, the first principle is to take precedence. Rawls argues that "social and economic inequalities, for example, inequalities of wealth and authority, are just only if they result in compensating benefits for everyone, and in particular for the least advantaged members of society." Moreover, "these principles rule out justifying institutions on the grounds that the hardships of some are offset by a greater good in the aggregate. It may be expedient but it is not just that some should have less in order that others may prosper" (pp. 14-15).

The concrete application of Rawls' theory can be demonstrated by reference to case 3.3, which involves the hiring, training and advancement of a member of a group that is disadvantaged in society and underrepresented in the public service. Rawls would argue that promoting Cary achieves basic liberty for her but does not infringe on the basic liberty of others. If Cary were not hired, one of society's most disadvantaged persons would be further disadvantaged. By hiring Cary, the government demonstrates its commitment to having its "positions and offices open to all." Finally, by hiring Cary, who is one of "the least advantaged members of society," the government is trying to ensure that its positions and offices are "open to all under conditions of fair equality of opportunity (Rawls 1971, p. 302). For public servants, a less complicated and more practical guide to the public interest may be found in Rawls' notion of "the veil of ignorance" mentioned in chapter 2. This is the notion that we should make decisions as if we didn't know what our lot in life is or will be. For example, in the sphere of employment equity, the decision maker would adopt the perspective of someone who didn't know whether he or she was going to be treated as an advantaged or disadvantaged person in the context of the employment equity regime that he or she creates.

CASE 3.3: PUBLIC INTEREST OR SELF-INTEREST?

In this case, Sean and Leslie chat about a colleague's recent promotion.

Sean: I just have to blow off steam – but I wouldn't want this to get around.

Leslie: Go ahead. I'm all ears.

Sean: Well, you know Cary. First, she gets a permanent job with the public service – no temporary position, no competition, no hassle. Then, she gets weeks and weeks of middle management training. Courses I'd love to attend, if I had the time and could get permission. So I'm minding memos, doing my job, paying my dues, while she's taking courses. Next I find out that she's being fast-tracked and will probably be a director within two years. Why? All because she's aboriginal and we've got the Indigenous Development Program. I know it's right and we need affirmative action and role models for our aboriginal people but... The bottom line is that I'm jealous. I'm more qualified and more experienced but I won't get offered the chance to compete for a director's position for a long time. There's less opportunity for advancement than there used to be. Frankly, I'm thinking of talking to the boss about it.

Leslie: Okay, I sympathize. But the other side of this is that aboriginal people have been shut out of the system. They need special programs so that managers will consider them. There's probably more racism out there than we realize. Besides, you may be better qualified than she is, but she is fully qualified for the job for which she was hired. Also, she might not be successful. She's trying to adjust to a new job, the course work is demanding, and she's afraid that other people in the office resent the assistance she's getting. Sometimes I wonder if she's being set up to fail. She's under a lot of pressure.

Sean: I wouldn't want that to happen to anybody. And I can see that her perspective on policy issues is needed. Plus her experience and contacts in the aboriginal political community are valuable, no question about it. But I still believe that I deserve a chance before she does.

Is Sean simply allowing his self-interest to blind him to the wider public interest?

Should individuals or groups be compensated for past discrimination or deprivation?

Is it fair to deny a member of a majority group what he or she would have normally received if affirmative action was not operating? What do you do when faced with developing policy or delivering programs in the face of such incompatible values?

Among the principles often singled out as the ultimate criterion for determining the public interest are those fostering rights such as liberty and equality, interpretations of which can be closely tied to particular political ideologies. We know that the ideological commitments of public servants can influence their recommendations and decisions on public policy (Kernaghan 1984, pp. 581-583), and we know that these commitments have a significant effect on policy decisions in such areas as the redistribution of income, employment programs and human rights. Do we want public servants emphasizing principles that foster a particular interpretation of liberty or equality as the overriding consideration in their decision-making calculus? Is it appropriate for them to inject an ideological bias into the policy process? What if this bias is not shared by their political superiors? Is it important that personal ideological perspectives be made explicit in public servants' decision making so that these perspectives can be openly weighed against others? Is the public interest to be found in the reconciliation of competing principles rather than in the application of a single dominant principle?

The Cost-Benefit Approach

This approach views the public interest as emerging from cost-benefit analysis, a technique used to evaluate policy options by determining for each option the ratio of benefits to costs or the difference between benefits and costs. The option that best serves the public interest is the one where the benefits exceed the costs by the greatest amount. This approach is a technically oriented variation on consequential ethical theory, which we described in chapter 2 as:

a pragmatic approach to making tough ethical choices which focuses on the particulars of the

situation, generally rejects making absolutist
statements about how to behave, attaches
no special significance to the protection of
individual rights, usually ignores a moral
agent's intentions and focuses instead on
impartial calculation of the effect of proposed
actions on all affected stakeholders.

Cost-benefit analysis is valuable in stimulating thought about alternative
ways of achieving government objectives and about the possible
consequences of various decisions. However, in its purest technical
form, cost-benefit analysis has some shortcomings as a reliable guide to
the public interest. As noted when we critically assessed consequential
analysis in chapter 2, the methodology associated with establishing
and measuring relevant costs and benefits can be demanding in a
complex policy setting. This approach can also rely too heavily on the
public servant's ability to anticipate the interests and preferences of
stakeholders.

The Procedural Approach

The procedural approach represents an effort to correct the latter flaw.
In parallel with developments in contemporary consequential analysis,
the procedural approach encourages the public servant to open up the
analysis of outcomes to the expression of interests and preferences
of those likely to be affected by a decision or action. It argues that the
public interest is found in the reconciliation of the conflicting interests
and preferences surrounding a particular issue through the use of
certain standards of procedure in the decision-making process. If these
standards (e.g., the democratic process, administrative due process)
are followed, the rights of those affected are protected by the process.
Glendon Schubert (1960) explains that "people accept democratic
decision-making processes because these provide the maximum
opportunity for diverse interests to seek to influence governmental
decisions at all levels...Decisions that are the product of a process of full
consideration are most likely to be decisions in the public interest" (pp.
204-205).

Advocates of this approach argue that there should be procedures
in the policy-making process to ensure that all groups affected by a
policy have access to government decision makers and that this access
is granted as equitably as possible. Public servants are encouraged to
ask such questions as these: Is the decision-making process fair to all
interests? Have I provided adequate access for individuals and groups
wishing to be heard? Have I provided all possible relevant information?

The Consensualist Approach

The cost-benefit approach emphasizes the importance of the interests and preferences of those affected by a decision; yet there are further objections to interpreting the public interest merely as the sum of individual or group interests. In the context of a discussion of the cost-benefit approach to the public interest, Mark H. Moore (1981) concludes that "the simple summation of individual preferences attached to effects fails to guide policy because it ignores legitimate social, as opposed to individual, values, and the distribution of gains and losses among individuals in different social positions" (p. 19).

The consensualist approach – as an extension of the procedural approach – attempts to remedy that perceived shortcoming. It reminds public servants that the public interest is broader than the sum of the interests of those who are well represented in the decision-making process. Account must be taken of the interests of individuals and groups who are unrepresented or underrepresented in the policy process (Goodsell 1990, pp. 106-107). The public interest is made up of more than private interests and self-interest; it must even take account of the interests of future generations (Pennock 1962, p. 180). Carol Lewis (2006) notes that "the moral responsibility here rests on future generations' vulnerability to current decisions with irreversible repercussions" (p. 698). She also notes the responsibility of public managers "to hear otherwise silent voices in the process by which the public interest is defined" (p. 698).

Anthony Downs (1962) asserts that the public interest is "closely related to the minimal consensus necessary for the operation of a democratic society. This consists of an implicit agreement among the preponderance of the people concerning two main areas: the basic rules of conduct and decision-making that should be followed in the society; and general principles regarding the fundamental social policies that the government ought to carry out" (p. 5). J. E. Hodgetts (1981) makes a similar argument in his assertion that mankind's pursuit of the public interest "has been a search for consensus — the hard core of accepted values and traditions that holds a community together, enabling it to pursue common objectives" (p. 218).

The consensualist approach prompts public servants who are seeking the public interest to ask themselves: Have I taken account of all affected interests and not just those of well-represented groups? Have I kept in mind the good of the community as well the interests of groups and individuals? Have I considered carefully enough the possible long-range effects of my decision?

Neutral Service and Avoiding Self-Interest

In addition to the practical advice flowing from the four public-interest tests explained above, public servants should keep in mind two other considerations. The first is the importance of neutral service; the second is the avoidance of self-interest.

Neutral Service

As explained earlier, the ethic of neutrality suggests that the public interest is the business of democratically elected political authorities, not of public servants. However, we have seen that public servants necessarily exercise power in the policy process and make judgments as to what the public interest requires in particular situations. Moreover, only a small proportion of decisions as to the content of the public interest can in practice be taken by political authorities. Under these circumstances, public servants are responsible for ensuring that ministers have the necessary information on the implications of policy decisions, including technical and financial implications that the minister needs to weigh against partisan and short-term considerations. Thus, it can be argued that public servants have an ethical as well as a legal or hierarchical obligation to contribute to the determination of the public interest.

The public servant who values neutral service highly is likely to emphasize accountability to hierarchical superiors so that his or her decisions will reflect the values of political authorities. Before making recommendations and decisions, this public servant will ask such questions as: Have I presented the options fairly and objectively to my superior? Does my advice reflect unduly my personal values? What does my superior want me to do in this case? What would my superior want me to do if he or she knew what I was doing?

Avoiding Self-Interest

It is naive to expect that most public servants will be motivated most of the time entirely, or even largely, by selfless considerations. Anthony Downs (1967) contends that "every official acts at least partly in his own self-interest, and some officials are motivated solely by their own self-interest" (p. 53). The challenge is to ensure that the reconciliation of competing values in the light of the public interest is not based unduly on self-interest.

Admittedly, the public interest is often difficult to discern, but it can usually be distinguished fairly easily, either instinctively or upon reflection, from self-interest. Certain kinds of self-serving behaviour, for example the use of public office for private gain, are readily recognized as contrary to the public interest. Other manifestations of self-interest, for example actions based primarily on considerations of career advancement, are less tangible. To avoid decisions based unduly on self-interest, public servants are encouraged to ask: What is my personal or private interest in this particular decision-making context?

Public servants make many decisions, ostensibly in the public interest, with which segments of the public disagree. Members of the public are more likely to view these decisions as legitimate if they are convinced that public servants are largely free from self-serving behaviour and if they believe that fair procedures have been followed. To what extent are the public servants in this chapter's three cases acting in their self-interest rather than in the public interest?

Searching for a Synthesis

None of the four approaches discussed above has, by itself, received general acceptance as an operational guide to determining the public interest. Yet each approach provides useful insights into the elements necessary for such a guide.

First, it is clear that no single principle is likely to win universal agreement as the ultimate criterion for determining the public interest. Thus, public servants will normally be required to seek an accommodation of competing principles. They must be especially mindful of their own dominant principles – and of their self-interest – so that their personal values do not overwhelm all other values.

Second, public servants should do the most comprehensive technical analysis of the costs and benefits of various decision alternatives that is possible in the circumstances. The greater the cost or risk to the public, the stronger the argument for a thorough cost-benefit analysis and reference to the precautionary principle. In the sphere of risk analysis, A. R. Dobell (1986) notes two extreme stances that responsible public servants should avoid. The first is to exaggerate "the clarity and certainty of the scientific facts relevant to a decision" so that the best decision seems overwhelmingly obvious. The opposite, and also unacceptable, stance is to exaggerate "the lack of factual knowledge available, asserting that questions of public risk are entirely issues of values, and referring every difficult risk decision to polls or referenda for resolution." He concludes that the senior public servant's responsibility is to reconcile "what the analyst sees as the public interest with what the constituency office feels as public pressure. This requires framing decision problems as clearly as possible, and taking seriously the educational role of the public servant...But in the final analysis, your responsibility as a public servant is to base your decisions and advice on the normative, scientific analysis of the public interest, not on the public opinion polls" (p. 617).

Third, solid technical analysis is not always enough. In many cases, to establish the most beneficial option or outcome, the interests and preferences of stakeholders need to be considered. Public servants should ensure that the procedures followed in obtaining information and consulting those affected by decisions are fair and open. Donald P. Warwick (1981) contends that "although the specific content of the public interest can never be established in any precise fashion, its absence can be noted in undue concessions to special interests and in violations of procedural safeguards designed to protect the public at large" (p. 112).

Finally, all stakeholders likely to be significantly affected by a decision should be identified and consulted. Competing values should be reconciled according to a broader conception of the public interest than the outcome of competition among diverse interests. This requires at the very least the consideration and reconciliation of interests beyond those of groups and individuals who are well represented in the decision-making process. From a duty ethics perspective, Kluge (1986) states the principle that "whenever the matter is of sufficient gravity that the reasonable and prudent person would want to be consulted,... the ethical public servant must attempt to involve the public by way of informed consent: by facilitating public awareness and engaging in consultation" (p. 621).

Conclusion

The concept of the public interest has a pervasive presence in public administration. It is a persistent theme in public service discourse, and it is formally embedded in many statutes, regulations and codes. In this chapter, we have seen that the public interest is a major consideration in the realms of policy advice and implementation and in risk analysis. In other chapters, we observe its close links to such central issues as conflict of interest, confidentiality, political neutrality and accountability. In that regard, note that the Province of Manitoba's *Civil Service Values and Ethics Guide* states that civil servants act in the public interest by:

- Resolving any conflict between our personal or private interests and our official duties in favour of the public interest

- Upholding both the letter and the spirit of the law

- Maintaining the confidentiality of information gained as a result of our work

- Being sensitive to the political process and acting in accordance with the traditions regarding political impartiality

- Being a careful steward of public resources and using them in an efficient, responsible and accountable manner. (Manitoba, 2007, p. 4)

In chapter 1 we used the language being used by governments in whistle blower protection legislation and policy across the country to help establish the moral responsibility of public servants to avoid offending the public interest by participating in any wrongdoing, including violations of the law, misuse of state resources, gross mismanagement and actions or inactions that were likely to cause significant harm to people or the environment. In this chapter, while reinforcing the obligation to avoid doing harm and exposing the public to indefensible risks, we argue further that to act in the public interest is not just to avoid wrongdoing but also to contribute to positively enhancing the public good. One can read the guidance provided by the Manitoba *Civil Service Values and Ethics Guide* as a somewhat more positive statement of the obligation to uphold the public interest and a useful companion to the directions about what to avoid found in whistle blower protection legislation. There are a number of different routes to establishing the public interest, reflecting the variety of general approaches to solving ethical problems, which we reviewed in chapter 2. We encourage readers to explore the possibilities of connecting these different approaches, seeing the ways in which such connections can strengthen the public-interest focus of the advice and decisions of public servants.

References

Alonso, P., & Lewis, G. B. (2001). Public service motivation and job performance: Evidence from the federal sector. *American Review of Public Administration, 31*(4), 363-381.

Amy, D. J. (1984). Why policy analysis and ethics are incompatible. *Journal of Policy Analysis and Management 3*(4), 573-591.

Boston, J., Bradstock, A., & Eng, D. (2010). Ethics and public policy. In J. Boston, A. Bradstock & D. Eng (Eds.), *Public policy: Why ethics matter* (pp. 1-17). Canberra: ANU E Press. Retrieved from http://epress.anu.edu.au/apps/bookworm/view/Public+Policy%3A+Why+ethics+matters/5251/ch01_intro.xhtml

Brewer, G. A., Selden, S. C., & Facer II, R. L. (2000). Individual conceptions of public service motivation. *Public Administration Review, 60*(3), 254-264.

Buchanan, J. M., & Tullock, G. (1962). *The calculus of consent: Logical foundations of constitutional democracy.* Ann Arbor, MI: University of Michigan Press.

Canadian Centre for Management Development. (1996). *A strong foundation: Report of the task force on public service values and ethics.* Ottawa: CCMD. Retrieved from http://publications.gc.ca/collections/Collection/SC94-72-1996E.pdf

Cassinelli, W. (1962). The public interest and ultimate commitment. In C. J. Friedrich (Ed.), *The public interest* (pp. 44-53). New York: Atherton Press.

Cochran, C. E. (1974). Political science and "the public interest." *Journal of Politics, 36*(2), 330-339.

Consumer Packaging and Labelling Act. (1985). In Statutes of Canada, R.S.C. 1985, c. C-38. Retrieved from http://laws-lois.justice.gc.ca/eng/acts/c-38/

Cousineau, S. (2012, September 29). The price that China must pay to win Nexen. *Globe and Mail*, p. F9.

Crewson, P. E. (1997). Public service motivation: Building empirical evidence of incidence and effect. *Journal of Public Administration Research and Theory, 7*(4), 499-518.

Denhardt, J. V., & Denhardt, R. B. (2003). *The new public service: Serving, not steering.* Armonk, NY: M. E. Sharpe.

Dilulio, J. D. (1994). Principled agents: The cultural bases of behaviour in a federal government bureaucracy. *Journal of Public Administration Research and Theory 4*(3), 277-320.

Dobell, A. R. (1986). The public servant as God: Taking risks with the public. *Canadian Public Administration, 29*(4), 601-617.

Donahue, A. K. (2008). Ethics and public policy. In E. M. Berman (Ed.), *Encyclopedia of public administration and public policy* (pp. 696-700) (2nd ed.). New York: Taylor & Francis.

Downs, A. (1962). The public interest: Its meaning in a democracy. *Social Research, 29*(1), 1-36.

Downs, A. (1967). *Inside bureaucracy.* Boston: Little Brown.

Dunn, W. N. (1983). *Values, ethics and the practice of policy analysis.* Lexington, MA: D. C. Heath.

Ellis, R. D. (1998). *Just results: Ethical foundations for policy analysis.* Washington, DC: Georgetown University Press.

Freedom of Information and Protection of Privacy Act. (1996). In Statutes of British Columbia, c. 165, s. 25. Retrieved from http://www.bclaws.ca/EPLibraries/bclaws_new/document/ID/ freeside/96165_00

Goodsell, C. T. (1990). Public administration as public interest. In G. L. Wamsley et al. (Eds.), Refounding public administration (pp. 96-113). Newbury Park, CA: Sage Publications.

Hamilton, M. R. (2007). Democracy and the public service. In R. C. Box (Ed.), *Democracy and public administration* (pp. 3-20). Armonk, NY: M. E. Sharpe.

Heintzman, R. (2004, September 25). *Opening keynote address, National Ethics Symposium,* St. Paul's University, Ottawa, ON.

Heintzman, R. (2008, December 2). *Armchair discussion and official launch of the values and ethics on-line course "Paving the Way."* Canada School of Public Service.

Heintzman, R. (2010). Loyal to a fault. *Optimum Online, 40*(1), 48-59.

Hodge, G. (1991). *Planning Canadian communities: An introduction to principles, practice, and participants* (2nd ed.). Scarborough, ON: Nelson Canada.

Hodgetts, J. E. (1981). Government responsiveness to the public interest: Has progress been made? *Canadian Public Administration, 24*(2), 216-231.

Hondeghem, A., & Perry, J. L. (2009). EGPA symposium on public service motivation and performance: Introduction. *International Review of Administrative Sciences, 75*(1), 5-9.

Hubbard, R. (2009). Speaking truth to power: A matter of imagination and courage. *Canadian Government Executive Magazine, 15*(1), 10-11.

Hubbard, R., & Paquet, G. (2009). Not in the catbird seat: Pathologies of governance. *Optimum Online, 39*(2), 11-20.

Kernaghan, K. (1984). The conscience of the bureaucrat: Accomplice or constraint? *Canadian Public Administration, 27*(4), 576-591.

Kluge, E-H. W. (1986). What is a human life worth? *Canadian Public Administration, 29*(4), 617-623.

Levine, G. J. (2009). *Municipal ethics regimes.* St. Thomas, ON: Municipal World.

Lewis, C. (2006). In pursuit of the public interest. *Public Administration Review, 66*(5), 694-701.

MacNair, M. D. (2006). In the name of the public good: "Public interest" as a legal standard. *Canadian Criminal Law Review, 10*(2), 175-204.

Manitoba. (2007). *Manitoba civil service values and ethics guide.* Retrieved from http://www.gov.mb.ca/csc/pdf/valueethic.pdf

Mitchell, J. (2007). *Can I really speak truth to power? Practical advice for new executives.* Notes for remarks by James R. Mitchell at the induction of new executives. Ottawa: March 27, pp. 1-6.

Moore, M. H. (1981). Realms of obligation and virtue. In J. L. Fleishman, L. Liebman & M. H. Moore (Eds.), *Public duties: The moral obligations of government officials* (pp. 3-31). Cambridge, MA: Harvard University Press.

New Brunswick. 2009. *New Brunswick public service values and conduct guide.* Retrieved at http://www2.gnb.ca/content/dam/gnb/Departments/ohr-brh/pdf/other/values_conduct_guide.pdf

Ontario Statutory Powers Procedure Act. (1990). In Statutes of Ontario, R.S.O. 1990, Chapter s. 22. Retrieved from http://www.e-laws.gov.on.ca/html/statutes/english/elaws_statutes_90s22_e.htm

Pennock, J. R. (1962). The one and the many: A note on the concept of the public interest. In C. J. Friedrich (Ed.), *The public interest* (pp. 177-182). New York: Atherton Press.

Perry, J. L. (1996). Measuring public service motivation: An assessment of construct reliability and validity. *Journal of Public Administration Research and Theory, 6*(1), 5-22.

Perry, J. L. (1997). Antecedents of public service motivation. *Journal of Public Administration Research and Theory, 7*(2), 181-208.

Perry, J. L., & Hondeghem, A. (Eds.). (2008). *Motivation in public management: The call of public service*. Oxford: Oxford University Press.

Perry, J. L., & Wise, L. R. (1990). The motivational bases of public service. Public *Administration Review, 50*(3), 367-373.

Rawls, J. (1971). *A theory of justice*. Cambridge, MA: Harvard University Press.

Saunders, D. (2012, September 29). The poor ain't what they used to be. *Globe and Mail*, p. F9.

Schubert, G. (1960). *The public interest*. Glencoe, IL: The Free Press.

Schubert, G. A., Jr. (1957). "The public interest" in administrative decision-making: Theorem, theosophy, or theory? *American Political Science Review, 51*(2), 346-368.

Science and Environmental Health Network. (2000, January). *The Precautionary Principle: A common sense way to protect public health and the environment*. Windsor, ND. Retrieved from http://www.mindfully.org/Precaution/Precautionary-Principle-Common-Sense.htm

Siegel, D. (forthcoming). *Leaders in the shadows: The leadership qualities of municipal Chief Administrative Officers*. Toronto: University of Toronto Press.

Siegel, D. (1994). Politics, politicians, and public servants in non-partisan local governments. *Canadian Public Administration, 37*(1), 7-30.

Somerville, M. (2012, September 29). The preposterous politics of female feticide. *Globe and Mail*, p. F9.

Thompson, D. F. (1985). The possibility of administrative ethics. *Public Administration Review, 45*(5), 555-561.

Treasury Board of Canada Secretariat. (2006). *Communications policy of the Government of Canada*. Retrieved from http://www.tbs-sct.gc.ca/pol/doc-eng.aspx?id=12316&section=text.

Treasury Board of Canada Secretariat. (2012). *Values and ethics code for the public sector*. Retrieved from http://www.tbs-sct.gc.ca/pol/doc-eng.aspx?id=25049&section=text#cha5

Vandenabeele, W. (2009). The mediating effect of job satisfaction and organizational commitment on self-reported performance: More robust evidence of the PSM-performance relationship. *International Review of Administrative Sciences,* 75(1), 11-34.

Warwick, D. P. (1981). The ethics of administrative discretion. In J. L. Fleishman, L. Liebman & M. H. Moore (Eds.), *Public duties: The moral obligations of government officials* (pp. 93-127). Cambridge, MA: Harvard University Press.

Wingspread Statement on the Precautionary Principle. (1998, January). Global Development Research Center. Statement drafted and finalized at Wingspread Conference Center, Racine, WI. Retrieved from http://www.gdrc.org/u-gov/precaution-3.html

Chapter 4

The Politically Neutral Public Servant

> To the extent that the public service is
> expected to be promiscuously partisan, that
> is, partisan for the government of the day for
> so long as it remains in power, impartiality is
> undermined. (Aucoin 2008, November, p. 12)

> [Public servants should] approach the question
> of political activity in the same manner that the
> Anglican prayer book prescribes for marriage:
> it is not by any to be entered upon...lightly or
> wantonly; but...discreetly, advisedly, soberly,
> and in fear of God. (Kroeger 1992, p. 6)

Since public servants are regularly advised that they have a duty to
be politically neutral, they need answers to two broad questions: what
are the appropriate relationships between elected officials and public
servants in the workplace, and to what extent should public servants
engage in political or advocacy politics away from the workplace? The
first question raises such issues as the links between merit, patronage
and political neutrality, the line between political sensitivity and political
partisanship, and what it means to be loyal to the government of the
day. The second question focuses to a large extent on how an optimum
balance can be struck between political rights and political neutrality.
Discussion of these several issues is often centred on the senior levels
of the public service, but political neutrality has important ramifications
at virtually all levels.

Defining the Duty

Political neutrality is a constitutional convention that provides that public
servants should avoid activities that are likely to impair, or seem to
impair, their political impartiality or the political impartiality of the public
service. This convention has been a central feature of the constitution
since Confederation.[2] "Clearly there was a convention of political
neutrality of Crown servants at the time of Confederation and the
reasoning in support of such convention has been consistent throughout
the subsequent years" (*OPSEU v. Ontario (A.G.)* 1980 31 O.R. (2d) 321).

---

2. For a detailed account of this evolution, see Juillet and Rasmussen (2008), especially
chapter 5.

The meaning of political neutrality can be explained by reference to the model set out below (revised from Kernaghan 1976). This model is an ideal-type[3] – it outlines the requirements for relations between politicians and public servants that would exist in an absolute sense in a Westminster-style government.

The major tenets of this model are as follows:

1. Politics and policy are separated from administration; thus politicians make policy decisions, public servants execute these decisions.

2. Public servants are appointed and promoted on the basis of merit rather than party affiliation or contributions.

3. Public servants provide forthright and objective advice to their political masters in private and in confidence; in return, political executives protect the anonymity of public servants by publicly accepting responsibility for departmental decisions.

4. Public servants execute policy decisions loyally irrespective of the philosophy and programs of the party in power and regardless of their personal opinions; as a result, public servants enjoy security of tenure during good behaviour and satisfactory performance.

5. Public servants do not engage in partisan political activities.

6. Public servants do not express publicly their personal views on government policies or administration.

Several points must be made about this model. First, tenets one through four relate primarily to political neutrality issues that arise in the workplace, whereas tenets five and six relate to issues that emerge away from work. Second, political neutrality in this pristine form has never existed in any government. The model provides a framework for analysis of the relationships between politicians and public servants rather than a set of objectives that public servants should strive to achieve fully. Indeed, achieving such objectives as excluding public servants from policy decisions, insisting on their unquestioning loyalty in implementation and restricting severely their political rights would be in line with the ethic of neutrality mentioned in chapter 1 according to which public servants do not exercise independent moral judgment. We have seen, however, that public servants are unavoidably involved

---

3. An ideal type is a theoretical tool that simplifies reality so as to provide conceptual clarity. The closer a government comes to achieving the requirements of the model, the closer it is to achieving political neutrality in an absolute sense.

in selecting and reconciling values in the course of giving advice and implementing policy. Third, the current practice of governments in Canada is significantly different from the tenets of the model. David Good (2008) warns that "the increasing public exposure of the failures of some practitioners to live up to even the most rudimentary aspects of the doctrine indicates that there is confusion over what is ideal in theory and what is actually possible in practice" (p. 81).

There are persuasive arguments for and against political neutrality. Those who are concerned with preserving political neutrality note its central place in the Canadian understanding of the Westminster model of government and its intimate links with the constitutional conventions of ministerial responsibility and public service anonymity. They also point to its importance in ensuring public service appointments and promotions according to merit and in fostering fair and impartial service to the public.

Others believe that existing rules and traditions concerning political neutrality are too restrictive. They note that undue emphasis on political neutrality suppresses individual rights (notably political rights). They assert also that many current interpretations of the duty to be politically neutral are outdated and unrealistic because relations among politicians, public servants and the public have changed, and continue to change. This chapter examines arguments on both sides of the debate.

The model shows that the overall duty to be politically neutral can be broken down into several more specific duties. Note that the various tenets of the model are interconnected, with the result that a change in one of them (for example, political partisanship) is likely to affect one or more of the others (for example, anonymity). The first component of the model is not considered here because we have already seen that politics, policy and administration are closely intertwined and that both politicians and public servants are involved in both policy making and policy implementation.

The political neutrality model can be adapted to non-partisan local governments (Siegel 1994, p. 13) to take account of the differences between parliamentary (federal and provincial) governments and local governments. Especially notable in local governments is the absence of a unified executive (there is no cabinet subject to collective ministerial responsibility) and the substantial openness in council-staff relationships (there is no tradition of anonymity in these relationships). As explained below, the adaptation of the political neutrality model to local governments requires revision of several, but not all, of its components.

Compared to their federal and provincial counterparts, local government councillors are in more direct contact with citizens and are the source of many policy proposals to remedy community problems. Municipal councillors also interact more closely and routinely with public servants than federal and provincial politicians do, partly to seek advice on policy development and partly because of their greater inclination to involve themselves directly in policy implementation. However, most councillors serve on a part-time basis, with limited time and little personal staff support. They are obliged to rely heavily on public servants for assistance in developing policy initiatives and to accept the dominant role of public servants in policy implementation. Municipal Chief Administrative Officers (CAOs) can be distinguished from other staff members by their greater involvement in developing new policies as opposed to implementing the existing ones. David Siegel (2010) argues that CAOs "must be separated from electoral politics, but operationally oriented, politically sensitive, and definitely involved in the politics of governing society" (p. 160).

References to the public servant's duty of political neutrality are set out – and often spread out – in a variety of official documents, including judicial decisions, legislation, value statements and codes of ethics. The Supreme Court of Canada has acknowledged "the existence of a convention of political neutrality, central to the principle of responsible government" (*Osborne v. Canada* 1991, 2 S.C.R. 69). The federal Guide for Ministers and Ministers of State, entitled *Accountable Government: A Guide for Ministers and Ministers of State*, notes that "[m]inisters have a responsibility for maintaining the tradition of the political neutrality of the public service" (Canada, Privy Council Office 2011, p. 44). Both the courts and other government institutions frequently use the terms "neutrality" and "impartiality" interchangeably. For example, the 2003 federal *Public Service Employment Act* (2003) recognizes "the right of employees to engage in political activities while maintaining the principle of political impartiality in the public service" (S.C. 2003, c. 22, s. 112). New Brunswick identifies impartiality as one of its five major Public Service Values, and its related Code of Conduct states that public servants do not engage in activities that impair their impartiality or make public statements incompatible with a politically impartial public service. Individual departments and agencies complement service-wide coverage of political neutrality with their own provisions. For instance, Parks Canada's Code of Ethics requires employees to "work within the laws of Canada and demonstrate political neutrality" (2009, n.p.). Examples of references in official documents to specific issues of political neutrality, such as political partisanship and public comment, are provided later in this chapter.

The Meritorious Public Servant

Political neutrality is closely linked to the issues of merit and patronage. It is a fact of political life in Canada that patronage appointments continue to be made and that the nature and extent of the practice varies from one government to another. As explained later, one rationale for continuing restrictions on partisan political activity is the desire to avoid a resurgence of patronage. Despite the existence of well-entrenched merit systems, there is continuing concern that the career prospects of public servants will be influenced by their involvement in high-profile partisan politics. Continuing efforts to prevent an increase in partisanship and patronage in public service staffing are motivated by a desire to avoid:

- dismissals due to partisan influence or, conversely, public servants currying favour for promotion and assignments ahead of the public interest and quality administration and advice (rewards and discipline could also be subject to partisan considerations);

- constant suspicion about the legitimacy of purchasing and contracting practices;

- protracted periods of turmoil during government transitions as large numbers of public servants are replaced;

- services to the public being influenced by partisan considerations (either delivery is aligned to a political ideology, or service is denied or varied, depending on the partisan history of the citizen);

- an absence of concern for qualifications in hiring, thereby jeopardizing the integrity of a professional public service;

- fewer checks and balances, with the principle of good government taking second place to partisan considerations; and

- elections and, by extension, democracy being greatly influenced by a governing party being able to call on the assistance of a partisan public service during campaigns (Canada, Public Service Commission 2008, p. 7).

Given the dominant role of public servants in managing the human resources process in general and the merit system in particular, it is important to remember that the duty to be politically neutral requires that public servants make appointments and promotions on the basis of merit rather than party affiliation or contributions. According to this duty, considerations of partisanship, like those of religion and other criteria unrelated to fitness for the job, should be excluded from hiring and promotion decisions. Merit systems cannot, however, eliminate the covert application of partisan considerations in appointments and promotions.

Many instances or allegations of patronage reported by the news media focus on appointments to the senior echelons of the public service where officials can have considerable influence on the content and administration of public policy. In some governments, however, partisan appointments extend well down the public service hierarchy and can do significant damage to public confidence in government. At the federal and provincial levels, prime ministers, premiers and ministers have increasingly large personal staffs of political advisors and can draw on the expertise of large political communications operations. The individuals in these positions are often hired as public servants and funded by the taxpayer. Many of them, however, have little experience of government and little awareness of the demands of political neutrality, which would, in any case, be antithetical to their roles.

In the municipal sphere, the merit-patronage component of the political neutrality model provides that "[p]ublic servants are appointed and promoted on the basis of merit rather than of relationships with any councillor or group of councillors" (Siegel 1994, p. 18). The absence of party politics in the local governments examined in this chapter means that there are fewer pressures and opportunities for political patronage than in the federal and provincial governments. Moreover, while local governments have a long history of personal patronage by individual councillors, this practice has been greatly reduced over the past several decades. Among the reasons for this decline are the need for competence in Canada's increasingly complex local governments, the development of professional credentials for many local government occupations, and the difficulty of concealing the exercise of patronage in the open hiring process that is characteristic of local governments.

The Responsible Minister and the Anonymous Public Servant

We turn now to an examination of the integral links between the constitutional conventions of political neutrality, ministerial responsibility and public service anonymity. Consider first the issue of ministerial responsibility.

There are two schools of thought on the relevance of the convention (or doctrine) of ministerial responsibility. Some commentators, the pragmatists, contend that the doctrine is a myth; others, the constitutionalists, view it as a key doctrine of our cabinet-parliamentary form of government (Wilson 1981, p. 196ff.). The different views on the meaning and application of ministerial responsibility can be effectively represented on a continuum ranging from those pragmatists who argue for a major reformulation of the doctrine to those constitutionalists who argue that all incursions on the operation of the traditional doctrine should be resisted.

The traditional model of political neutrality requires that the responsible minister be complemented by the anonymous public servant. Ministers are expected to take public credit and public blame for departmental actions so as to protect the anonymity of their officials. Public servants themselves are expected to protect their anonymity by providing frank and impartial advice to ministers in private and in confidence and by refraining from activities that will involve them – or appear to involve them – in partisan politics. Like the conventions of political neutrality and ministerial responsibility, however, public service anonymity has in practice been somewhat eroded. Is the duty of anonymity still a useful and realistic one?

Public servants receive conflicting signals as to the current meaning of public service anonymity. In general, they are expected to preserve their anonymity, but at the same time they are required to perform tasks that undermine it. In support of their ministers, they now appear regularly before legislative committees where their policy views and policy contributions sometimes become evident. Moreover, increased emphasis on public participation in government decision making has brought more public servants into direct and frequent contact with members of the public, either in public forums or in private offices. The policy influence of public servants is often evident during their consultations and negotiations on behalf of their ministers with pressure-group representatives. The higher visibility of public servants resulting from the combined impact of these developments is compounded by the increased focus of the news media on the activities and influence of public servants. Public servants' use of the Internet is further eroding their anonymity. For example, their government e-mail addresses are now available to the general public.

It has been suggested also that governments' freedom of information legislation is reducing public service anonymity because more documentary information on the decisions and recommendations of public servants has become available. An offsetting consideration is that the names of the public servants involved are usually blacked out on such documents. In addition, most of the politically sensitive material is excluded from disclosure.

Ministers differ in the importance they attach to public service anonymity and to the traditional requirements of ministerial responsibility. Some ministers are more inclined than others to permit public servants to interact with legislators, members of the public, pressure-group representatives and the media. Some ministers have gone so far as to identify and criticize publicly officials allegedly guilty of maladministration or providing poor advice. Paul Thomas (forthcoming) has observed that "the naming, blaming and shaming of individual public servants" under the Harper Government did damage to the "reputations and careers of public service professionals, as well as to the tradition of an anonymous, neutral public service" (n.p.). Such incidents not only severely strain the doctrine of ministerial responsibility, they also diminish public service morale because public servants, as part of their commitment to anonymity, and to keeping their jobs, cannot usually respond publicly to such allegations.

The role of public servants in the political process often brings them into the public spotlight. The convention of ministerial responsibility provides some direction in that it still requires that public servants limit their public activities to explaining government policies, while leaving ministers to defend these policies. When public servants drift over the sometimes indistinguishable line between the explanation and the defence of policy, they may be perceived as having entered the partisan political arena. In this context, their comments and identities will receive much greater publicity.

What should public servants do if obeying their minister's (or their administrative superior's) instructions will involve them in activities that will significantly diminish their anonymity? Should they resist the instructions only if the activities would involve them (or appear to involve them) in partisan politics? Can they justify their resistance on the grounds of ministerial responsibility and political neutrality? Does loyalty to the minister and the government of the day override considerations of anonymity?

In the municipal realm, the doctrine of ministerial responsibility does not apply. Still, public servants are expected to give "forthright and objective advice to their political masters in an open and honest manner. When they are required to make recommendations, they present all available options in a balanced manner. In return, politicians recognize that administrators are using their best administrative judgment and do not criticize them in public for providing honest and forthright advice" (Siegel 1994, p. 26). Municipal staff do not provide their advice in private and in confidence, nor do they look to elected officials to preserve their anonymity. There can be considerable tension between administrators and councillors, especially when the council is divided on an issue. Nonetheless, councillors are expected to take careful account of the professional advice of administrators and to refrain from criticizing them in public.

The Loyal Public Servant

Traditionally, security of tenure for public servants has required that they serve loyally and impartially whatever political party is in power. The 2012 federal *Values and Ethics Code for the Public Sector* requires public servants to show respect for "the Canadian parliamentary democracy and its institutions by...loyally carrying out the lawful decisions of their leaders and supporting ministers in their accountability to Parliament and Canadians" (Treasury Board of Canada Secretariat 2012, n.p.). In return, public servants have traditionally been assured of security of tenure during good behaviour and satisfactory performance. There is now substantial debate, however, as to exactly what the duty of loyalty requires of public servants and how well they fulfill this duty. Moreover, the guarantee of security of tenure has become more tenuous, especially in times of financial constraint and staff cutbacks. In this section, we ask what the duty of loyalty means and how public servants can walk the narrow line between political sensitivity and political partisanship.

Public servants are expected to serve successive governments with equal loyalty. They are, in short, expected to be political chameleons whose colour changes with a change in the political complexion of the governing party. Loyalty means that public servants are neutral in relation to the government and the opposition in the sense of being non-partisan. They are, nevertheless, expected to apprise their minister of the political consequences of pursuing various courses of action. They are expected to be politically sensitive rather than politically partisan (see case 4.1).

Does loyalty to the government mean the same thing as loyalty to the government of the day? The Supreme Court of Canada has declared that "as a general rule, federal public servants should be loyal to their employer...The loyalty owed is to the Government of Canada, not the political party in power at any one time...[T]here is a powerful reason for this general requirement of loyalty, namely, the public interest in both the actual, and apparent, impartiality of the public service" (*Fraser v. Canada* 1985, p. 470). However, Peter Aucoin (2008, November) identified the emergence in recent years of "promiscuous partisanship." He argued, in regard to Canada and other Westminster systems, that political executives are expecting a level of loyalty that goes beyond the traditional duty of public servants to give advice in an impartial and confidential manner. "The expectation is not that they engage in the partisan-political process, for example, at elections or political rallies. Rather, it is that they be promiscuously partisan, that is, agents of the government of the day in relation to stakeholders, organized interests, citizens, media and parliamentarians" (Aucoin 2008, November, p. 19). The pressure on public servants to be loyal in this sense is heightened in a minority government context, where the political environment is especially tense and politicians are especially sensitive to any perceived disloyalty by public servants. However, the pressure persists when a minority government becomes a majority one. Canada's federal Conservative Party Government has been criticized for its partisan exploitation of public servants, especially by drawing them "into partisan communications, directives, events, activities and maintaining websites to promote the Conservative brand" (May 2011, December 10). Under the Conservatives, the line between partisan political communications and professional administrative communications "has become blurred and controversial as the pre-occupation with generating favourable publicity and avoiding negative news spills over from the political centre of government into the administrative culture of the senior ranks of the public service" (Thomas 2013, p. 80).

Some public servants believe that their ultimate loyalty (or responsibility) is not to the government but to the public, to the public interest, or to their own conscience. Are public servants bound to obey governments or ministers who act outside the law or who take decisions that the public servant's conscience cannot bear? Surely the answer must be no, but for their own sake public servants must be sure of their ground before they disobey their minister's instructions. Judicial decisions have identified three situations in which public servants may make exceptions to the duty of loyalty (Treasury Board of Canada Secretariat 2005):

1. the Government is engaged in illegal acts;

2. Government policies jeopardize life, health or safety; or

3. the public servant's criticism has no impact on his or her ability to perform effectively the duties of a public servant or on the public perception of that ability.

As noted in chapter 1, many governments across the country have ensconced such limitations on loyalty in the definitions of what would constitute "wrongdoing" found in recent whistle blower protection legislation.

CASE 4.1: DRAWING THE LINE

A conversation is overheard between two public servants.

Donna: The minister's going to love this program. It'll be very popular and will undoubtedly increase the government's standing in the polls. It will also make the department look very good.

Martin: It's not our job to make the government look good. Our concern should extend only so far as to give the best advice possible. You shouldn't be concerned about the political implications of your advice.

Donna: Well, that goes with the territory. We work closely with politicians in devising policy. If we do a good job, the government looks good. That's the way it is. We work for political masters.

Martin: You're going too far, Donna! Not every policy that is advisable is going to be politically popular. Public servants who become fixated by the popularity of the government are ignoring their professional responsibilities.

Donna: You're exaggerating, Martin. The public service must help the government make good decisions. An essential component of policy making is political feasibility. In that sense, I suppose you could say that the public servant must support the party in power. That's what we're here for.

Martin: Yes, but there's a fine line between political sensitivity and political partisanship, and you've stepped over it.

Whose side would you take in this debate, Donna's or Martin's? Does the public servant's duty of loyalty to the minister mean that he or she should do anything required to keep the minister out of trouble and the government in power? Is there a line between political sensitivity and political partisanship? How would you characterize it? Is the kind of public service Donna seems to support a politically neutral public service?

Municipal public servants are expected to "execute policy decisions loyally, irrespective of their personal opinions; as a result, public servants enjoy freedom from public criticism by councilors and security of tenure during good behaviour and satisfactory performance" (Siegel 1994, p. 29). Municipal employees are in a more difficult position than public servants at other levels of government because their advice to elected officials is given in public. When council's decisions do not reflect that advice, it is understandable that both councillors and citizens may wonder whether employees will be able to implement those decisions impartially and effectively. However, once the council has made a decision, it is the employees' professional responsibility to implement the decision to the best of their ability, regardless of their personal feelings. This will help to ensure, but not guarantee, that employees will escape public criticism from councillors and that they will keep their jobs if a faction of council or a newly elected council wants them gone.

Political Staff

Public servants have to consider not only the appropriate extent of their own loyalty but also the loyalty issues raised by the role of political appointees who advise and assist political executives such as ministers and mayors. These appointees are known variously as political staff or exempt staff (because they are exempt from staffing and other controls that apply to departmental public servants). The intended role of exempt staff is to provide political executives with partisan political advice that cannot be provided by politically neutral public servants. Over the past two decades in particular there has been a steady increase in the number and influence of political staff, some of whom have become as influential as public servants in giving policy advice to political executives – and in some instances even more influential (Aucoin 2008, November; Benoit 2006).

There is tension between public servants and political staff, in part because the latter are perceived, often correctly, as having little experience and knowledge of government. In official terms, political staff do not have formal authority over public servants and are not supposed to interpose themselves between public servants and political executives. Increasingly, however, political staff have been reaching down the hierarchy, often in an informal manner, to interact with public servants and influence administrative action (Benoit 2006; Dutil 2006, June).

Problematic relationships between public servants and political staff have provoked calls for rules of conduct in this sphere. The federal government's response is contained in *Accountable Government: A Guide for Ministers and Ministers of State* (Canada, Privy Council Office 2011), which stipulates that exempt staff have no role in departmental operations; they cannot legally exercise the delegated authority of ministers; and they are not permitted to give orders to departmental public servants. Moreover, the Guide states that exempt staff must "respect the non-partisanship of public servants and not seek to engage them in work that is outside their appropriate role," and that they "have an obligation to inform themselves about the appropriate parameters of public service conduct, including public service values and ethics, and to actively assess their own conduct and any requests they make to departmental officials in the light of those parameters" (p. 46).

Since these rules are subject to interpretation, public servants can sometimes be placed in a difficult position in their relations with political staff. Liane Benoit (2006), in her detailed study of federal political staff for the Gomery Commission, observed that the practice of political staff giving directions to departmental officials "is subtle, reasonably pervasive, and in many instances a practical necessity" (p. 237). She concluded that "[a]s long as all sides stick to their respective roles, the system, by and large, bumps along with an acceptable degree of efficacy, efficiency and propriety" (p. 196). This is not always the case, however. In 2013, for example, the British Columbia government was immersed in a scandal when political staff in the Premier's Office were revealed to have tried to engage ordinary public servants, ministerial political staff, BC Liberal caucus staff and Liberal Party staff to collectively support a rather cynical plan to win votes for the ruling Liberal Party in "ethnic" communities in the upcoming election (British Columbia, Deputy Minister to the Premier 2013).

The following case provides a basis for considering how far a public servant should go in cooperating with ministerial staff.

CASE 4.2: WE LIVE IN A POLITICAL WORLD

Kate, a professional economist and statistician, is responsible for preparing the regular quarterly report on the employment situation in the province for the Department of Labour. It's getting close to an election and the department employees can feel the pressure to make the economic situation look as rosy as possible.

A couple of days after she has produced the draft of the employment report in the standard format, her boss comes into her office and closes the door. He says that he shared the draft report with the minister's office and has had some pressure from a senior staffer in the office to put a more "positive" spin on the deteriorating unemployment situation. What he suggests is that she replace the unemployment graph at the front of the report with an employment graph showing that there was a small growth in new jobs in the last quarter. He also recommends that she narrow the scale on this graph so that the growth in jobs looks more substantial. When Kate protests this change in the way they report, he agrees to include the unemployment data for the last quarter towards the end of the report but asks Kate to broaden the scale of that graph so that the increase in unemployment does not appear to be as significant as it really is.

Kate says that she is uncomfortable with "spinning" the report in this manner because the media and the casual reader could easily draw the wrong conclusions. It might also create mistrust in the financial community that depends on the data in the report. Her boss tells her to relax and get on with the redrafting. "We live in a political world" he says, as he goes out the door.

Should Kate do as she is instructed?

The Public Servant's Political Rights

The next two sections of this chapter examine the implications of political neutrality for public servants when they are away from the workplace. The focus is on the extent to which public servants can exercise political rights. The challenge is to find the optimum balance between the enjoyment of political rights and the need for political neutrality. The arguments provided below on each side of this issue can be considered in relation to case 4.3 on political partisanship and case 4.4 on public comment.[4]

The argument most often presented for extending political rights is that public servants should enjoy the same freedoms of speech and association as other citizens. Proponents of this view argue that these freedoms are guaranteed under section 2 of Canada's Charter of Rights and Freedoms. The other side of this argument is that the present restrictions are reasonable limits in a free and democratic society under section 1 of the Charter. Opinions on this issue range from the view that public servants should enjoy full political rights to the view that these rights should be strictly limited so as to preserve the reality – and the appearance – of a politically neutral public service.

Another argument for extending the political rights of public servants is that restrictions on these rights deprive the public in general and political parties in particular of valuable information and insights on public affairs. The argument is also made that restrictions on the political rights of public servants limit the involvement in partisan politics of a large percentage of the most educated citizens in the labour force. Moreover, these restrictions are viewed as artificial in that they only limit public displays of partisanship; they do nothing to reduce the partisan beliefs or feelings that public servants may have. Finally, it is suggested

---

4. An extended discussion of these arguments can be found in Kernaghan (1976).

that knowledgeable and skilled persons whose talents are needed in government will be unwilling to accept employment if their political rights are unduly restricted.

The arguments against the expansion of political rights are primarily arguments in favour of political neutrality. "In a democratic society it is desirable for all citizens to have a voice in the affairs of the State, and for as many as possible to play an active part in public life. Yet the public interest demands the maintenance of political impartiality in the public service and of confidence in that impartiality as an essential part of the structure of government in this country" (Starr and Sharp 1984, p. 46). Thus it is commonly argued that the participation of public servants in partisan politics or in public comment undermines public confidence in the impartial conduct of the public's business.

Similarly, both ministers and members of the opposition need to have confidence in the loyalty and impartiality of public servants; otherwise, ministers will be inclined to make more patronage appointments, especially at the senior levels of the public service, and opposition members, when they form the government, will be inclined to replace these appointees with their own supporters. Indeed, the argument is frequently made that a substantial expansion in the political rights of public servants will lead to an increase in patronage appointments at all levels of the service and that this will undermine the merit system of appointment and advancement and reduce government efficiency and effectiveness. A final concern about the expansion of political rights relates to political partisanship rather than to public comment. This is the concern that if public servants are permitted to engage in a wide range of partisan political activities, they are more vulnerable to exploitation by superiors seeking support for a specific political party or candidate. Consider the case of an Alberta deputy minister who sent a message to employees suggesting which candidate they should support in the 2011 Conservative Party leadership race.

The resolution of the political rights–political neutrality issue lies in accommodating these conflicting viewpoints. The Supreme Court of Canada has asserted that "freedom of expression is a deep-rooted value in our democratic system of government...but it is not an absolute value...All important values must be qualified, and balanced against, other important, and often competing values" (*Fraser v. Canada* 1985, p. 462-463). The real question, then, is not whether there should be limits on the political rights of public servants, but what the extent of these limits should be. The challenge is to provide the fullest possible measure of political rights that is compatible with the maintenance of the political impartiality of the public service. On the basis of these considerations, we shall discuss the appropriate balance first between political neutrality and political partisanship and then between political neutrality and public comment.

The Non-Partisan Public Servant

The term "partisan political activities" includes a broad range of activities from voting to standing for election. These activities can be divided into two main categories: low-profile activities (e.g., voting, being a member of a political party, attending political meetings); and high-profile activities (e.g., soliciting financial contributions, door-to-door canvassing).

Rules on the political activity of public servants can be depicted on a continuum running from the extreme position of no restrictions to the other extreme of political sterilization, but in Canada, no government's rules fall at either extreme. Indeed, the issue is not whether there should be some restrictions on partisan political activity but rather how permissive or restrictive the rules should be. The details of the differences among the political-activity regimes of Canada's federal, provincial and municipal governments cannot be reviewed here, but it is important to note the central elements on which there is substantial agreement. Most public servants are permitted to engage in such low-profile activities as attending political meetings and contributing money to support a political candidate or a political party. Some jurisdictions, however, restrict certain public servants from such high-profile activities as soliciting funds for a political party or candidate on the grounds that these activities are more likely to undermine the confidence of the public and elected officials in the political neutrality of the public service. The great majority of public servants are permitted to seek nomination and election to public office, and in some jurisdictions they are reinstated after losing a bid for nomination or election. Most jurisdictions impose greater restrictions on public servants in senior and sensitive positions, including a prohibition against seeking public office.

The argument is often made that public servants should have an unrestricted right to engage in partisan politics unless they have policy-making responsibilities or perform sensitive duties in such areas as human resource management or regulation. The line of reasoning on the other side is that the cumulative impact of the participation of large numbers of public servants in high-profile partisan politics may undermine the confidence of the public or elected officials in the impartiality of the public service.

CASE 4.3: SECOND-CLASS CITIZENS?

This conversation takes place between Dave, a provincial public servant, and Andrea, a friend who is a candidate in the upcoming provincial election.

Andrea: I'd like you to come to work for me as my campaign manager.

Dave: You know my position. I'm a government employee. I can't get involved in a political campaign.

Andrea: You're an engineer. How much influence could you possibly have on government policy making?

Dave: Very little, granted. But the logic is that if I publicly declare my political loyalties it would appear that I'm less capable of doing my job impartially. And even the appearance of partisanship is unacceptable.

Andrea: Public servants aren't second-class citizens, Dave. You have rights and freedoms just like everyone else. Aren't you going to stand up for yourself?

Dave: I can't, Andrea. I knew what I was doing when I took this job. I knew I would have to make some concessions. I can contribute to your campaign, but I just can't work on it.

Is it justifiable for Dave's rights as a private citizen to be curtailed in this way because of his employment in the public sector? What are the downside risks to the public service of allowing political activity among public servants? What is the appropriate extent of political activity for a public servant? Are concerns about impartiality with respect to advice and service delivery relevant to an engineer? Might whole groups in the public service be safely allowed more political rights?

Seeking nomination and election to public office while on leave of absence is a high-profile activity in which most public servants are, nonetheless, permitted to engage. Thus, public servants, despite public identification with a particular political party, can be reinstated in the public service after losing a bid for nomination or election. Is it consistent to permit the return of public servants involved in such a high-profile political activity while restricting the political activity of public servants involved in less visible activities? Or is the leave of absence and reinstatement policy justified by the small number of public servants involved and by the undesirability of the alternative – an absolute prohibition on the right of public servants to seek political office?

Central concerns about the overt partisan affiliation of public servants and its effect on loyalty and on the merit system have been succinctly summarized as follows:

> If a Minister began to consider whether A, on account of his party views, might be more capable of carrying out his policy than B, the usefulness of B would be limited and the opportunities of A would be unfairly improved. This would become known, and a tendency to trim the sails to the prevailing wind would be one consequence. Another would be cynicism about the reasons for promotion very damaging to morale...The danger...may result from only small beginnings, but once begun, it produces a snowball effect, which is difficult, if not impossible, to check. Once a doubt is cast upon the loyalty of certain individuals or upon the equity of the promotion machinery, an atmosphere of distrust may rapidly pervade an office and affect the arrangement of the work and damage the efficiency of the organization (United Kingdom 1949: para. 3).

The right of federal public servants to engage in a broader range of partisan political activities was significantly extended by the Supreme Court's decision in *Osborne v. Canada* (1991). The Court struck down the political-activity provisions of the *Public Service Employment Act* (2003) (PSEA) except for their application to deputy heads and the requirement that public servants seek leave to be a political candidate. The Court viewed the restriction on political activity as an unreasonable limit of freedom of expression. While the Court acknowledged the importance of preserving political neutrality, it noted that "a great number of public servants...in modern government are completely divorced from the exercise of any discretion that could be in any manner affected by political considerations." In addition, the Court found that the Act was "over inclusive and went beyond what is necessary to achieve the objective of an impartial and loyal civil service." The Court also ruled that restrictions on political activities should be geared to such considerations as the nature of the work being performed, the visibility of the political activity in question, and the public servant's role and responsibilities.

Parliament responded to the Court's decision in 2003 when it adopted the new PSEA that came into force at the end of 2005. The

Act's preamble stresses the importance of a merit-based, non-partisan public service, and section 112 recognizes "the right of employees to engage in political activities while maintaining the principle of political impartiality in the public service." Public servants are permitted to engage in any political activity "as long as it does not impair, or is not perceived as impairing, the employee's ability to perform his or her duties in a politically impartial manner." The political activity of deputy heads, however, is limited to voting.

Similarly, in the Province of Ontario, the 2006 *Public Service of Ontario Act* created a "specially restricted public servants" class (s. 85, para. 2) that restricts the activities of persons in senior and sensitive positions to voting, attending all-candidates meetings, contributing money to a political party or candidate, and campaigning for or standing as a candidate for municipal election if that would not constitute a conflict of interest.

The extent of disagreement as to what public servants can legally do in the sphere of political activities has been reduced, but it is important to ask whether it is sufficient for a responsible public servant simply to adhere to the law or the written rules. Should public servants look to the spirit as well as the letter of the law? It is certainly possible to act legally while acting unethically. Take the example of a welfare caseworker who during the evening engages legally in door-to-door canvassing for votes in the same neighbourhoods where he or she visits clients during the day. Is it reasonable to expect public servants to ask themselves not only whether an action is legal but also whether it is ethical?

Common sense suggests that public servants may on some occasions be well advised to refrain from participating in the considerable range of partisan political activities to which they are now legally entitled. The federal Public Service Commission has noted that "[r]epeated involvement by public servants in political activities could potentially harm their perceived political impartiality or that of their department" (Canada, PSC 2010, March 2, n.p.). Arthur Kroeger (1992), a former federal deputy minister, has noted:

> In cases where individuals are identified, or
> even suspected, of having party connections of
> the wrong kind, there is only so much deputy
> ministers can do to protect them...[T]here
> will of course still be consenting adults in the
> public service who are prepared to accept the
> consequences of ending up on the wrong side

after an election. For the others, however, I
would suggest they approach the question of
political activity in the same manner that the
Anglican prayer book prescribes for marriage:
it is not by any to be entered upon...lightly or
wantonly; but...discreetly, advisedly, soberly,
and in the fear of God. (p. 6)

The Public Service Commission has also observed that "Internet
social networking technologies can blur the public and private lives of
public servants and lead to perceptions that they are making political
statements" (Canada, PSC 2010, March 2, n.p.). For example, a
junior-level federal employee working in the Privy Council Office openly
supported a political party on a social networking website. The Public
Service Commission concluded that the employee's activities could be
perceived as impairing his ability to perform his duties in a politically
impartial manner and ordered corrective action. It is not surprising
that the torrent of communications flowing between Canadians through
such means as text messaging and Facebook includes messages from
public servants that raise questions not only of appropriate political
partisanship but also of appropriate public comment. Indiscretion is
not, however, limited to the young. A forty-six-year-old public relations
attaché employed by the federal Department of Foreign Affairs was
reported to have made disparaging remarks on Facebook about the
prime minister and government policy (Weston 2009, November 10).

For municipal governments, political neutrality requires that
"public servants do not engage in partisan political activities or any
type of electoral politics at the local level, and avoid involvement at the
federal or provincial levels as well" (Siegel 1994, p. 21). The extent of
permissible political activities varies among local governments, but in
general local governments have extended the political-activity rights
of employees since the 1991 Supreme Court decision in Osborne
mentioned earlier. Most governments permit employees to engage
in activities such as posting lawn signs and supporting a candidate's
campaign but prohibit high-profile activities while at work, such as
soliciting campaign contributions and wearing campaign buttons. The
City of Thunder Bay (2002) adopted a tiered system (similar to that of
Ontario) that classifies employees into the three categories of Senior
Management (severely restricted in respect of political activity), Division
Managers (somewhat restricted) and All Other Employees (largely
unrestricted). Municipal employees are typically required to obtain a
leave of absence to stand for election to federal or provincial office. If
they seek municipal office, however, they are usually required to resign
their government post.

As suggested for federal and provincial employees, municipal employees may be ill advised to engage in all of the political activities that are permitted. Consider, for example, the possible effect on employees' career prospects if the current mayor should encounter them when visiting the campaign headquarters of an opponent. Consider also the fate of municipal employees engaged in high-profile provincial politics at the time of a serious provincial-municipal dispute.

The political-rights issue is further complicated by public servants' involvement in "non-partisan" political activities. Among these activities is being an executive or a member of an organization that advocates environmental protection or tax reduction and that challenges government policy. A celebrated example here involves a public servant who was dismissed from her position in the Official Languages Support Program of Heritage Canada when she became president of a Quebec sovereigntist organization. The Public Service Staff Relations Board recognized her advocacy work as incompatible with her position, but reinstated her to a different job (Canada, Public Service Staff Relations Board 2006).

The Discreet Public Servant

The traditional duty of public servants to be politically neutral requires that they not engage publicly in critical comment on government policies and programs. Critical comment needs to be distinguished, however, from the broader concept of public comment. Many forms of public comment (for example, the description or explanation of government structures, processes, policies and programs) are acceptable or required activities connected with public servants' formal responsibilities. Beyond these activities are riskier types of public comment, such as recommending reforms in government machinery or speculating in public on future government policy. Participation in these activities can occasionally diminish the anonymity or perceived neutrality of the public service or damage its reputation.

Government approval for public comment reduces the risk for public servants. For example, a pilot project in the federal Department of Foreign Affairs and International Trade (Lambert 2010, October 11) encouraged public servants to post responses online that corrected perceived misinformation circulated by groups opposed to Canada's seal hunt. The public servants involved in this project were required to reveal their government position and to refrain from entering into debates.

Public servants' expression of public criticism can have significant consequences for anonymity, ministerial responsibility and political neutrality. At first glance, it may appear crystal clear that public servants cannot with impunity be permitted to criticize government policies or programs. But is it reasonable to forbid public servants to engage in criticism that is unrelated to their official duties or to the policies or programs of their own department (see case 4.3)? What if their comments relate to the policies or programs of another government, for example, comments by a provincial public servant on a federal government policy? What are the circumstances under which public servants should be allowed to engage in public criticism of government? Should we be surprised that an employee of the Canadian Security Intelligence Service was disciplined for describing his workplace as a "rat hole" to a journalist who published this description in a newspaper (Canada, Public Service Staff Relations Board 2002)?

Some assistance in answering these questions has been provided by the Supreme Court of Canada. The Court has stated that "an absolute rule prohibiting all public participation and discussion by all public servants would prohibit activities which no sensible person in a democratic society would want to prohibit." However, "freedom to criticize the Government...is not an absolute freedom...[W]hereas it is obvious that it would not be 'just cause' for a provincial Government to dismiss a provincial clerk who stood in a crowd on a Sunday afternoon to protest provincial day care policies, it is equally obvious that the same Government would have 'just cause' to dismiss the Deputy Minister of Social Services who spoke vigorously against the same policies at the same rally." We have a "tradition surrounding our public service [that] emphasizes the characteristics of impartiality, neutrality, fairness and integrity...[E]mployment in the public service involves acceptance of certain restraints. One of the most important of those restraints is to exercise caution when it comes to making criticisms of Government." Finally, the court noted that "a public servant may actively and publicly express opposition to the policies of a government...if, for example, the Government were engaged in illegal acts, or if its policies jeopardized the life, health or safety of the public servant or others, or if the public servant's criticism had no impact on his or her ability to perform effectively the duties of a public servant or on the public perception of that ability" (*Fraser v. Canada* 1985, pp. 467, 468, 471, 470.) Similar language has been used to describe the practice of whistle blowing (discussed in chapter 6), that is, the exposure of government wrongdoing involving such activities as violations of the law or threats to the public's safety or health.

CASE 4.4: NO COMMENT

The following heated exchange takes place between Paul and Erica, his supervisor, in a federal government department.

Erica: First you send a letter to the editor; next you appear as featured speaker at an anti-metric rally, and now television! Do you have anything to say for yourself before I begin an action to suspend you, Paul?

Paul: Yes, I certainly have. As a Canadian citizen, I have a fundamental right to free speech, which is guaranteed by the Charter of Rights and Freedoms. If I don't agree with government policy, I have a right to say so, just like everyone else.

Erica: As a public servant your responsibility is to act with professionalism and impartiality.

Paul: Which I have done. My criticism of the government's metric policy is completely unrelated to my work in this department. I am convinced that I have in no way jeopardized my ability to perform my duties.

Erica: On the contrary, your conduct is going to make it difficult for the minister to have confidence in our department; it is likely to undermine public confidence in our department. I must warn you, Paul, that unless you stop your public criticisms of government policy, you risk losing your job.

Whose position would you defend in the above exchange? Why? Would you argue that a public servant should give up some freedom of speech as a part of his or her job? What are the appropriate boundaries of public comment? Is the subject matter of the comment the key issue here?

Many governments provide advice on permissible public comment in their codes of conduct. British Columbia's *Standards of Conduct for Public Service Employees* states that "employees are free to comment on public issues but must exercise caution to ensure, that by doing so, they do not jeopardize the perception of impartiality in the performance of their duties...[C]are should be taken in making comments or entering into public debate regarding their ministry policies" (British Columbia, Public Service Agency 2003, n.p.). Even comment intended as constructive criticism of government may be perceived by political or administrative superiors as grounds for dismissal or other disciplinary action. Broadly worded advice to "exercise caution" and "take care" can have a chilling effect on public servants' willingness to engage in public comment. Even more chilling have been the federal Government's efforts to stifle dissent by dismissing several public servants who publicly criticized its policies (Gergin 2011). On rare occasions, public servants signal their dissent by resigning. The head of Statistics Canada resigned in protest against a minister's claim that the agency agreed with the government's decision to scrap the mandatory long-form census questionnaire.

Should governments spell out in specific terms the appropriate bounds of public comment? Is this feasible? Should public servants be able to seek advice when they are uncertain as to how far they can go? These several questions can be considered in relation to the concrete situation set out in case 4.4. In addition, readers can refer to a lengthy report by the Treasury Board of Canada Secretariat on the duty of loyalty, which deals primarily with the extent to which public servants can engage in criticism of the government (2005).

Municipal public servants, like their federal and provincial counterparts, are restricted in their public expression of personal views on their government's policies or administration. An Alberta court has summed up the widely accepted position on this issue as follows:

> A municipal employee must not engage in activities that attack the municipal government policies or activities and if a municipal employee does so, he displays a lack of loyalty to the municipality that is inconsistent with his duties as a municipal government employee. (*Bishop v. Trochu (Town)* 1998, A.J. No. 1279 at para. 35 (Q.B).)

Given the close interactions between municipal councillors and employees, it is appropriate to caution employees that they should not attack "personalities" either.

Advances in information and communication technologies, including Web 2.0 tools, have impacted the issue of public comment. The City of Calgary defines a public statement as a declaration made by a city employee "in any public forum, which relates to the City of Calgary, its employees and/or its business units and includes statements made in weblogs (blogs), in online forums, on social networking sites, in wikis and elsewhere in the public record" (Calgary, Corporate Services 2008, March 11, p. 2). Among the City's key requirements for employees outlined in its public relations policy are these:

- Do not defame, and / or speak negatively of The City, City personnel or The City's business units when making public statements...

- If you write online, be prepared for your text to exist online in perpetuity once you publish it...

- When posting information on public websites, blogs, discussion forums or wikis on work that you do in a City capacity, or when participating in discussions about The City, identify yourself as a City of Calgary employee.

- When making a public statement as a private citizen on matters not related to your work, do not identify yourself as a City employee. (p. 2-3)

Conclusion

The policies and practices of governments in Canada vary significantly from the requirements of the idealized model of political neutrality explained earlier in this chapter. The extent of this variation differs from one government to another, and even from one department to another within a single government. Moreover, not only public servants but also judges, legislators, journalists and academics are uncertain or in disagreement as to the meaning of the public servant's duty to be politically neutral. The task of defining this duty is complicated by the fact that some of the rules bearing on political neutrality, including those affecting political rights, are in a state of flux.

The duty of political neutrality is commonly justified by reference to its status as a constitutional convention supporting the closely related conventions of ministerial responsibility and public service anonymity. But has too much emphasis been placed on preserving these conventions in their traditional form? Are further departures from the various components of political neutrality desirable or feasible? We have noted that the meaning and application of ministerial responsibility and public service anonymity are the subject of substantial debate. Moreover, political neutrality is respected in Canada's municipal governments and in governments like that of the United States that are not based on ministerial responsibility. The similarity of the arguments for political neutrality in both federal/provincial and municipal governments shows that factors other than constitutional conventions are in play. These arguments are a complex mix of constitutional and ethical considerations. It is important, therefore, to contemplate the extent to which the duty of political neutrality can be justified by reference to broadly based ethical standards and, in particular, the three approaches to ethical justification outlined in chapter two.

Consider, for example, the need to find an appropriate balance between political neutrality and political rights. Consequentialists would assess, for all affected stakeholders, the extent to which restricting the political rights of public servants would have good outcomes (e.g., preserving public trust in government, discouraging patronage) or bad outcomes (e.g., reducing freedom of expression, depriving the public of informed opinion on public affairs). Duty theorists would assess whether the freedom of expression associated with extensive political rights is more important than political neutrality. They would apply the criteria of the categorical imperative by asking whether the rules enforcing political neutrality could be made universal, whether the rules offend rationality by depriving others of their rights and whether we would like to have the rules applied to ourselves. Virtue ethicists would look to public servants who have, ideally, internalized respect for political neutrality as a fundamental democratic value and who understand the need to balance that value with other values.

Chapter 2 concludes with a discussion of the steps that a responsible public servant should take to reach a reflective equilibrium when faced with a moral dilemma. The scenario outlined there includes a clash between the public servant's duty of loyalty to the government – an important dimension of political neutrality – and his duty as set out in whistle blower protection legislation to report a threat to public safety. Reference to the convention of political neutrality alone does not provide a satisfactory resolution to the dilemma. Thus the public servant is encouraged to delve into his or her ethical toolkit to apply the three ethical theories to the dilemma. While it is unlikely, in the event of such a controversial moral dilemma, that one ethical theory will clearly outshine the others, the process should assist public servants to determine the extent of political neutrality that is compatible with responsible public service.

References

Aucoin, P. (2008, November). *New public management and the quality of government: Coping with the new political governance in Canada*. Paper presented at conference on New Public Management and the Quality of Government, University of Gothenberg, Sweden.

Benoit, L. (2006). Ministerial staff: The life and times of Parliament's statutory orphans. In Commission of Inquiry into the Sponsorship Program and Advertising Activities. *Restoring Accountability: Research Studies Volume 1,* pp. 145-240.

Bishop v. Trochu (Town). (1998). A.J. No. 1279 at para. 35 (Alta. Q.B).

British Columbia, Deputy Minister to the Premier. (2013). *The review of the draft multicultural strategic outreach plan.* Retrieved from http://www.cbc.ca/bc/news/bc-130314-dyble-report.pdf

British Columbia, Public Service Agency. (2003). *Standards of conduct for public service employees.* Revised September 2003. Retrieved from http://www.llbc.leg.bc.ca/public/pubdocs/bcdocs/364448/standards_of_conduct.pdf

Calgary, Corporate Services. (2008, March 11). *Public statements and media relations policy.* MP-001. Retrieved from http://www.calgary.ca/docgallery/bu/hr/policy/public_statements_and_media_relations_policy_mp001.pdf

Canada, Privy Council Office. (2011). *Accountable government: A guide for ministers and ministers of state.* Retrieved from http://pm.gc/grfx/docs/guidemin_e.pdf

Canada, Public Service Commission. (2008, July). *Public service impartiality: Taking stock.* Retrieved from http://www.google.ca/search?output=search&sclient=psy-ab&q=public+service+impartiality+taking+stock&btnK=

Canada, Public Service Commission. (2010, March 2). *Symposium on safeguarding a non-partisan public service in the 21st century: Political activity case studies.* Ottawa, ON.

Canada, Public Service Staff Relations Board. (2002). *Simard v. Canadian Security Intelligence Service*, 166-20-30345 (2002 PSSRB 52).

Canada, Public Service Staff Relations Board. (2006). *Gendron v. Treasury Board (Department of Canadian Heritage)*, 166-02-34747 (2006 PSLRB 27).

City of Thunder Bay. (2002). *Staff code of conduct relating to political activity.* Retrieved from http://ctbpub.thunderbay.ca/ctbapps/ctb_p&p.nsf/0/79fff69b2f442c8985256a32006a8683?OpenDocument

Dutil, P. (2006, June). *Working with political staff at Queen's Park: Trends, outlooks, opportunities.* IPAC Executive Brief. Retrieved from http://www.ipac.ca/documents/WorkingwithPolStaff064.pdf

Fraser v. Canada (Public Service Staff Relations Board). (1985). 2 S.C.R. 455.

Gergin, M. (2011). *Silencing dissent: The Conservative record*. Ottawa: Canadian Centre for Policy Alternatives.

Good, D. A. (2008). An ideal model in a practical world: The continuous revisiting of political neutrality and ministerial responsibility. In D. Siegel & K. Rasmussen (Eds.), *Professionalism and public service: Essays in honour of Kenneth Kernaghan* (pp. 63-83). Toronto: University of Toronto Press.

Juillet, L., & Rasmussen, K. (2008). *Defending a contested ideal: Merit and the PSC of Canada 1908-2008*. Ottawa: University of Ottawa Press.

Kernaghan, K. (1976). Politics, policy and public servants: Political neutrality revisited. *Canadian Public Administration, 19*(3), 432-456.

Kroeger, A. (1992). On being a deputy minister. *Policy Options, 13*(4), 3-6.

Lambert, S. (2010, October 11). Bureaucrats wade into online debate about Canada's seal hunt. *Globe and Mail*. Retrieved from http://www.theglobeandmail.com/news/national/bureaucrats-wade-into-online-debate-about-canadas-seal-hunt/article4328716

May, K. (2011, December 10). Public service, government need 'moral contract'to stop partisan exploitation of bureaucracy. *The Ottawa Citizen*. Retrieved from http://www.ottawacitizen.com/news/Public+service+government+need+moral+contract+stop+parti san/5842683/story.html

New Brunswick. (2009). *New Brunswick public service values and conduct guide*. Fredericton: Province of New Brunswick. Retrieved from http://www.google.ca/search?hl=en&output=search&sclient=psy-ab&q=new+brunswick+values+and+conduct+guide+public+service&btnK=

OPSEU v. Ontario. (1980), supra note 16 at para. 99. Appeal from a judgment of the Ontario Court of Appeal [1980], 31. O.R. (2d) 321, 118 D.L.R. (3d) 661.

Osborne v. Canada (Treasury Board). (1991). 2 S.C.R. 69.

Parks Canada. (2009). *Code of ethics of the Parks Canada Agency*. Retrieved from http://www.pc.gc.ca/eng/docs/pc/guide/code/page01.aspx

Public Service Employment Act. (2003). In Statutes of Canada, c. 22, s. 112.

Public Service of Ontario Act (2006). In Statutes of Ontario, c. 35, Part V, p. 85, s. 2: Rules for political activity of specially restricted public servants.

Siegel, D. (1994). Politics, politicians, and public servants in non-partisan local governments. *Canadian Public Administration, 37*(1), 7-30.

Siegel, D. (2010). The leadership role of municipal chief administrative officers. *Canadian Public Administration, 53(2), 139-162.*

Starr, M., & Sharp, M. (1984). Ethical conduct in the public sector: Report of the Task Force on Conflict of Interest. Ottawa: Supply and Services Canada.

Thomas, P. G. (forthcoming). Two (not three) cheers for bureaucracy: Canada's public service. In A. G. Gagnon & J. Bickerton (Eds.), *Canadian Politics* (6th ed.). Toronto: University of Toronto Press.

Thomas, P. G. (2013). Communications and prime ministerial power. In J. Bickerton & B. G. Peters (Eds.), *Governing: Essays in honour of Donald J. Savoie* (pp. 53-84). Kingston: McGill-Queen's University Press.

Treasury Board of Canada Secretariat. (2005). *Duty of loyalty.* Retrieved from http://www.tbs-sct.gc.ca/rp/icg-eng.asp

Treasury Board of Canada Secretariat. (2012). *Values and ethics code for the public sector.* Retrieved from http://www.tbs-sct.gc.ca/pol/doc-eng.aspx?id=25049&section=text#cha5

United Kingdom. (1949). *Report of the committee on the political activities of civil servants.* (Cmd. 7718).

Weston, G. (2009, November 10). Kicked in the tweets: Diplomat's Facebook exposure wakes feds up to social networking. *Ottawa Sun.* Retrieved from http://www.ottawasun.com/comment/columnists/greg_weston/2009/11/10/11692211-sun.html

Wilson, V. S. (1981). *Canadian public policy and administration.* Toronto: McGraw-Hill Ryerson.

Chapter 5

Conflict of Interest

> The use of [public] office to satisfy private
> desires or to effect private gain is not a private
> action but a public crime. (Dobel 1999, p. 187)

> Because maintaining the public trust is a
> crucial aspect of administrative responsibility,
> the appearance of conflict of interest may be
> sufficient to jeopardize faith in the integrity of
> government. (Cooper 2006, p. 140)

Conflict of interest is one of the most common forms of unethical conduct in the public sector. It is certainly the type that is best known to the general public and that arouses the most controversy outside government. Conflicts of interest are pervasive in society, and they affect not only government organizations but also business and not-for-profit ones as well. However, this chapter is concerned solely with conflicts of interest in government and focuses on public servants rather than politicians.

What is a conflict of interest? Has its meaning changed over time? How can the public servant's duty to avoid conflicts of interest be fulfilled? How can a real conflict of interest be distinguished from an apparent conflict and from a potential conflict? Why should we be concerned about conflicts of interest? What are the various forms of conflict of interest? These are the major questions considered in this chapter.

Defining the Duty

It is important to define and explain the term "conflict of interest" because there is much disagreement and confusion about its meaning. Traditionally, conflict of interest has been seen as a situation in which a public official uses public office to enhance his or her personal interests. The *Code of Conduct and Ethics for the Public Service of Alberta* captures the essence of this approach when it states that public servants are in a conflict of interest if they "take part in a decision in the course of carrying out their duties, knowing that the decision might further a private interest of the employee, their spouse or minor child" (Alberta, Personnel Administration Office 2005, p. 10). But what do we mean by a private interest? Until recently, the focus has been almost exclusively on financial gain. Examples include accepting or soliciting a benefit (e.g., box seats at a hockey game) from someone with whom one does business as a public servant; using government resources (e.g., office supplies) for personal purposes; making private investments based on insider information (e.g., confidential information about the location of a new government-sponsored high tech park); or moonlighting at a second job (e.g., preparing lectures for a part-time university teaching position) when one is supposed to be working at one's public service job.

More recently, codes of conduct have begun to come to grips with the degree to which personal interests can be broader than simple financial gain. The federal *Policy on Conflict of Interest and Post-Employment* notes that "[c]onflict of interest does not relate exclusively to matters concerning financial transactions and the transfer of economic benefit. While financial activity is important, conflicts of interest in any area of activity can have a negative impact on the perceived objectivity of the public service" (Treasury Board of Canada Secretariat 2012a, Appendix B). According to the 2005 Bellamy Inquiry into the City of Toronto's computer-leasing scandal, a conflict of interest "should be considered in its broadest possible sense. It is about much more than money. Obviously, a conflict of interest exists when a decision-maker in public service has a personal financial interest in a decision. But conflicts of interest extend to any interest, loyalty, concern, emotion, or other feature tending to make the individual's judgment less reliable than it would normally be" (Bellamy 2005, p. 39).

What does this mean in practical terms? A public servant may gain in popularity rather than in the pocketbook by appointing friends or relatives to government posts. Similarly, a public servant who passes along confidential information that friends and relatives can use to their economic advantage may achieve no personal economic benefit. An immigration officer who promises special treatment to an immigrant in return for sexual favours receives no financial benefit. Yet an Immigration and Refugee Board judge was sentenced to 18 months in prison for offering to grant refugee status to an applicant in exchange for sex (Bell 2010, December 16).

Conflict of interest may even be interpreted to include the use of public office for partisan gain. Consider, for example, the case of a public servant who provides confidential information to the party in political opposition in order to enhance his or her partisan objectives. Note also that the City of Calgary's (2004, September 21) *Conflict of Interest Policy* advises employees to "conduct political activity during non-work time and outside of the workplace" (p. 5). Finally, the term "conflict of interest" may be extended to conflict between one's official duties and conduct in one's private life. An example of this type of conflict is the social worker who abuses his or her spouse.

The notion of personal interest has also been greatly expanded over the years to recognize that a public servant may be in a conflict of interest not only if he or she is paying attention to his or her own narrow interests – financial or otherwise – but also if he or she is focusing on the interests of a spouse, partner, child, relative, friend, or a past or present business associate. This expansion of the concept of private interest has been driven in most jurisdictions by the increasing willingness of the media to draw attention to any possible personal connection – however remote – between a public official and those who might benefit from a government action. There have even been instances of a public servant being accused of conflict of interest because of involvement with decisions that might favour a particular community in which the public servant once resided or a voluntary sector organization with which the public servant was previously involved.

Not all refinements of the notion of private interest have served to widen the concept of personal interest. Several codes of conduct stress that a private interest does not include a matter "that is of general application" or one that affects a public servant as "one of a broad class of the public." That is to say, you are not in a conflict of interest as a public servant if you take part in a government action to lower taxes for all citizens of the province, yourself included, provide a subsidy to all farmers if you happen to be a farmer or to increase the pay of public servants across the board. A private interest can also be trivial and not require the public servant to declare it or recuse himself or herself from decision making or implementation. An example might be a situation in which the public servant owns a very small number of shares of a company that could be affected by a regulatory decision in which the public servant would participate.

Beyond the issue of the nature of a private interest, definitions of conflict of interest (contained in legislation or codes of conduct) over the past two decades have put more emphasis on the performance of one's public duties and less emphasis on receiving inappropriate benefits, whatever form they might take (Langford 1991-92). The Conflict of Interest guidelines for Saskatchewan public service employees take a balanced approach, describing a conflict of interest as:

> a situation in which a public employee, either
> for himself/herself or some other person(s),
> attempts to promote a private or personal
> interest which results or appears to result in:

> - an interference with the objective exercise of his/her duties in the public service
>
> - a gain or an advantage by virtue of his/her position in the public service. (Saskatchewan, Public Service Commission 1994, p. 1)

But some jurisdictions go much further, defining conflict of interest entirely in terms of the temptation that a public servant might feel to subvert the performance of his or her public duty. For example, the British Columbia Standards of Conduct states:

> A conflict of interest occurs when an employee's private affairs or financial interests are in conflict, or could result in a perception of conflict, with the employee's duties or responsibilities in such a way that:
>
> - the employee's ability to act in the public interest could be impaired; or
>
> - the employee's actions or conduct could undermine or compromise:
>
>   - the public's confidence in the employee's ability to discharge work responsibilities; or
>
>   - the trust that the public places in the BC Public Service. (British Columbia, Public Service Agency 2008, p. 3)

The conflict of interest debate is increasingly focusing on situations in which the personal interests (financial and otherwise), past experiences, business and personal associations, outside activities, beliefs and even the future employment of government employees might erode public confidence in the fairness of the government's decision-making processes and the fitness of a public official to hold office. The focus of concern has shifted from the action of pocketing a personal financial benefit to worrying that official duties will be carried out fairly. There is now more concern about the damage to the reputation of the organization as a place where all members of the public will be treated fairly. In short, conflict of interest has become more about the ideal of creating a level playing field where all citizens, groups and interests can expect fair (i.e., impartial) treatment. It is particularly noteworthy that this focus does not require any action by a public servant to advance his or her interests. The conflict exists when the public servant goes to work on an issue in circumstances in which "the public employee has a private or personal interest sufficient to influence or appear to influence the objective exercise of his [or her] public duties" (Kernaghan 1975, p. 13). We are preoccupied more "with the need to enhance the legitimacy of the state and its officials in the eyes of the public than with staunching the flow of inappropriate benefits to individual officials" (Langford 1991-92, p. 29).

There are several complications in dealing with the public servant's duty to avoid conflict of interest. First, there are many variations of conflict of interest, ranging from accepting a bribe or influence peddling, which are prohibited by the *Criminal Code*, to such activities as improper use of government property, moonlighting and accepting benefits. As a result, many public servants are sometimes genuinely perplexed as to whether certain activities constitute a conflict of interest. Precisely what kinds of business involvement are incompatible with one's official duties? Can government property be used to assist an organization like the Red Cross? What forms of outside employment are permissible? The ethics rules set out by some governments are too vague to provide much practical guidance on such questions, but other governments specify in considerable detail the forbidden types of conflict of interest and provide hypothetical examples of each. In the area of accepting benefits, for example, Saskatchewan's Conflict of Interest guidelines for public service employees (Saskatchewan, Public Service Commission 1994) not only set out criteria to define outside employment (e.g., self-employment, activities from which there is a monetary reward) but also provide examples of activities which are considered to be outside employment (e.g., farming, freelance journalism, consulting work).

A second complication is that the application of conflict of interest rules varies not only from one government and one department to another but also from one public servant to another. The City of Toronto's *Conflict of Interest Policy* (2000) provides that only "executives, managers and employees who give professional advice or assistance or who work on program policies or budgets...may not appear before Council or a city committee on behalf of a private citizen other than himself/herself, his/her spouse, his/her parents, or his/her minor children, where the employee is either paid, or is involved in any way in the issue/policy" (n.p.). A third and closely related complication is that opinions change over time as to what activities constitute conflict of interest. For example, certain forms of moonlighting by public servants are more permissible than they used to be.

A final complication, which is considered separately below, is the difficulty of distinguishing a *real* conflict of interest from an *apparent* one and from a *potential* one.

Real, Apparent or Potential Conflict?

Many public officials are involved in conflict of interest situations in the normal course of carrying out their official responsibilities. In most cases, however, their involvement is in an apparent or a potential conflict of interest rather than in a real conflict. The wrongdoing lies not in mere involvement in a conflict of interest situation but in not taking the necessary steps to avoid a real conflict. A federal commission of inquiry (the Parker Commission) observed that "at least three prerequisites have to be established before a public office holder can be said to be in a position of *real* conflict of interest. They are: the existence of a private interest; that it is known to the public office holder; and that it has a connection or nexus with his or her public duties or responsibilities that is sufficient to influence the exercise of those duties or responsibilities" (Canada 1987, p. 25). The federal *Policy on Conflict of Interest and Post-Employment* explains succinctly that "a real conflict of interest exists at the present time, an apparent conflict of interest could be perceived by a reasonable observer to exist, whether or not it is the case, and a potential conflict of interest could reasonably be foreseen to exist in the future" (Treasury Board of Canada Secretariat 2012a, Appendix A).

An apparent conflict of interest is one that is deduced from appearances. In a lengthy treatment of this subject, the federal Treasury Board of Canada Secretariat (2006) asserts that "[p]ublic servants are required to be as concerned with preventing apparent conflicts of interest as they are with preventing real and potential conflicts of interest" (n.p.). The Parker Commission asserted that "an apparent conflict of interest exists when there is a reasonable apprehension, which reasonably well-informed persons could properly have, that a conflict of interest exists" (Canada 1987, p. 35). For example, a public servant who awards contracts to a firm that employs one of his or her relatives may appear to be involved in a conflict of interest even though there is no actual wrongdoing. Justice Mahoney of the Federal Court of Canada has provided the following test for determining the existence of apparent conflicts of interest: "Would an informed person, viewing the matter realistically and practically and having thought the matter through, think it more likely than not that the public servant, whether consciously or unconsciously, will be influenced in the performance of his [or her] official duties by considerations having to do with his [or her] private interests?" (Quoted in Canada, Public Service Staff Relations Board 1986, December 22, pp. 64-65). Consider the case of an employee of the Canadian Food Inspection Agency (CFIA) who was suspended because he used his annual leave to work in the musk ox harvest for a meat marketing company that was regulated by the Agency, even though in the past the Agency had told him not to do this. The adjudicator upheld the suspension because the employee could use his knowledge of CFIA regulations to help the meat company, and this created an apparent conflict of interest (Canada, Public Service Labour Relations Board 2007).

A potential conflict of interest is one that may develop into an actual conflict. For example, a public servant who is in a position to influence the fate of grant applications from a firm in which he or she holds shares has a potential conflict of interest. The Parker Commission explained that "the potential for conflict exists as soon as the public office holder can foresee that he or she has a private economic interest that may be sufficient to influence a public duty or responsibility. As soon as a real conflict of interest is foreseeable, the public office holder must take all appropriate steps to extricate himself or herself from the predicament." Under most codes of conduct, "all appropriate steps" include disclosure of the potential conflict to a supervisor or another more senior official and recusal (withdrawal) from further involvement in the activity in which the individual has personal interests that could influence the performance of his or her public duty. The Commission noted further that "if the caution signs are ignored and the public office holder proceeds to discharge any duty or responsibility of the particular public office that could affect or be affected by the private interest, the line is crossed and a situation of real conflict ensues" (Canada 1987, p. 30).

Each allegation or possibility of conflict of interest must be considered carefully in the light of the explanations provided above. Cases 5.1 and 5.2 provide practice in determining what kind of conflict, if any, is involved.

Despite the broad interpretation that can be given to the term "conflict of interest," most conflicts that attract public attention do involve economic benefits for public officials. Moreover, it is much easier to discern and to regulate economic benefits than those of an emotional or psychological nature.

It is sometimes argued that a person is only in a real conflict of interest position if he or she actually benefits from the situation. The contention is that public officials who try, without success, to use their public office for private gain are not guilty of wrongdoing. This is an unduly narrow interpretation. A key consideration is that the official is actively seeking to advance his or her personal interests. The penalty imposed on public servants who fail in efforts to seek private advantage from their public office will usually be less than for those who succeed; the fact remains, however, that even the attempt to secure such benefits constitutes misconduct. Are we likely to have any more trust in public officials who fail rather than succeed in their efforts to use their public office for personal enrichment?

There is also disagreement over the importance that should be attached to apparent conflicts of interest. Is it appropriate in some instances to answer conflict of interest allegations with the argument that what may appear to some people to be a conflict really is not? Or is the threat to public trust and confidence in government so important that even the appearance of conflict must be removed? Consider the case of meteorologists working for the Atmospheric Environment Service of the federal Department of the Environment. Some radio stations like to employ such meteorologists outside their working hours to provide weather forecasts. The department tends to look favourably upon such off-duty work because it means that the public receives weather forecasts from trained meteorologists. However, off-duty meteorologists, especially if they are supervisors, may receive or appear to receive preferential treatment from their co-workers in the government weather office when they are preparing their weather broadcasts. Where does the public interest lie in such circumstances?

The expansion in the meaning of conflict of interest has been accompanied by uncertainty among public servants as to what is a conflict and what is not. We shall see in chapter 8 that there has been a corresponding expansion in the number of statutes, regulations and guidelines designed to explain, deter and punish conflicts of interest. In recent years, governments have become increasingly risk-averse, so that even the prospect that a private interest could create an appearance of conflict can be enough to warrant disclosure and withdrawal.

Why Be Concerned about Conflicts of Interest?

It is sometimes suggested that concern about conflicts of interest is a luxury in the sense that we have, in Western democratic countries, cleaned up the worst forms of corruption and can now focus on comparatively mild forms of misconduct, including the appearance of and the potential for misconduct. Conflict of interest can be viewed as "a matter that only an otherwise secure and established society can afford to worry about. Only when grosser larcenies in government have been reduced to tolerable limits – only when outright venality is uncommon enough to shock – is it possible for a government to concentrate on potential for evil and try to head off corruption at its sources" (Canada, Task Force on Conflict of Interest 1984, p. 22). It is often suggested also that compared to the shocking level of corruption in some Third World countries, the concern about conflicts of interest in developed countries such as Canada is a luxury.

Since the Second World War, the level of corruption surrounding many governments in the Western world has significantly diminished, in part because of the increase in laws, regulations and guidelines forbidding the use of public office for private gain. But can governments in Canada afford to treat conflict of interest as a luxury item to which resources need to be devoted only occasionally? Politicians and public servants whose careers have been critically affected by involvement – or allegations of involvement – in conflict of interest would answer no. So, it appears, would members of the general public, especially after reading frequent newspaper reports of alleged conflict of interest and corruption. For example, the Canada Revenue Agency experienced, over an eight-year period, an annual average of almost 60 cases involving conflict of interest, breach of trust, falsification or destruction of documents, fraud, inappropriate off-duty conduct, abuse of authority, and unauthorized access or disclosure of confidential information (Leblanc 2012, April 29).

A primary reason for concern about conflicts of interest is that they reduce public trust and confidence in the integrity and impartiality of government. In this respect, the appearance of a conflict can be as damaging as an actual conflict. Whether members of the public are motivated by genuine commitment to high ethical standards in government or by envy of those in a position to benefit from conflicts of interest, there is no doubt that public expectations regarding the ethical standards of government officials have gradually become greater. This public concern has been stimulated by media coverage of instances and allegations of conflict of interest, which in turn have prompted many politicians to seek out cases of actual or apparent conflicts of interest involving their political opponents with a view to using adverse media coverage for political advantage. Some journalists and politicians have been reckless and irresponsible in their allegations against government officials, but others have exposed and publicized serious ethical offences.

Increased concern in contemporary society about conflicts of interest has come about in large part from the realization that public servants now have more opportunities to put private benefit before public duty. These opportunities arise from the increased scale and complexity of government and the expansion of bureaucratic power in the policy process. Public concern has been accompanied by changed attitudes toward some of the variations of conflicts of interest discussed below. For example, while the practice of moonlighting has become more permissible, post-employment practices (the kinds of activities one can engage in after leaving office) have become more tightly regulated. The slowing of growth in government in periods of economic downturn means that public servants have fewer opportunities for promotion and that their jobs are likely to be less permanent. The detrimental effect of these developments on morale has been aggravated by the public's negative image of the public service. It is not surprising, then, that more public servants should feel less committed to their job and that they should increasingly engage in activities for remuneration outside government as a hedge against losing or quitting that job. In some cases, public servants may feel that the financial and psychological rewards from serving the public are inadequate and that they are, therefore, justified in using their public office for private gain.

The revelation of even a few conflict of interest offences is important because the publicity they receive can have a negative effect on public trust and confidence in government that is out of proportion to their number and gravity. Given the low public regard in which many members of the public hold government officials, there is an inclination to conclude that the few offences that are revealed are only the tip of the iceberg. The news media tend to give more publicity to conflicts of interest involving politicians than those involving public servants, but the reputation of public servants suffers along with that of politicians as a result of the spillover effect on appointed officials of the ethical offences of elected officials. Is it reasonable to expect high ethical performance by public servants when elected officials, especially cabinet ministers, do not provide a role model worthy of emulation?

A former senior public servant, whose experience was that "nearly all" of the many ministers under whom he worked were "meticulous and upright," provided the following anecdote about one who was not:

> Another minister was angry with me because
> I returned a case of wine or spirits that had
> been sent to me by someone in the business
> who might have asked a favour of the
> government with which it was negotiating for
> support. The minister was not about to send
> back the cases of wine he had received. I had
> to advise him that I felt bound to record my

disapproval. He was furious because the files
would contain the evidence of his indiscretion.
Although he failed to have the evidence
removed, he kept his prizes and wasn't publicly
discovered. The industry got what it was after,
I should add. (Ostry 1987, December, p. 3)

To what extent are the normative ethical theories examined in
chapter 2 helpful in informing public servants' actions in respect of
conflict of interest? Proponents of duty ethics, which focuses on the
nature of the act rather than on the consequences, would argue that
public servants who engage in conflicts of interest violate the rules
of right behaviour in the workplace. Moreover, Kant's categorical
imperative prompts us to ask whether we would accept the notion of
everyone engaging in conflicts of interest; whether it is fair that some
public servants should use their public office for personal gain; and
whether (from behind a veil of ignorance) we would condone conflicts
of interest if we didn't know whether we would ever be in a position to
benefit from one. On the other hand, some conflict of interest rules
restrict the freedom of public servants by imposing a post-employment
regime restricting their mobility rights, and questions of fairness arise
from rules requiring public servants to disclose not only their own
financial interests but also those of family members.

The consequences of public servants' involvement in conflicts of
interest discussed earlier in this chapter suggest that the application of
consequential ethical theory would render an overwhelmingly negative
view of such involvement. However, it can be argued that engaging in
conflict of interest can in some cases be benign or, occasionally, even
a positive force. Some writings on corruption present a positive view of
conflict of interest as a means, for example, of bypassing burdensome
government regulations and thereby promoting efficiency. Unethical
behaviour can exist even when there is no obvious clash of interests –
there can be a "compatibility of interest" when a public servant pursues
the public interest and his or her private interest at the same time
(Canada, Task Force on Conflict of Interest 1984, p. 29).

Proponents of the virtue ethics approach would expect the virtuous
public servant to deal with conflicts of interest by reference to such
values as integrity and fairness. For example, the federal *Values and
Ethics Code for the Public Sector*, in a section on integrity, advises
public servants to take "all possible steps to prevent and resolve any
real, apparent or potential conflicts of interest between their official
responsibilities and their private affairs in favour of the public interest"
(Treasury Board of Canada Secretariat 2012b, n.p.). The BC Standards

of Conduct set similar advice in a broader context by informing public servants that the government recognizes their right "to be involved in activities as citizens of the community" (British Columbia, Public Service Agency 2008). It can be argued that the management of conflict of interest should focus on serving the public interest rather than aggressively pursuing petty conflicts of interest in a manner that assumes that public servants are inherently weak and self-interested and that undermines the public service's image of integrity and fairness.

Variations on a Common Theme

Continuing problems in the conflict of interest sphere arise in part from the fact that there are so many variations of this offence. It is useful to visualize each variation on a separate continuum running from "black" conflicts through various shades of grey to "off-white" conflicts. For example, the variation known as accepting benefits ranges along the continuum from bribery – through the acceptance of gifts or entertainment of varying but substantial value – to the acceptance of benefits of nominal value. Other types of conflict of interest such as moonlighting are usually grey-area conflicts that normally do not approach the black pole of the continuum. It is notable also that as the seriousness of offences moves them toward the black pole, a decision has to be made as to whether the offence should be handled within the government as an administrative infraction or treated as a violation of criminal law. For example, public servants may simply be reprimanded for accepting benefits of slightly more than nominal value, but they may be prosecuted under the *Criminal Code* for accepting a large bribe.

Conflicts of interest can be divided into the following eight categories: self-dealing, accepting benefits, influence peddling, using government property, using confidential information, outside employment, post-employment and personal conduct. Some of these categories require lengthier treatment than others because of the comparative difficulty of defining and regulating them.

The first three of these variations of conflict of interest are similar in that they involve situations where public servants use their public office to bring about decisions that favour themselves, their family or an organization in which they have an interest.

Self-dealing

Self-dealing refers to a situation in which one takes an action in an official capacity that involves dealing with oneself in a private capacity and that confers a benefit on oneself. An obvious example is a public servant who awards a contract to a company that he or she owns. In an early case, a chief of security services for the Department of the Secretary of State rented electronic surveillance equipment from a firm in which he was a partner (Jefferson 1977, July 15). More recently, the notion of "self" in self-dealing has been expanded to include one's spouse, family members, friends and past and present business associates. For example, a public servant in Consulting and Audit Canada (CAC) was suspended for participating in contracting activities involving the firm of a person with whom he had both a family and a personal relationship (Canada, Public Service Labour Relations Board 2008). Consider whether any of the participants in case 5.1 are involved in a conflict of interest.

CASE 5.1: ALL IN THE FAMILY

The following conversation takes place between two middle managers in a provincial Department of Regional Industrial Expansion.

Mike: I understand that you've had a request for financial assistance from a computer manufacturer.

Frances: We've been flooded with requests lately, Mike. This has been a bad year for this province. But I think I know the company you mean. It's in Spruceville, isn't it?

Mike: Yes, that's the one. They've been in touch with me, and apparently they're in a real crisis situation. Frankly, Frances, they're afraid that they'll have to shut down if they don't get some financial help soon.

Frances: That doesn't sound good. But I just received their application this week. With the pile of applications on my desk right now, it'll be another month or two at least before I get to it.

Mike: That'll be too late. The owner of the firm is married to my sister, so I told him I'd look into the situation. I think their financial situation is critical enough to justify putting their application near the top of the pile.

Is Mike in a real, apparent, or potential conflict of interest situation here? Is the firm's reported dire financial situation a sufficient justification for Mike to involve himself in the application vetting process? How should Frances respond to Mike's request? How would the average citizen react to this situation? Would the case be handled any differently if Mike was not related to the owner of the firm? Should information about the firm's critical financial situation be ignored because of the source of the information?

Accepting Benefits

As noted above, the acceptance of benefits can take the form of bribery at the one extreme and the receipt of benefits of nominal value at the other. A wide range of benefits can be conferred on public servants, including gifts, meals, free travel, paid vacations, entertainment and money.

Cases in which a public servant accepts benefits that are of such magnitude that the fitting response is prosecution under the *Criminal Code* are comparatively easy to handle. The real difficulty comes with benefits that fall into the grey area, such as meals associated with a business meeting, a bottle of liquor at Christmas time, an evening at the theatre, an honorarium for a speech or a gift that may be perceived as having more than nominal value. More recently, offers of the keys to a condominium or tickets to an Ottawa Senators hockey game have been replaced by fully paid opportunities to take part in a "professional development workshop" at a high-end resort. Is this likely to be an educational experience or an opportunity to spend quality time with the corporate sponsors who also want your organization to buy their data management software or change a regulation in their favour? An informal guideline that is reported to have existed in earlier and simpler times was that public servants should only accept a gift that they could consume within a 24-hour period. The inadequacy of such a guideline is obvious in the case of a developer who shortly after New Year's Eve ran into a senior regional official at a liquor store. "[T]he red-faced official was cashing in two trolley carts full of liquor that he had received as gifts" (Ferguson and King 1988, October 26 to November 3).

The nature of the problem can be illuminated by the efforts of governments to regulate the acceptance of benefits. Is the best solution to prohibit the receipt of gifts of any kind? This approach has the virtue of simplicity, but is it sensible and feasible? Most governments permit the receipt of casual benefits such as small gifts or hospitality. For example, Alberta's Code of Conduct and Ethics for the Public Service provides that:

> Employees shall not accept fees, gifts or other benefits that are connected directly or indirectly with the performance of their public service duties, from any individual, organization or corporation, other than
>
> > a. the normal exchange of gifts between friends;

b. the normal exchange of hospitality between persons doing business together;

c. tokens exchanged as part of protocol;

d. the normal presentation of gifts to persons participating in public functions. (Alberta, Personnel Administration Office 2005, p. 9)

Some governments try to define what "nominal" value means by setting a limit of, say, one hundred dollars. Is this limit too high or too low? What constitutes a benefit of nominal value? The City of Toronto's *Conflict of Interest Policy* (2000, n.p.) permits exceptions to a strong prohibition against accepting gifts by allowing "promotional gifts or those of nominal value e.g., coffee mug or letter opener with the company's logo or the occasional lunch." But what about a government purchasing agent who accepts many gifts, none of which is valued at more than a hundred dollars? And what about public servants whose influence can be bought for the price of an expensive lunch?

Public servants involved in certain commercial or diplomatic activities with persons from foreign countries where the giving of gifts is normal practice would have genuine problems with a limit of one hundred, or even two hundred dollars. Compare the situation of a public servant from the Business Development Bank who is invited to dine at the home of a businessperson seeking a loan to that of a public servant from the Department of Foreign Affairs and International Trade who is invited to dine at the embassy home of a foreign diplomat whose country is seeking a loan. Should the rules on accepting benefits be tailored to the public servant's level and responsibilities in the public service? Could the same objective be achieved by requiring due authorization from administrative or political superiors before any benefits are accepted? The federal *Policy on Conflict of Interest and Post-Employment* provides that "where it is impossible to decline gifts, hospitality or other benefits...or where it is believed that there is sufficient benefit to the organization to warrant acceptance of certain types of hospitality" (Treasury Board of Canada Secretariat 2012a, sect. 2.3), a public servant shall seek written direction from their Deputy Head. The Deputy Head will then notify the public servant in writing whether the gifts, hospitality and other benefits are to be declined or retained by the department, donated to charity, disposed of, or retained by the public servant concerned.

Influence Peddling

Influence peddling is the practice of soliciting some form of benefit from individuals or organizations in exchange for the exercise of one's official authority or influence on their behalf. It is closely related to the practice of accepting benefits. However, it is a more active form of conflict of interest in that it involves the *solicitation* of benefits. It is also a *Criminal Code* offence. A blatant example of this offence is the Citizenship and Immigration Canada employee who allegedly solicited money from prospective immigrants in exchange for approving their applications for residence (Bell 2010, December 16).

Using Government Property

Public sector codes of ethics often provide that employees should not use government property of any kind, without authorization, for activities unrelated to their official duties. The private use of government property can take a multitude of forms. It can range from relatively minor offences, such as taking pencils home or using a government office for non-government purposes, to major offences such as using government computers or front-end loaders for a private business. The City of Calgary's Acceptable Use of City Technology Resources Policy (Calgary, Corporate Administration 2004, September 21) advises employees to avoid such things as:

- Accessing Internet web sites, using City technology resources that have any content that could be considered inappropriate.

- Using City technology resources for a private business or a non-City job.

- Using your computer or other technology resources to send or receive large amounts of personal e-mails.

- Letting personal use of City technology resources adversely affect your work. (p. 3-4)

An absolute prohibition on the use of government property for private purposes is, like an absolute ban on accepting benefits, an administratively convenient approach. It is not necessarily, however, the most sensible one. A more flexible approach would permit public servants to seek permission to use government property for private purposes in such exceptional circumstances as providing space for a Red Cross blood drive or a United Way fund-raiser. The important point here is that government property not be used for personal gain. But how far should this restriction be carried? Is it appropriate for municipal employees to take scrap lumber home from a department of public works yard if it would otherwise be burned? Should the same opportunity be made available to the general public? Consider case 5.2 in light of these questions.

CASE 5.2: A MOVING TALE

The following discussion takes place between Gerry, a maintenance worker in the Department of Public Works, and his friend Pierre.

Pierre: Hey, Gerry. You agreed to help me move this weekend and I agreed to rent the truck, but I can't find a truck for rent anywhere. Why don't we use your government vehicle?

Gerry: Yikes! It's not my government vehicle; it's the government's government vehicle.

Pierre: Don't worry. Nobody will know and if anybody made a fuss, I could explain that I absolutely had to move this weekend. In fact, the government would probably be happy to help me out because I was a victim of the recent flood and had to move to emergency housing. I'm not permitted to stay there beyond this weekend.

Gerry: Well, I suppose that I wouldn't be in a conflict of interest since I won't be getting any financial gain from using the truck. But I'm not really sure about the rules – and since it's already Friday evening, I can't seek advice from the office.

Is this a real conflict of interest or an apparent one? For this situation to constitute a conflict of interest, does Gerry have to receive personal financial benefit? Is it appropriate for Gerry to use the vehicle during these unusual emergency circumstances? Do you think that most citizens would approve of Gerry's use of the vehicle? Given Gerry's uncertainty as to whether there is a rule prohibiting such use, should Gerry simply act in what he thinks is the public interest?

Using Confidential Information

What is involved here is the use for personal or private purposes of a particular form of government property, namely, confidential information. The offence lies in using information, including information about decisions made by other public servants, for private gain. As we will see in chapter 6, there are serious consequences for public servants who disclose, without authorization, confidential government information.

The consequences are likely to be even more serious if the information is used for the private benefit, especially the economic benefit, of the public servants or their friends and relatives.

The Statement of Principles of the Institute of Public Administration of Canada (1987) provides that "public employees should not seek or obtain personal or private gain from the use of information acquired during the course of their official duties which is not generally available to the public" (p. 2). Public servants can, however, use with impunity information that is available to the general public. But does this really create an equitable situation for public servants and the general public with respect to the use of government information? Is it not possible, for example, for public servants to take advantage of advance information by accumulating funds that they can invest immediately upon the public announcement of a government contract for a particular firm? How would you handle the case of a public servant who, on the basis of "insider knowledge," invested in a company a few weeks before information about a large government grant to the company was made available to the general public? This kind of activity is difficult to regulate.

Should we worry less about such insider trading than about other kinds of conflict of interest because the benefits to the public servant cost the taxpayer nothing? How concerned should we be about a Department of Agriculture employee who uses statistics collected on crops to speculate on grain futures before these statistics are released to the public? To what extent is our concern about such behaviour motivated by envy and to what extent is it motivated by the need to preserve public confidence in the integrity of public officials?

Outside Employment

Outside employment, or moonlighting as it is often described, refers to the work or activity in which a person engages outside normal working hours for additional remuneration. While such activity may be conducted on a full-time basis (for example, driving a taxi for a full shift each evening), it usually involves part-time work and includes a wide range of activities, such as working for a non-governmental organization (for example, a business or an educational institution), running a business, or consulting. Moonlighting problems are similar in the public and private sectors, but the damage to reputation is greater in the public sector. John Langford (1991) notes the consequent "corrosive effects on public confidence and the legitimacy of government...To discover that public officials are abusing their position of trust by doing less than a full day's work or by using confidential information or government resources to enhance their incomes, does little to endear the state to the citizen" (p. 65).

Among the benefits to the employer claimed for moonlighting are better employee morale, less frustrated employees, increased skill development and lower turnover rates. Conflict of interest problems arise when the moonlighting activities of public servants clash with the performance of their official duties. More specifically, moonlighting may need to be restricted:

- if the activity is in direct competition with the employer;

- if the employee's work performance is affected;

- if the employer's property is being used to engage in the activity;

- if confidential information is being used by the employee;

- if the employee is using his/her position to solicit business; or

- if the employee's activity could be perceived by the public to be a conflict of interest (Taylor and Filmer 1986, p. 595).

There are some obvious links between conflict of interest in the moonlighting sphere and other types of conflict, including the use of government property, the use of confidential information, and influence peddling. Moreover, the *appearance* of conflict is a common problem with respect to moonlighting activities.

CASE 5.3: BY THE LIGHT OF THE MOON

This conversation takes place between two public servants who work in the procurement office of a large federal department.

Manjeet: A group of four of us have decided to start a consulting company on the side to run seminars telling businessmen how to deal with government, and, in particular how to get contracts from the department.

Arlene: Who's involved?

Manjeet: Me and three colleagues in the office.

Arlene: And what exactly are you going to offer?

Manjeet: We'll outline the various contract regulations, rules, policies, procedures, restraints and constraints affecting the process. We're also going to offer advice for maximizing opportunities to sell goods and services to the government. The fee will be quite reasonable; about $200 per person.

Arlene: My goodness! Surely you know you're not allowed to use information acquired during the course of your public service employment in that way!

Manjeet: That's true only if the information we're providing is not generally available to the public. All the information we're planning to give out is readily available from the department if anyone bothers to ask for it.

Are Manjeet and his colleagues involved in a conflict of interest? If so, is it a real, apparent or potential conflict? Is the integrity of the contracting-out process threatened by such an activity as this? Does the fact that the information they would be providing is available to the public alter your view of the case? How do you think this situation would be viewed by the average citizen?

Case 5.3 provides a basis for assessing the virtues and disadvantages of moonlighting and for examining its links to other types of conflict. Consider also the case of a federal public servant working for the Department of Employment and Immigration as an employment counsellor (Canada, Public Service Staff Relations Board 1987, July 24). The Public Service Staff Relations Board found that this public servant had contravened the federal conflict of interest guidelines by trying, during normal office hours, to sell vacuum cleaners to clients of the department, by persuading a client to provide cheap labour for the painting of his house, and by releasing information about a client to the police and threatening to release the same information to a welfare agency. In another case, the Board upheld the firing of an auditor at the Canada Customs and Revenue Agency who violated the department's Conflict of Interest Code by continuing to prepare income tax returns for remuneration after he began his employment with the department (Canada, Public Service Staff Relations Board 2003a).

While it is generally acknowledged that the use of confidential information is unacceptable in the conduct of moonlighting activities, there is more debate about the use of information in the form of knowledge and experience that has been acquired on the job. Is there anything wrong with a public servant using knowledge of government structures and procedures in a part-time business? Does it make a difference if this knowledge is readily available to the public from the government? Examine these questions in relation to case 5.3.

Post-Employment

Post-employment is sometimes described as subsequent employment or future employment.[5] It constitutes a conflict of interest when public servants use, or appear to use, information and contacts acquired while in government to benefit themselves or others after they leave government. The federal *Policy on Conflict of Interest and Post-Employment* states that "[a]ll public servants have a responsibility to minimize the possibility of real, apparent or potential conflict of interest between their most recent responsibilities within the federal public service and their subsequent employment outside the public service" (Treasury Board of Canada Secretariat 2012a, Appendix B).

There are several possibilities for wrongdoing here. After public servants move out of government, they may use confidential information for personal benefit through self-employment (for example, as a consultant) or they may use such information for the benefit of a private or third-sector organization by which they are employed. Much of the concern here is focused on former public servants being engaged in lobbying or supporting lobbyists, whether they are in-house, industry associations or "gun for hire" consulting companies. The practice of "switching sides" – that is, taking up employment in the private or not-for-profit sector that involves working on a matter for which the public servant was responsible in his or her government position – is considered to be especially offensive. In recent years, concern about post-employment practices has increased because public servants are moving more frequently between public and private sector jobs, and some of them have cozy connections with business firms. Public servants may also benefit by receiving privileged access or preferential treatment from their former colleagues. One variation of post-employment offence, often referred to as "securing a soft landing," can occur even before public servants leave government in that some public servants may enhance their prospects for profitable private employment by granting preferential treatment to certain firms or organizations.

Media coverage of public servants who have moved to private sector jobs, notably in industry lobbying organizations, has set off alarm bells about possible conflicts of interest. For example, the air administrator of the Canadian Air Transportation Administration at

---

5. For a lengthy examination of the post-employment issue in Canada and elsewhere that focuses mainly on political office holders but includes ethics analysis in general, see Oliphant Commission (Canada. Commission of Inquiry into Certain Allegations Respecting Business and Financial Dealings between Karlheinz Schreiber and The Right Honorable Brian Mulroney 2010).

Transport Canada became the president and chief executive officer of the Air Transport Association of Canada; a deputy minister of forests in British Columbia became president of the Council of Forest Industries in that province; and an assistant deputy minister of mineral policy in the federal Department of Energy, Mines and Resources became managing director of the Mining Association of Canada.

A 2011 municipal case demonstrates the complications that arise in this sphere. Geoff Rathbone, Toronto's General Manager of Solid Waste Management Services, had recommended the contracting-out of some garbage collection and recycling. When he resigned to become a vice-president of a large waste management company, the Public Works chair threatened to ban the company from bidding on the contract. The City's Municipal Code prohibited senior officers from lobbying their former colleagues for one year after leaving the city, but contained no rule requiring that information acquired while in government be kept confidential. The company said that Mr. Rathbone would have no association with the bid and two potential competitors for the contract not only expressed no concern but also praised Rathbone's sterling reputation. One competitor observed that "[t]he appearance is a bit odd but the underlying facts don't bear that (suspicion of advantage) out" (Rider 2011, May 9).

Among the several variations of conflict of interest, the post-employment problem is one of the most difficult to regulate. The difficulty arises in large part from the fact that the persons being regulated are *former* public servants; once public servants have left the government, the range of penalties that the government can apply to them is more limited. The federal government has acknowledged this limitation:

> Technically, once a public servant has left the Public Service, there are no simple measures that a department can use to check whether that public servant is respecting the post-employment compliance measures to which he or she is subject. The onus for compliance is on the individual in question. Once an individual has left office, he or she is no longer a public servant, hence managers no longer have any authority over him or her (Treasury Board of Canada Secretariat 2004, n.p.).

As a result, governments try to discourage public servants from using their public office unethically (for example, through influence peddling) to attract job offers in the first place. Some governments require that public servants report to their superiors any job offers they receive, especially from persons with whom they have, or had, official business. In the federal government, ministers and public servants are responsible for ensuring that former public officials do not take advantage of their previous position.

Efforts are also made to discourage public servants from accepting a private sector job in which they hope to use their specialized public service knowledge to earn a high salary. A common disincentive is to prohibit public servants from engaging for a period of time (for example, one or two years) in any employment that would conflict, or appear to conflict, with their official responsibilities. This "cooling off" period not only discourages public servants from leaving government in the first place, it also minimizes the value of confidential information that they possess and it reduces the likelihood of a private employer obtaining a competitive advantage from the use of such information. Because public servants may be unaware of the precise post-employment restrictions placed on an ex-colleague, the burden of sorting out whether or not to do business with that ex-colleague can be an onerous one. Some post-employment regimes also threaten to "blackball" firms that hire ex-government employees during cooling-off periods.

The problem of distinguishing between confidential information and information in the form of knowledge and experience that was discussed in the context of moonlighting is also a central consideration here. Could a persuasive argument be made that public servants, like their private sector counterparts, should have the right to move from one job to another on the basic of their competence and reputation? How can an appropriate balance be struck between the right of public servants to move between public and private sector employment and, on the other hand, the need to prevent abuse of confidential information and preserve public trust in the integrity of public officials? An analysis of case 5.3 will provide useful practice in answering such questions.

In addition, the Post-Employment Good Practices Framework (adapted and abbreviated from Kernaghan 2007, p. 13-14) outlined below provides guidance for the implementation of a post-employment regime. Among the major elements of an effective regime are these:

1. The post-employment regime contains the instrument (or instruments) needed to deal effectively with current and anticipated post-employment problems.

2. The post-employment instrument (or instruments) is linked, where feasible, with instrument(s) dealing with conflict of

interest in general and with the government's overall values and ethics regime.

3. The post-employment regime covers all of the important risk areas for post-employment conflict of interest.

4. The length of the time limits imposed on the activities of former officials is proportionate to the gravity of the post-employment conflict of interest threat that the officials pose.

5. The enforcement sanctions for post-employment offences are clear and appropriate, and are consistently and equitably applied.

This is an area of conflict of interest very much in flux. As governments downsize in the face of tough employment conditions, there is reluctance to enforce post-employment rules too strictly. It is also relatively easy for departing public servants to disguise what they actually do to help private or not-for-profit organizations in their relations with government. There are also gaps in the coverage of post-employment regimes. Most conspicuously, such regimes do not generally apply to the movement of a public servant from one public agency to another. But this can represent serious potential conflicts of interest. In one case, for instance, the deputy minister of health left the federal government to become head of a large provincial health authority, which depends on the health ministry for its funding. These regimes also do not cover personnel exchanges between government and the private and not-for-profit sectors. The placement of a senior energy official in an equally senior position in a large oil and gas firm regulated by government is portrayed as an excellent opportunity for both parties to learn more about each other rather than a situation rife with potential conflicts of interest.

CASE 5.4: THE INSIDE TRACK

The following conversation takes place between Natasha and Mario, two officials of the Ministry of Justice.

Natasha: What are we going to do about the new contract that's come up?

Mario: That work would have been Smith's responsibility.

Natasha: Yes, but she left us about a month ago and has returned to private law practice. Before she left, though, she developed a contracting-out process for programs of this kind.

Mario: Good. Have you received any bids?

Natasha: Yes, we have. Actually, we've received quite a few. In fact, one of the bids came from the law firm that Smith just joined.

Mario: Well then, that firm would seem to be the logical choice for handling this contract. Smith knows exactly what's expected and she knows all the players.

Natasha: Yeah, that's true, but it may not look so good giving the contract to someone who set up the process and worked here until a month ago.

Mario: Hell, are you suggesting that we have to exclude the best-qualified firm because one of their lawyers worked for us? Who'd work for the public service under those conditions?

Would Mario be acting irresponsibly in hiring Smith's law firm? Is Smith in a conflict of interest situation? What limits should be placed on the relationship an ex-public servant can have with his or her ex-department? Can you justify limiting the freedom of ex-public servants?

Personal Conduct

Is a public servant's personal life any of the government's business? Can a public servant be in a real or an apparent conflict of interest because of improper or questionable conduct in his or her private life? Could drug or alcohol addiction be deemed to be "a situation in which a public official has a private or personal interest sufficient to influence or to appear to influence the objective exercise of his or her official duties?" What about wife or child abuse? Does improper conduct have to become public knowledge before the public servant's administrative superiors can take official notice of it, or is it sufficient for administrative superiors simply to know that improper conduct has occurred?

By the early 1990s, the meaning of conflict of interest had expanded to include such non-economic private activities of public servants as:

- the pattern of their friendships and acquaintances;

- the sexual predilections of them and their spouses;

- their political or religious affiliations;

- their alcohol and drug usage;

- their personal financial management practices; and

- their other "lifestyle" idiosyncrasies of behaviour (Langford 1991-92, p. 31)

The personal conduct of public servants is obviously an area where government must tread warily for fear of infringing on the public servants' right to privacy. But are public servants entitled to the same privacy as other citizens? Does the power that public servants exercise in the development and implementation of public policy justify greater concern about their personal conduct and greater encroachments on their privacy? Should we be more concerned about the conduct of elected than of appointed officials? Would that make sense when many public servants exercise more power in the public policy process than many elected officials, especially backbench legislators and municipal councillors? How important to the consideration of personal conduct is the public servant's level of influence or authority and the type of issues for which he or she is responsible?

These are difficult and complicated questions, yet on occasion they must be answered. Certainly the sphere of personal conduct is likely to give rise to more disagreement than most other types of conflict of interest. It seems reasonable to argue that in at least two circumstances a public servant's personal conduct, outside government, may constitute a conflict of interest. The first circumstance is when a public servant's conduct (for example, drug or gambling addiction) makes him or her vulnerable to pressure to use his or her public office improperly. The second circumstance is when the public servant's conduct brings significant discredit to the government or to a particular department and thereby undermines public trust in public officials. On the other hand, could a convincing case be made that the public and indeed the government only have a legitimate interest in the public servant's personal conduct in private life if that conduct actually affects adversely the performance of his or her official duties? The problem is that "[t]he ways in which private lives may be relevant [to official duties] are complex" (Thompson 1987, p. 129). It has been argued that:

> if integrity is required of a public servant
> in the performance of his duties, the same
> requirement applies to his conduct in
> private life, particularly, if he occupies a
> fairly high position in management. When
> a public servant in such a position engages
> in activities prohibited by law or considered
> of questionable morality by the general

> public, this constitutes an offence which in
> turn becomes...a breach of discipline liable
> to a sanction (Canada, Public Service Staff
> Relations Board 1976, December 19, p.
> 31-32).

Implicit in this argument is the suggestion that we should be more concerned if a public servant who regularly engages in fist fights in a local bar is a law enforcement officer than if he or she is a janitor. Similarly, we should be more distressed if a public servant addicted to drugs is a deputy minister than if he or she is a file clerk. The federal Public Service Staff Relations Board upheld the termination of a correctional officer who was arrested for possession of drugs. The adjudicator ruled that this was misconduct incompatible with the officer's duties in that he had tarnished the Department's image and rendered himself incapable of performing his duties in the sphere of corrections (Canada, Public Service Staff Relations Board 2003b).

It is clear that each case of questionable or improper personal conduct involving public servants needs to be carefully considered on its merits. "It is...not possible to discover a set of rules that would determine in advance the kinds of activities that should constitute the private life of a public official" (Thompson 1987, p. 124).

Conclusion

At several points in this chapter, we have asserted or implied the need for conflict of interest rules. These rules are designed to prevent real, apparent or potential conflicts of interest from arising and to provide a basis for handling them when they do arise. The federal Task Force on Conflict of Interest (1984) observed that "in an earlier time...the public was more prepared to give the benefit of the doubt to a minister or public official. In other words, there was confidence that such officials would give precedence to their public duties over their private interests. This is no longer so. The public has come to expect positive measures designed to remove or minimize the conflict of interests" (p. 22).

Governments across Canada at all levels have responded to this desire for positive measures with an unprecedented number and variety of conflict of interest rules. The form of these rules varies from one jurisdiction to another and includes statutes, regulations and guidelines. Conflict of interest rules often form part of a code of ethics or a conflict of interest code that prohibits the several forms of conflict explained in this chapter. Among the techniques used are rules requiring disclosure of assets and specific potential conflicts of interest; divestment of one's assets and business connections; and the arrangement of a blind, frozen or retention trust for one's assets. The utility of such rules and of codes of conduct in general is examined in chapter 8.

There is a need for continuing vigilance to ensure that public trust in the impartiality and fairness of administration is not undermined and that even a small number of public servants do not use their public office for private or personal gain. There is, however, legitimate concern that the rights of responsible public servants are sometimes unduly diminished by conflict of interest rules. This concern has grown as a result not only of the expanded scope and volume of the rules but also of the increased emphasis on removing apparent as well as real conflicts. While public trust and confidence in government requires that most apparent conflicts be removed, allegations of conflict occasionally flow from an excessive zeal. Those public servants who draft, endorse and enforce the rules should ask themselves whether they would want the same rules applied to them.

References

Alberta, Personnel Administration Office. (2005). *Code of conduct and ethics for the public service of Alberta*. Retrieved from http://www.assembly.ab.ca/lao/library/egovdocs/2005/alpe/158311.pdf

Bell, S. (2010, December 16). Immigration employee arrested on bribery charges. *National Post.* Retrieved from http://news.nationalpost.com/2010/12/16/immigration-employee-arrested-on-bribery-charges

Bellamy, D. (2005). *Toronto computer leasing inquiry.* Vol. 2. Toronto: City of Toronto.

British Columbia, Public Service Agency. (2008). *Policy statement - Standards of conduct*. Retrieved from http://www.bcpublicserviceagency.gov.bc.ca/policy/HR_policy/09_Standards_Conduct.htm

Calgary, Corporate Administration. (2004, September 21). *Administration policy: Code of conduct,* HR-LR-005.

Canada. Commission of Inquiry into Certain Allegations Respecting Business and Financial Dealings between Karlheinz Schreiber and The Right Honorable Brian Mulroney. (2010). *Volume 3: Policy and consolidated findings and recommendations*. Ottawa: Minister of Public Works and Government Services Canada. Chaired by Justice Jeffrey J. Oliphant. Retrieved from http://publications.gc.ca/collections/collection_2010/bcp-pco/CP32-92-2-2010-2-eng.pdf

Canada. Commission of Inquiry into the Facts of Allegations of Conflict of Interest Concerning the Honourable Sinclair M. Stevens. (1987). *The Parker Commission.* Ottawa: Supply and Services Canada. Chaired by Justice W. Parker.

Canada, Public Service Labour Relations Board. (2007). *Frank Duske and Canadian Food Inspection Agency,* 166-32-35998 (2007 PSLRB 94). Retrieved from http://pslrb-crtfp.gc.ca/decisions/fulltext/2007-94_e.asp

Canada, Public Service Labour Relations Board. (2008). *Frank Brazeau and Deputy Head (Department of Public Works and Government Services),* 566-02-378 and 379 (2008 PSLRB 62). Retrieved from http://pslrb-crtfp.gc.ca/decisions/fulltext/2008-62_e.asp

Canada, Public Service Staff Relations Board. (1976, December 19). *Legault and Treasury Board (Post Office Department).*

Canada, Public Service Staff Relations Board. (1986, December 22). *John H. Spinks and Jack G. Threader v. Treasury Board.*

Canada, Public Service Staff Relations Board. (1987, July 24). *Max Bilkoski and Treasury Board (Employment and Immigration Canada).*

Canada, Public Service Staff Relations Board. (2003a). *Gordon Oliver and Canada Customs and Revenue Agency,* 166-34-31255 (2003 PSSRB 43). Retrieved from http://pslrb-crtfp.gc.ca/decisions/fulltext/31255_e.asp

Canada, Public Service Staff Relations Board. (2003b). *Gilbert Dionne and Treasury Board (Solicitor General of Canada – Correctional Service),* 166-2-30053 (2003 PSSRB 69). Retrieved from http://pslrb-crtfp.gc.ca/decisions/fulltext/30053_e.asp

Canada, Task Force on Conflict of Interest. (1984). *Ethical conduct in the public sector.* Ottawa: Supply and Services Canada.

City of Toronto. (2000). *Conflict of interest policy.* Retrieved from http://www. toronto.ca/calldocuments/conflict_of_interest_policy.htm

Cooper, T. L. (2006). *The responsible administrator: An approach to ethics for the administrative role* (5th ed.). San Francisco: Jossey-Bass.

Dobel, J. P. (1999). *Public integrity.* Baltimore: Johns Hopkins University Press.

Ferguson, J. & King, D. (1988, October 26 to November 3). Behind the boom: The Story of York Region (eight-part series). *Globe and Mail*.

Institute of Public Administration of Canada. (1987). *IPAC statement of principles regarding the conduct of public employees*. Toronto: IPAC. Retrieved from https://www.ipac.ca/documents/PRINCIPLES2.pdf

Jefferson, J. (1977, July 15). Rented from own firm: Ex-security chief. *Globe and Mail*.

Kernaghan, K. (1975). *Ethical conduct: Guidelines for government employees*. Toronto: Institute of Public Administration of Canada.

Kernaghan, K. (2007). *Public integrity and post-public employment: Issues, remedies and benchmarks*. Paris: OECD.

Langford, J. W. (1991). Moonlighting and mobility. *Canadian Public Administration, 34*(1), 62-72.

Langford, J. W. (1991-92). Conflict of interest: What the hell is it? *Optimum 22*(1), 28-33.

Leblanc, D. (2012, April 29). Documents reveal hundreds of 'high-risk misconduct' cases at CRA. *Globe and Mail*. Retrieved from http://www.theglobeandmail.com/news/politics/documents-reveal-hundreds-of-high-risk-misconduct-cases-at-cra/article4104022

Ostry, B. (1987, December). Ethics and public service. *IPAC Bulletin* 10. Toronto: IPAC.

Rider, D. (2011, May 9). City garbage boss's move to private firm stirs concern. *Toronto Star*. Retrieved from http://www.thestar.com/news/article/988449–city-garbage-boss-s-move-to-private-firm-stirs-concern

Saskatchewan, Public Service Commission. (1994). *Conflict of interest*. Human Resource Manual, section PS 801A. Retrieved from http://www.cs.gov.sk.ca/801

Taylor, M. H., & Filmer, A. E. (1986). Moonlighting: The practical problems. *Canadian Public Administration, 29*(4), 592-597.

Thompson, D. F. (1987). *Political ethics and public office*. Cambridge, MA: Harvard University Press.

Treasury Board of Canada Secretariat. (2004). A*RCHIVED - Values and ethics code for the public service: Questions and answers*. Retrieved from http://www.tbs-sct.gc.ca/gui/intcd02-eng.asp

Treasury Board of Canada Secretariat. (2006). *Apparent conflict of interest*. Retrieved from http://www.tbs-sct.gc.ca/rp/acipr-eng. asp?format=print

Treasury Board of Canada Secretariat. (2012a). *Policy on conflict of interest and post-employment*. Retrieved from http://www.tbs-sct. gc.ca/pol/doc-eng.aspx?section=text&id=25178

Treasury Board of Canada Secretariat. (2012b). *Values and ethics code for the public sector*. Retrieved from http://www.tbs-sct.gc.ca/pol/ doc-eng.aspx?section=text&id=25049

Chapter 6

Confidentiality, Transparency and Privacy Protection

A public service which holds tight to a culture
of secrecy is a public service ripe for abuse.
(Information Commissioner of Canada 1998, p. 4)

[P]eople appear to want and value privacy, yet
simultaneously appear not to value or want it.
(Nissenbaum 2010, p. 104)

We live in a time in which information is a powerful force for both good
and evil. Governments play pivotal roles in an information society as
generators, repositories and distributors of enormous amounts of data
critical to the making and administration of public policy, the privacy of
employees, citizens and organizations, and the capacity to hold public
officials to account. Moreover, the technological tools available to
governments to collect, integrate, analyse, store, and share (or hide)
information are becoming more powerful. As a result, public servants
are faced with difficult and rapidly evolving questions about how to
manage information in an ethically defensible manner.

In this chapter we will be looking first at the tug of war between
the obligations of transparency and confidentiality. Within and between
these contradictory obligations lurk very difficult dilemmas which afflict
public servants at all levels of government in Canada. In a liberal
democratic society, how does one justify keeping vital information
from the public and from other participants in policy-making and
administrative processes? How compelling are traditional confidentiality
rules in the context of the "open government" demands being placed on
public servants to engage clients and citizens, the need to work closely
with partners across agency, government and sectoral boundaries, the
new engagement opportunities presented by Web 2.0, and the emerging
obligation to blow the whistle by disclosing the risks of serious harm to
the public interest? What is the nature of a public servant's proactive
duty to provide information, separate from reactive obligations arising
from freedom of information legislation? Is it ever appropriate to
mislead the public by providing false or distorted information?

The iconic obligation to protect the privacy of employees, clients,
citizens and organizations providing sensitive information to government

also creates ethical dilemmas for public servants. Under freedom of information legislation, the protection of privacy is traditionally one of the limitations placed on public servants' obligation to share information with the public. But the very notion of privacy and the well-established principles governing the collection, manipulation, storage and dissemination of sensitive personal and corporate information set out in privacy legislation are under increasing pressure from demands for enhanced security of the country and workplace as well as the health and safety of citizens and the environment. They are also being undermined by the perceived benefits flowing from the surveillance, data-matching and dissemination opportunities provided by rapidly changing information and communications technology and the willingness of citizens to embrace that technology on a daily basis in their personal lives. How sustainable are traditional privacy claims and rules in the face of contemporary threats and practices? In this rapidly shifting environment, what is the nature of the public servant's duty to protect the privacy of individuals and organizations about which it holds sensitive information? Is privacy a right and, if so, how significant is it?

Confidentiality and privacy are ethical problem areas in which the moral intuitions of public servants about how to act in specific situations are often distant from the traditional rules governing their behaviour. This chapter examines what it means to deal responsibly with government information in a society variously preoccupied by the power of knowledge, the collection, integration and sharing of information, the need for accountability and the perplexing demands of personal informational privacy.

Confidentiality: The Prime Directive

The duty not to disseminate without authorization information which is obtained in the course of one's work is an obligation recognized and enforced by individual governments through the common law, oaths of office, the *Criminal Code*, the *Security of Information Act* (1985), freedom of information legislation, non-disclosure provisions of specific statutes, codes of conduct, and special policy directives by individual governments. All of this reflects a pervasive political and bureaucratic "culture of secrecy" (Reid 2002, p. 32) and "tight control of information" (Thomas 2011, p. 1) which, despite increasing pressures for transparency, has taken hold at the federal level and in varying degrees at the provincial and municipal levels.

Oaths and Laws

While the accumulated case law provides for exceptions where there is a public interest in disclosure, overall, tribunals and courts have established a significant duty of confidentiality and loyalty for public servants (Treasury Board of Canada Secretariat 2012a). This duty is complemented and recognized more specifically with respect to government employees in the oath of office that they take when joining government service, which almost always includes an undertaking to maintain confidentiality. For example, the Government of Canada requires through its oath of office that public servants not disclose or make known without due authority any matter that comes to their knowledge by reason of holding office (Department of Justice Canada 2012a). To this wide-ranging prohibition, public servants must add restrictions on disclosure emanating from the *Criminal Code* and the *Security of Information Act*. The former provides the opportunity for prosecutors to use the sections related to offences against the administration of law and justice to treat unauthorized disclosure of information by a public servant in exchange for a benefit as a fraud on the government (Department of Justice Canada 2012b). The latter replaced the infamous *Official Secrets Act* in 2001 and provides significant sanctions for the unauthorized disclosure by any public servant and, in particular, by "persons permanently bound to secrecy," of "special operational information" (e.g., confidential sources of intelligence, targets of covert surveillance, military operations) and other information the government is "taking measures to safeguard," the release of which would cause damage to the Government of Canada (Treasury Board of Canada Secretariat 2003a). The Act also contains provisions designed to criminalize leakage and even receipt (by journalists, for instance) of virtually any "official" government document (Forcese 2009, p. 17-18).

Ironically, freedom of information legislation in every jurisdiction across the country contains clauses forcing or allowing public servants to refuse to disclose information for a wide variety of reasons, including the possibility that it would be harmful to international relations, national security, the economic interests of the government, law enforcement, intergovernmental relations, Cabinet confidences, policy and legal advice from officials, negotiations, third-party business interests, the conservation of heritage sites, personal privacy, etc. In recent years, Canadian governments have proposed and, in at least one case (Newfoundland and Labrador 2012), enacted further limitations on what are described as frivolous, vexatious and systematic requests as well as access to such items as third-party business information and a wider range of Cabinet records including policy proposals, research reports and briefing notes. Exemptions were further strengthened at the federal level by the passage of the *Anti-Terrorism Act* in 2001, which permits the restriction of disclosure of security information provided by foreign governments (Roberts 2006, p. 136). Many Canadian jurisdictions also use legislation to place more specific disclosure restrictions on employees working in certain areas (taxation, immigration, statistics, health records, security, etc.). Most of these latter restrictions relate to the protection of privacy.

Codes of Conduct Stress Secrecy

Public service codes of conduct or special guidelines often further reinforce the non-disclosure duty. The *Conflict of Interest Policy* for City of Toronto employees, for instance, states that:

> Employees may not disclose confidential or privileged information about the property, or affairs of the organization, or use confidential information to advance personal or others' interests. Employees cannot divulge confidential information about the city's employees without those employees' written authorization. (City of Toronto 2000, n.p.)

The *Code of Conduct and Ethics for the Public Service of Alberta* refers to confidentiality only briefly in the context of rules about public statements by public servants. The Code reminds public servants of the non-disclosure obligations flowing from their oath of office and states that: "[t]he responsibility for maintaining the confidentiality of information or documents includes the responsibility for ensuring that such information or documents are not directly or indirectly made available to unauthorized persons" (Alberta Corporate Human Resources 2011, s. 16[2]). In British Columbia's Standards of Conduct, public servants are cautioned that:

> Confidential information, in any form, that employees receive through their employment must not be disclosed, released, or transmitted to anyone other than persons who are authorized to receive the information. Employees with care or control of personal or sensitive information, electronic media, or devices must handle and dispose of these appropriately. Employees who are in doubt as

to whether certain information is confidential must ask the appropriate authority before disclosing, releasing, or transmitting it. (British Columbia, Public Service Agency 2008, n.p.)

Guidelines and Policies Reinforce Non-disclosure

To clarify terms such as "confidential," "protected" and "sensitive," codes are supplemented in many jurisdictions by information-security guidelines for public servants providing detailed instructions concerning the classification, management and protection of restricted information. Classification is usually based on the degree of harm the release of information would cause. At the federal level, for example, information which could cause injury to the national interest (defined as the "social, political and economic stability of Canada") can be classified as top secret, secret, and confidential. There is also a category of information labeled "designated," which refers to information held by government that cannot be disclosed because disclosure is restricted under provisions of access to information and privacy legislation as noted above. Such information is classified as Protected C (extremely sensitive), B (particularly sensitive) and A (low sensitivity) (Treasury Board of Canada Secretariat 2009). In Alberta, information is classified as restricted, confidential, protected, or unrestricted (Alberta Government Services 2005); in Ontario, classified information is denoted as high, medium or low sensitivity (Ontario Ministry of Government and Consumer Services 2008). As a general rule, information that is not classified as unrestricted requires authorization by a superior before it can be disclosed. Many public servants would not usually have access to information classified as highly sensitive, top secret or secret.

The obligation of confidentiality is still further strengthened by policy directives issued by governments in response to specific concerns about the information being disseminated by appointed officials. For example, in 1990, the federal Privy Council Office cautioned public servants to limit their provision of information to parliamentary committees to "explanations" and "factual information" and to avoid defending complex policy matters or the administration of their department or programs. Public servants were also cautioned that no classified information or "other confidences...beyond that normally accessible to the public" should be provided without the permission of the minister (Privy Council Office 1990, n.p.). Similar cautions are contained in the more recent Communications Policy, which states that spokespersons for government agencies must be designated and:

> (a)t all times must respect privacy rights, security needs, matters before the courts, government policy, Cabinet confidences and ministerial responsibility. When speaking as an institution's official representative, they must identify themselves by name and position, speak on the record for public attribution, and confine their remarks to matters of fact concerning the policies, programs, services or initiatives of their institution. (Treasury Board of Canada Secretariat 2012b, s. 20)

The policy also provides opportunities for a federal department to block public servants from speaking publicly about their work. Spokespersons must be "designated" by their department and "receive instruction, particularly in media relations" before they do so. There have been numerous complaints about federal scientists being denied the right to respond to media inquiries in a timely manner, speak at academic conferences or publish research on controversial issues such as health, climate change and fisheries (CBC News, 2010, September 20; Greenwood 2013). In more recent years the ultimate control of sensitive public communications at the federal and provincial levels has tended to shift from the departmental level to central public affairs offices reporting to the prime minister or premier (Thomas 2013).

Finally, with the increasing use of social media tools by government, federal public servants are warned in *Guidelines for External Use of Web 2.0* that: "[only publicly available information must be shared externally, unless you are specifically authorized otherwise." The Guidelines advise public servants wishing to use a social media site for official purposes that they must have permission to create a profile and engage the public only with the support and under the direction of their agency's "designated official responsible for Web 2.0" (Treasury Board of Canada Secretariat 2011, n.p.). Similar restrictions apply in other jurisdictions such as Alberta (Alberta Public Affairs Bureau 2010). This degree of control is bound to create tension as public servants make more use of social media in a digital environment which embraces the assumption that information is a commodity to be shared freely and quickly in exchanges with networks of clients, stakeholders and engaged citizens.

Transparency: Far from a Duty

On the other side, *transparency* has been a trending value of governments at all levels in Canada since the passage of access to information legislation in Nova Scotia in 1977, Quebec in 1982 and Ottawa in 1983. Over the years, freedom of information (FOI) laws have been adopted by all provincial and territorial governments and in most jurisdictions extended to a wider universe of public sector organizations (e.g., Crown corporations, health authorities, regulatory bodies, universities) and regional and municipal government institutions, including police forces, school boards, etc. These FOI regimes are generally designed to give individuals, corporations and other organizations operating in Canada "the right to access information that is contained in government records" (Treasury Board of Canada Secretariat 2012c, n.p.). The formal process of requesting information under FOI legislation is intended to complement the right to informally request and receive from any government institution information that is not specifically exempted from disclosure. The regimes are almost entirely *reactive* in character in that a public servant's formal obligation to disclose information is triggered by a written application from an individual or organization, which is in most cases presented by a fellow employee in the department or agency tasked with coordinating the fulfillment of formal access requests. There is usually a fee associated with the application. Requests that are denied in full or in part or for which an apparently unreasonable fee is charged can be appealed to a freedom of information commissioner.

One significant boost to transparency found in a number of provincial FOI laws is the *proactive* obligation placed on the head of a public body to disclose without delay to the public or those likely to be affected "information (a) about a risk of significant harm to the environment or to the health or safety of the public or a group of people, or (b) information the disclosure of which is, for any other reason, clearly in the public interest" (British Columbia 1996, s. 25). In other FOI regimes, including the federal legislation, similarly stated public interest disclosure obligations are discretionary (Tromp 2008, ch. 5).

Many governments across the country have created policy directives providing guidance to public servants on how to manage disclosure obligations under FOI laws. The federal government, for example, has issued a *Policy on Access to Information* designed to ensure "sound management and decisions in responding to requests from applicants" seeking information. The policy emphasizes the importance of providing "complete, accurate and timely responses...without regard to the applicant's identity"; "exercising discretion...in a fair, reasonable and impartial manner"; "[e]nsuring that every reasonable effort is made to help applicants"; and keeping exemptions "limited and specific" (Treasury Board of Canada Secretariat 2008a, n.p.).

Freedom of Information Laws Are Not a Panacea

Unfortunately, FOI laws have not proved to be the boon to transparency that was anticipated (Rees 2012). Over the years, exemptions and exclusions – especially those related to national security after 9/11 – have been more broadly interpreted. "Overclaiming" related to the sensitivity of information, secret evidence rules for court proceedings and heavy redaction of released text have become commonplace (Forcese 2009). Large access fees are often demanded, and lengthy delays in dealing with information requests – especially politically sensitive ones – are regular occurrences (Roberts 2002). Ministers' and prime ministers/premiers' offices have become more active in influencing and managing decisions about the release of information to individuals or organizations that might embarrass the government (Roberts 2005, Thomas 2013). Fewer records are kept of controversial activities and meetings, and management of records – especially of electronic exchanges – has become less reliable (Tromp 2008). A particular concern in this area is the use by public officials of private cell phones to conduct government business. Finally, more governmental activities have been transferred to private and not-for-profit organizations not subject to FOI laws (Roberts 2001).

Whistle Blower Legislation and Policy

The legislated obligation to share information does not end with the FOI laws operating at all levels of government in Canada. As noted in chapter 1, public servants across the country are increasingly being provided in whistle blower protection legislation and policy with the right (except in British Columbia where it is an obligation) to disclose evidence of violations of law, gross mismanagement, misuse of government resources, or substantial and specific threats to public health and safety to superiors or designated departmental disclosure officers. However, the strong emphasis in all of these regimes is on *internal disclosure* to superiors who may – at most – be obliged to share the information about a confirmed wrongdoing with the public (FAIR 2013).

Canadian whistle blower protection regimes only become vehicles for wider transparency if a public servant determines that the complaint about wrongdoing is not being dealt with adequately within his or her department or agency. Then, the public servant is generally allowed

– but not obligated – to share the information only with a senior government official outside of his or her chain of command (e.g., the deputy minister of the environment, an integrity commissioner, a public health officer), an oversight agency (e.g., the auditor general) or the police.

Most importantly from a transparency perspective, whistle blower protection laws in Canada do not *obligate* a public servant to disclose information about wrongdoing directly to the public. Federal public servants are warned in the *Public Servants Disclosure Protection Act* (2005) that a "disclosure made to the public – for example the media – will not be a protected disclosure (i.e. it will not provide you with the protection offered by the Act) unless there is not enough time to make it in using the internal or PSIC (Public Service Integrity Commissioner) processes and you believe that there is a serious breach of federal or provincial laws, or an imminent risk of a substantial and specific danger to the life, health and safety of persons or the environment." The Act further cautions "that in making a disclosure, you should provide only as much information as reasonably necessary to make the disclosure, and you must follow regular procedures for handling, communicating and storing the information securely" (Treasury Board of Canada Secretariat 2013a, s. 3). The Nova Scotia legislation is more explicit about the kind of information that should not be released in the course of making a wrongdoing public (*Public Interest Disclosure of Wrongdoing Act* 2010). Such guidelines suggest that a public servant must exercise a complex judgment call before publicly disclosing a perceived wrongdoing and also ensure that any release of information in support of the allegation of wrongdoing does not violate rules of confidentiality related to sensitive information discussed earlier in the chapter.

Such warnings cast a pall over the prospect for public disclosure by whistle blowers. In addition, it is well understood by public servants that whistle blowing is usually characterized as an act of disloyalty by colleagues and superiors, an act which often provokes retaliation – especially when disclosures are public (Dworkin and Baucus 1998). New whistle blower protection regimes establish processes to safeguard public servants from retaliation, but protection levels vary in effectiveness and there is still plenty of evidence of attempts at organizational vengeance against whistle blowers (Alford 2001; FAIR 2013; Lewis 2008). Protection that is seen to be inadequate by public servants represents a further blow to the prospects for public disclosure.

Open Government and Digital Technologies

Since the beginning of the new millennium, Canadian public servants have increasingly been confronted with commitments to "open government" by the politicians they serve. Prime Minister Harper's Conservative Party identified transparency and accountability as its highest priorities in its 2006 election platform (Conservative Party of Canada 2006). Premier Redford of Alberta created an associate minister of accountability and transparency with a mandate to develop transparency legislation when she came into office in 2012 (Alberta Government 2012). Mike Savage promised a new era of transparency and openness when he successfully ran for mayor of Halifax in 2012 (Fraser 2012, October 20). Such commitments can result in narrowly focused disclosure initiatives such as whistle blower legislation, obligations to report on travel and hospitality expenses, and demands that lobbyists report on their communications with public officials. But such commitments have also begun to produce more significant new initiatives in the area of proactive information release, with a stronger emphasis on citizen engagement in the development of priorities, policies and budgets, the implementation of programs and the evaluation of their effectiveness. Digital technologies are key factors in these developments, providing both the online platforms for massive, accessible and user-friendly "data dumps" by government and Web 2.0 social media tools for interconnectivity, interaction and crowd-sourcing. The ability to take advantage of such initiatives ultimately conjures up the vision of "Citizen 2.0" – empowered to engage, innovate, organize, challenge and even co-produce services (Barkat et al. 2012; Morison 2010; Roy 2013).

The movement to engage the citizen more effectively seems most developed at the municipal and regional levels. For example, Vancouver used web-based software to share information and solicit ideas, votes and comments on how to "green" the city. A team of public servants reviewed and reacted online to ideas as part of the process of creating an action plan for presentation to council (Vancouver 2012). Edmonton has led the way in establishing an open data system as part of its open government initiative (Edmonton 2013). At the federal and provincial levels, the talk about open government is slowly translating into the kind of information sharing and informed dialogue anticipated by the protagonists of citizen engagement. The federal government launched an Open Government Strategy in 2011 featuring Open Information, Open Data and Open Dialogue initiatives (Canada 2013). Open Information will obligate public servants to "proactively release information on government activities on an ongoing basis," mostly online. The Open

Data initiative will focus on making geo-spatial and non-geospatial data sets publicly available through a government data portal. Finally, the Open Dialogue initiative will move the existing Consulting with Canadians website (Canada 2011) on to a new Web 2.0 "citizen engagement platform that federal organizations can use to conduct public consultations" (Canada 2013, n.p.). Some provincial governments (e.g., Ontario and British Columbia) are making parallel efforts to leverage web-based platforms to provide information and engage citizens (British Columbia 2012; Ontario Ministry of Government Services 2010). But, as noted earlier, Canadian federal and provincial public servants are being asked to participate in these initiatives in the context of relatively restrictive sets of policies governing the type of information they are permitted to share and the degree of discretion they may exercise in their online dialogues with stakeholders and the public. Some governments at the municipal level in Canada and governments in other jurisdictions, Australia for instance, appear to be providing considerably more latitude to their public servants to engage and inform the public using Web 2.0 platforms (Australian Department of Finance and Deregulation 2010; Australian Public Service Commission 2012).

What Codes of Conduct Say

While initiatives like these may foreshadow the adoption of a more proactive obligation for public servants to inform and engage citizens more comprehensively, at this point such an obligation is far from written in stone. A review of the federal Consulting with Canadians website (Canada 2011) suggests that the more traditional top-down model of consultation is still the rule, allowing limited opportunities for citizens to react to draft government agendas or plans – "where commitments have been made and ideas hardened" (Turnbull and Aucoin 2006, p. 1), few signs of opportunities to engage in dialogue with the drafters themselves and even fewer signs that citizens' inputs have made a difference. Moreover, political commitments to open government are only rarely matched by parallel commitments to proactive transparency or openness in codes of conduct for public servants. The Nova Scotia code focuses on responsibility and transparency in pursuit of the core value of accountability (Nova Scotia Public Service Commission 2009). The 2003 federal *Values and Ethics Code for the Public Service* contained the following conflicted message: "Public servants should also strive to ensure that the value of transparency in government is upheld while respecting their duties of confidentiality under the law" (Treasury Board of Canada Secretariat 2003b, n.p.). But even this half-hearted endorsement of the value of transparency disappeared in the more recent version of the Code, which doesn't mention any duty of transparency or openness at all (Treasury Board of Canada Secretariat 2012d). Finally, the City of Vancouver *Code of Conduct* sets a very high standard, which could be held out as a benchmark for Canadian governments at all levels:

> Council officials, staff and advisory body members have a duty to be as open as possible about their decisions and actions. This means communicating appropriate information openly to the public about decision-making processes and issues being considered; encouraging appropriate public participation; communicating clearly; and providing appropriate means for recourse and feedback. (Vancouver 2011, p. 2)

But powerful pro-transparency statements like this are the rare exception. Most codes of conduct don't establish any duty of transparency. Overall, when public servants in Canada survey the messages sent to them by their employers about confidentiality and transparency, the weight of obligation as expressed in law, policy, codes of conduct and administrative culture is still clearly on the side of secrecy and information control. In a world increasingly dominated by information-sharing networks such as WikiLeaks, Human Rights Watch, the World Economic Forum, the Alliance for Climate Protection and Wikipedia, most public services above the municipal level are still restricted by a web of rules and practices antagonistic to the values of transparency, participation and collaboration. Information management may provide one of the clearest illustrations of a continuing gulf between public and private morality.

For and Against Secrecy

If we exclude, for the moment, considerations related to the protection of privacy, what arguments can be mustered for and against the presumption of secrecy, which seems to dominate Canadian public administration? Sissela Bok (1983) argues that underlying what is, for the most part, a consequentialist approach to the defence of secrecy is an "esoteric rationale" which suggests that secrecy is even more justifiable for governments than it is for individuals – that governments have a right to keep the "secrets of rule" or "mysteries of state" from the people (p. 172).

Failing the persuasiveness of a doctrine flowing from the divine right of kings, other more results-oriented rationales for secrecy are at hand. In essence, these are arguments rooted in a concern about government's capacity to carry out its role effectively. Secrecy is essential to make and implement plans, to negotiate, and to protect citizens from enemies. The long shadow of these traditional rationales is easily visible in the types of exemptions and exclusions which are commonplace in contemporary freedom of information legislation.

Secrecy and Anonymity

But let us look at these rationales a little more closely. In Canada and other countries that have adopted the Westminster model of government, the consequential concern about the ability to make and implement plans has become intertwined with a constitutional rationale for secrecy. Our system of responsible cabinet government at the federal and provincial levels, it is argued, won't work unless cabinets, their committees, ministers and supporting bureaucracies are allowed in secrecy to develop, discuss and argue about the widest possible set of policy alternatives before choosing one, sealing the various compromises, closing ranks, and applying the convention of collective ministerial responsibility for that decision. Similarly, as we have discussed in chapter 3, the views and roles of public servants in the decision-making process must be kept dark to protect their anonymity and further buttress the notions of collective and individual ministerial responsibility. Anonymity, in this sense, can be thought of as a constitutionally protected virtue of a public servant at the federal or provincial level. As Gordon Robertson (1972) put it:

> It has always been recognized as fundamental
> to the principle of ministerial responsibility
> for policy that confidentiality be maintained
> about advice received from officials. It is the
> Ministers who decide: the policy is theirs. It
> does not matter whether it was devised by
> officials, or whether they argued for or against
> it. The principles would not last long, nor
> would the anonymity of the public service,
> if Cabinet documents became publishable
> without some prescribed and substantial
> delay. (p. 12)

Secrecy and Effectiveness

Of course, the consequential justification for secrecy does not draw the line at the protection of cabinet documents related to policy development. A strong argument is also made for protecting government's capacity to deliver policy. Effectiveness in implementation often calls for stealth, which, in turn, depends on secrecy. The details of a criminal investigation cannot be made known to the public without being made known to the criminals. Other values, such as fairness and equity, may also be at stake. The regulatory regime for a new tax policy cannot be displayed prematurely for fear that some crafty citizens or corporations will negate the intention of the new taxes. For the same reasons, the decision-making process leading to an adjustment of interest rates must be kept secret until the government is ready to move.

This logic is easily extended to the whole realm of negotiation. A government cannot bargain successfully with unions, corporations, or other levels of government, it is argued, if its bottom line and strategy are widely known. The ultimate realm of secrecy, of course, is information about a government's relationships and negotiations with foreign governments or groups and its preparation for defence or attack. As Sissela Bok (1983) points out: "At the root of the rationale for military secrecy is the imperative of self-preservation...And because a degree of military secrecy is so fundamental to survival, it can call on greater sacrifices than all other rationales for secrecy" (p. 192). The Internet's capacity instantly to distribute information worldwide reinforces the logic of suppressing the release of any information (e.g., diplomats' memos on the abuse of Afghan detainees; soldiers' blog postings on the vulnerability of military vehicles to roadside bombs) that might increase the level of risk faced by our military, diplomatic or foreign aid personnel. There is nothing like the threat of an outside enemy to buttress a government's argument that even the normal concerns about the intentional concealment of information have to be put aside.

Overall, then, democratic governments argue that to govern effectively they must hide a good deal of information from the citizens they represent. Thus public servants are confronted with a strong message to keep their mouths shut, their e-mail and social media activities muted and their file drawers locked unless otherwise instructed. But what about the arguments on the other side? What kind of case can be made for a presumption of disclosure rather than secrecy?

The Right to Information

The most telling argument against secrecy in a democratic society is its impact on the distribution of power and, ultimately, the right of citizens to participate meaningfully in the democratic process. Secrecy gives power to those who hold the information and removes it from the uninformed. Without information, citizens lose their capacity both to influence public policy making and to hold governments to account. Widespread public participation and accountability are both essential features of a healthy democracy. Donald Smiley (1978) argued that "information must be so distributed that public debate is not a 'dialogue of the deaf' between those who don't know and those who won't tell" (p. 23). Since the outset of the push for freedom of information legislation, therefore, there has been an increasing tendency to characterize access to government information as a basic right of a citizen in a democratic society (Florini 2007a; Ontario. Commission on Freedom of Information and Individual Privacy 1980, vol. 2).

The relationship between information and meaningful participation is obvious and goes well beyond concern for creating an informed electorate ready to cast their ballots intelligently. Groups or individual members of the public who are immediately affected or merely concerned about the development of government policy in a particular area are in no position to join the debate and argue their case persuasively if they do not have access to the array of information which the government has gathered to support its proposals. The more recent citizen engagement and deliberative democracy movements extend the right to know still further to embrace extensive two-way interaction and dialogue (Sheedy 2008). This more robust right to information requires elected and appointed officials to establish forums and processes designed to provide relevant information to potentially affected citizens and groups; elicit opinions and preferences on the nature of the problem, potential solutions, resources required and implementation priorities related to the policy or program being examined; and allow for dialogue informed by evidence among stakeholders representing different positions in an atmosphere of mutual respect and equality among officials, stakeholders and the wider citizenry (Cohen 2003). This inflation of the right to information represents a significant departure from the more traditional notion of citizen participation defined in terms of one-way flows of information, voting, responding to polls and voluntarily taking part in consultative activities designed, initiated and controlled by government.

Transparency and Effectiveness

While a rights perspective on transparency may be a good place to start, there are parallel consequential arguments that are equally powerful (Florini 2007b). Providing the information required for citizens and groups to participate more fully in the decision-making process reduces the distrust of government and increases its efficiency. The

Ontario Commission on Freedom of Information and Individual Privacy (1980) argued that:

> the effect of public awareness of and
> participation in the decision-making processes
> may reduce the intensity of protracted public
> debate concerning proposed government
> initiatives. It is simply inefficient for
> governments to make decisions and to devote
> considerable resources to the development
> of programs only to have them subsequently
> either rejected by an angry public or subjected
> to the expense and delay of prolonged
> reconsideration and inquiry. (p. 81)

Our contemporary approach to policy making is one in which groups and individuals make mutual adjustments in order to achieve as many of their desired ends as possible. "What makes mutual adjustment work is the wide availability of relevant information, so each mutual adjuster can figure out what the others might do under varied conditions and give forth useful signals about his or her own behavior" (Cleveland 1985a, p. 190). This logic is equally compelling as we move from government to governance and try to maximize the performance of partnerships that governments create among their own agencies and with other governments and organizations in the private and not-for-profit sectors. Information sharing is the key lubricant of all of these contemporary relationships. In short, the argument is that the benefits of making more information available in most circumstances considerably outweigh the costs.

Similarly, the accountability of government officials for actions taken cannot survive and prosper without the free flow of information between government and its citizens. Secrecy means that individuals and institutions that have a right within our model of responsible democratic government to scrutinize the performance of government often lack the information required even to formulate relevant questions. A citizen, an oversight agency or a legislative committee cannot examine government actions if data about the implementation of policy are withheld or only reluctantly and partially made available when specifically requested. Despite the traditional focus of accountability on elected officials, this concern is perhaps even more relevant to public servants than politicians. It is the former who breathe life into policy decisions of the latter, and it is the identification of those who exercise discretionary authority under legislation and knowledge about how they exercise that authority that are the key building blocks of an administrative accountability regime, as we shall explore in more detail in chapter 7.

A system that fosters confidentiality about the operation of government might also be fostering abuse of administrative power. In any case, it is clearly public perception – reinforced by the media – that an unduly secretive government must have something to hide. That something, as often as not, includes incidents of waste of resources, negligence with respect to the health or safety of the public, conflicts of interest or misdirection of funds.

There are a number of consequentialist arguments in favour of greater openness but not directly related to the democratic values of participation and accountability. David Curzon (1977) argues that secrecy can endanger the efficacy of the decision-making process in government. Keeping information within a small circle of decision makers and advisors can hide the fact that the premises upon which a decision is based are simplistic, biased or just plain wrong. If the premises are faulty, then the decision is unlikely to be effective. Secrecy can hide the fact that the objectives influencing a decision may represent the personal interests of officials or a small group or class in the community (Curzon 1977). Secrecy can also keep from view the fact that a very limited number of alternative courses of action were considered or that the thinking about the problem was bounded by ideology or the limited imaginations of the few participants. Anyone who has taken part in decision making under conditions of secrecy will appreciate how ignorance, lack of imagination or willful blindness can damage the effectiveness of government.

Defensible Whistle Blowing

Consequential arguments are also at the heart of the defence of whistle blowing, a form of disclosure that is being transformed from an extreme act of dissent to a core obligation or right of a responsible public servant. Increasingly, governments at all levels across the country recognize that it is unacceptable for a public servant to ignore activities or omissions of government that harm the public interest by violating the law, misusing resources or creating serious risks to public health or safety or the environment. But, regardless of its new status, whistle blowing is not without moral complexities. Public servants must make difficult judgments about the significance of the harm that they are considering disclosing. Is their judgment supported by solid evidence that the wrongdoing is serious and ongoing or imminent, or is there a possibility that their judgment is clouded by personal or political prejudice? The whistle blower must also be conscious of the fact that an accusation unsupported by compelling evidence may be unfair and damaging to the individuals implicated.

The strong emphasis placed on internal disclosure by virtually all whistle-blowing regimes raises further concerns. While internal disclosure is in accord with the strong cultural pressure to solve problems "within the family," it can represent a significant deterrent to lower-level public servants unfamiliar with the bureaucratic world beyond their own unit. It takes moral courage to take an accusation up through the hierarchical chain, especially as some whistle-blowing regimes require the public servant to inform the administrative head of the department or agency about the problem before going outside the organization – a further step that requires even more courage in view of the evidence that providing protection from retaliation has proved to be a difficult task (Organization for Economic Cooperation and Development [OECD] 2012; Ramirez 2007). The potentially high personal cost of revealing yourself as a whistle blower might also force to the surface a difficult choice between following the open internal disclosure route set out in most whistle-blowing regimes and "leaking" the information surreptitiously (Bok 1983, p. 223). Finally, there is the question of where the public servant's responsibility to prevent a particular harm ends. For instance, is he or she obligated to continue to report incidents of the same kind of wrongdoing if his or her supervisor has indicated that the practice in question will be stopped in due course?

The Virtue of Candour

Finally, openness is cherished not only because of its contributions to democratic and effective government but also because it is tied closely to a central value for a number of professions commonly found in the public service. The codes of conduct of lawyers, doctors, social workers, and health science administrators, for example, place great emphasis on the notion of a free flow of information between professional and client. As Michael Bayles (1981) notes, "The responsibility of candor is at the heart of the professional-client relationship" (p. 72). There are relatively few instances, Bayles argues, in which a professional would be justified in withholding or manipulating information and, thereby, interfering with the client's capacity to make informed judgments and properly consent to a proposed government action.

Deception, Disinformation, Propaganda, and Censorship

The reference to information manipulation in the context of the professional virtue of candour raises a wider issue. The clash between the duty of confidentiality and the duty of transparency extends not only to the more obvious question of whether or not to provide certain government information to individual citizens or groups but also to the acceptability of the related practices of deception, disinformation, propaganda and censorship. The ethical dilemmas associated with such practices are often overlooked because they are traditionally directed towards "enemy" nations or criminals. But it is a mistake to write such activities off as ethically benign. In almost all instances they raise the same concerns as the more common forms of information concealment.

In our ordinary relationships with friends, family and partners, deception or lying (the practice of intentionally misleading another) is generally portrayed as a serious moral transgression because of the enormous benefits we all gain from being able to trust that others are telling us the truth (Bok 1978). However, public servants are often faced with situations in which they may be asked to participate in deception. For example, elaborate "sting" operations by law enforcement and security officials will involve the deception of suspected gang members or terrorists to tempt them to display their criminal or violent intent. The debate about the line between the encouragement of the potential criminal or terrorist and the entrapment of the innocent is in part a debate about the legitimate use of deception.

One of the most common forms of deception is *disinformation*, which Sissela Bok (1983) characterizes as "the spreading of false information to hurt adversaries. Common in wartime, and increasingly used by contending secret service networks even in peacetime, it now flourishes in the media, as governments try to influence public opinion against one another and against domestic adversaries" (p. 187). The sense of ethical unease which may develop when using deception to fight crime or terrorism often evaporates when the practice of *disinformation* is considered. Consider, for example, the extensive campaign waged by the federal government against the "yes" forces in the sovereignty-association referendum in Quebec in 1980. Federal public servants were heavily involved in what became a no-holds-barred political brawl. In such circumstances, intentionally "pumping up" the government's position and distorting the likely effects of your opponent's strategy may seem defensible to some. But this is a slippery slope, with public servants becoming increasingly caught up in the everyday deceptive and manipulative efforts of government communications staff to put a positive "spin" on its position and discredit the position of its opponents across a wide range of domestic issues (Roberts 2005; Thomas 2013). Ironically, Richard Mulgan (2007) attributes the increasing willingness of public servants to support disinformation efforts to the effect of freedom of information laws, which he argues "places officials under greater pressure to compromise with the truth in the interests of not undermining the credibility of their political masters" if their advice is made public (p. 585). Regardless of the pressures, public servants have to consider carefully the rights of the individuals who will be affected, the degree to which such practices degrade their political neutrality (see chapter 3) and the longer-term corrosive effects of the practice of disinformation on the level of public trust in government and the media.

Parallel arguments can be made about *propaganda* and *censorship*. Again these are practices that in wartime have been justified as reasonable and necessary to demoralize the enemy, buoy one's own citizens, and keep strategic information from falling into the hands of the opposing side. But whether used in wartime or applied domestically (outside the context of concerns about the survival of the nation), such practices are merely variations on previously explored themes of secrecy and disinformation. As such, they raise the full panoply of rights and consequences arguments associated with the tension between disclosure and confidentiality. In addition, censorship directed not at information of strategic significance but rather at material thought to be seditious or immoral raises significant rights issues associated with freedom of expression.

Final Thoughts on Secrecy and Transparency

Overall – from the perspective of consequences, the right to information and the fostering of key values such as participation, accountability and candour – a strong set of arguments can be made to reverse the "culture of secrecy" and shift the balance between confidentiality and transparency in favour of the latter. This would seem to suggest that beyond the existing legislated obligation to disclose some information when requested, public servants should have a positive duty to proactively disclose information held by government in circumstances in which the public interest would not be demonstrably harmed. But, despite political and legal commitments to transparency and the opportunities for information sharing presented by the Internet, an expanded duty of openness will never be fully embraced by public servants if it remains a career-shattering and potentially illegal move. A "culture of transparency" will only become a reality if proactive sharing of information becomes the default position supported by more senior public service managers and their political masters.

Mindful of both the legitimacy of many demands for government information and the obviously heavy-handed quality of many confidentiality rules, public servants regularly struggle with disclosure dilemmas. If information is power, or at least a prerequisite for exercising power, then public servants are often put in the position of deciding who will have it and who won't.

The following cases pick up on some of the issues raised in the discussion of the tension between confidentiality and openness. Case 6.1 focuses on the defensibility of an informal information-sharing initiative that a public servant takes to get around formal confidentiality rules.

CASE 6.1: THE REAL WORLD OF CONFIDENTIALITY

Harry is a new member of a provincial treaty negotiating team engaged in land claims negotiations with a BC First Nation and the federal government. He is curious about the lengthy conversation that his chief negotiator, Bob, just had with his federal counterpart.

Harry: What was going on there? It sounds like you were giving the chief federal negotiator a very full account of our proposed resource revenue-sharing strategy and the rationale for it. Isn't that protected information?

Bob: You're right, it was a very full account and I was drawing heavily on a protected ministry analysis. We have to have the Feds onside before we can put an offer on the table, and we can't build the support we need without giving them the whole story. .

Harry: Have you received authorization to do that?

Bob: Not really. When the chief negotiators talked to the deputy minister about it he didn't want to know. All he said was: "do what you have to do to get results." If I restricted information only to those people authorized to see it, these negotiations would never get anywhere. The only way I get solid information about mandates and strategies from the Feds is if I share. In fact, you shouldn't even have access to some of the stuff you've been reading. You're not cleared to see it. But you wouldn't be much use to me if I didn't keep you fully in the picture. The same goes for The First Nation negotiators and our stakeholder advisory groups. The third parties just wouldn't work with us if I restricted them to the information they are supposed to get. The real world is far more open than the confidentiality rules suggest.

Can you defend Bob's approach to confidentiality?

The second case deals with the issue of deception and the nature of the proactive duty a public servant has to help members of the public to understand what is really happening with an issue in which they have a considerable stake.

CASE 6.2: I ANSWERED THE QUESTION

Two directors in the health ministry are chatting before the weekly management meeting.

Stefan: I saw the news clips on that public meeting you attended on surgical wait times. You really got away with murder.

Sheila: Come on, Stefan. I didn't really lie. But if they don't ask the right questions I am sure not going to volunteer anything.

Stefan: But it is pretty misleading to compare our stats with other provinces since we don't count the time before the patient gets to see the specialist into the total wait time. In some cases, that can be the longest part of the wait.

Sheila: Look, every province does the calculation differently. If you just use our published numbers we look pretty good. It's not my job to go out of my way to explain the differences in the calculation method. Why should I make trouble for the minister on this issue?

Stefan: That's an interesting question. When I last looked, you weren't a member of the governing party.

Sheila: I'm not. But I am a team player. This is a tough issue and we aren't going to gain the confidence and support of the minister going forward if we go out of our way to show how bad things are at the moment. If I get asked the right question I will provide the right answer. But, otherwise, I am just reading the lines prepared by the communications folks.

Is this an acceptable position for a public servant to take when answering questions from citizens and stakeholders?

The third case looks at the tough questions faced by a public servant who sees another public servant committing or counseling what she thinks is a wrongdoing. It would be helpful to use a specific piece of whistle blower legislation or policy as a resource in answering the questions posed.

CASE 6.3: *THIS IS WRONG!*

The following conversation takes place between an employee of the provincial Ministry of Natural Resources and a colleague.

Doug: You look upset, Ellen. What's up?

Ellen: I've been ordered to prepare the paperwork to justify allowing the ACME mining company to start open-pit mining in an area where we haven't even had time to do a proper environmental impact study. They gave me some quickie consultant's report showing that the environmental impact will be minimal, but the study isn't worth the paper it's written on, in my view.

Doug: What exactly are you saying?

Ellen: I'm saying that we aren't following the rules here, Doug. Under the existing regulations, which I have the responsibility to administer, ACME can't have a permit without a proper environmental impact certificate from this branch. There must be some reason they're pushing this through.

Doug: Have you taken this up with your boss?

Ellen: Yes, I went to see her and told her what had happened.

Doug: What did she say?

Ellen: She said to go ahead and do as I've been told. Then I took it to the Assistant Deputy Minister, and he let me know that it would be inadvisable to raise the matter again. When I asked why, he just pointed upstairs.

Doug: Are you going to leave it at that, Ellen?

Ellen: I don't know. I'm not sure what more I can do inside the ministry. I am concerned enough about it at this point to send the story to my MLA.

Doug: I'd think pretty carefully before I did that.

What is the nature of the wrongdoing in this case? Is Ellen's evidence strong enough to support her disclosure of the situation? Has she done enough to alert more senior officials in her own ministry? If not, in the circumstances she faces, how and to whom should she report the situation? Under what circumstances would it be defensible for Ellen to provide the information to an individual or agency outside the ministry?

Privacy: An Overview of the Ethical Issues

A government's emphasis on secrecy is a reflection of its concern about its own privacy. In a sense, therefore, we have been focusing to this point on the nature of the public servant's duty to protect the privacy of government and its decision makers. But public servants also have a widely accepted duty to protect the privacy of individuals, private and not-for-profit sector organizations and other governments that interact with the government for which they work. In the discussion that follows we will focus primarily on the informational privacy of individuals, as opposed to their spatial (ability to limit searches of your premises) and bodily (ability to control what is done with your body) privacy (British Columbia Civil Liberties Association 2012a). In recent years, influenced by debates in the United States, "privacy as control over information about oneself has come to be viewed by many as also including protection against unwarranted searches, eavesdropping, surveillance, and appropriation and misuse of one's communications" (DeCew 2012, n.p.). The duty of confidentiality and the duty to protect individual informational privacy are obviously closely linked. In fact, informational privacy protection is one of the key justifications for the duty of confidentiality and the limits placed on disclosure in FOI legislation.

But the duty to protect informational privacy clearly raises ethical questions that range well beyond the issue of how much of the personal information held by governments should be publicly disclosed. What kind of information is it appropriate for a government to be collecting about its citizens? How should it be allowed to collect such information (i.e., what forms of surveillance and coercive acquisition are appropriate)? When is the consent of the individual required? What limitations should be placed on the way a government uses and secures this information? While a citizen's claim to informational privacy might appear to be a motherhood issue, troubling questions have emerged about what a duty to protect personal information should mean in the 21st century. In addition, this is an issue that is being radically transformed by two external forces: changes in surveillance and data management technologies, on the one hand, and wider cultural shifts with respect to the meaning and significance of personal privacy, on the other.

Messages about Privacy Protection

Although privacy is thought of by many as a fundamental human right – and recognized as such in the United Nations Universal Declaration of Human Rights, it is almost completely ignored in Canadian federal and provincial human rights charters. Article 5 of the Quebec *Charter of Human Rights and Freedoms* (Quebec 2013) maintains that "every person has a right to respect for his private life," while the *Canadian Charter of Rights and Freedoms* is limited to references to "the right to be secure against unreasonable search and seizure" (Department of Justice Canada 1982, s. 8). While court decisions have recognized the "quasi-constitutional status of the protection of personal information" (Flaherty 2008, p. 6), the legitimacy, nature and limits of a "right of informational privacy" are far from clear.

References to protection of privacy in codes of conduct for public servants in Canada are rare and, where they exist, tend to focus on the duty to comply with relevant FOI and privacy legislation and to keep information about employees confidential. However, whether referenced in a code of conduct or not, informational privacy protection is legislated for most public servants in Canada. All Canadian privacy protection legislation is *to varying degrees* modeled on internationally accepted Fair Information Practices adopted by the Organization for Economic Cooperation and Development (OECD 2013) and reflected in the Canadian Standards Association Model Code for the Protection of Personal Information created in 1996 and reaffirmed in 2001 (Consumer Measures Committee 2011). The CSA Code focuses on how organizations collect, use and protect personal information, as well as on the right of individuals to access their own personal information, and if necessary, to have it corrected. It sets out the following principles:

1. Accountability. An organization is responsible for personal information under its control and shall designate an individual or individuals who are accountable for the organization's compliance with the following principles.

2. Identifying Purposes. The purposes for which personal information is collected shall be identified by the organization at or before the time the information is collected.

3. Consent. The knowledge and consent of the individual are required for the collection, use, or disclosure of personal information, except where inappropriate.

4. Limiting Collection. The collection of personal information shall be limited to that which is necessary for the purposes identified by the organization. Information shall be collected by fair and lawful means.

5. Limiting Use, Disclosure, and Retention. Personal information shall not be used or disclosed for purposes other than those

for which it was collected, except with the consent of the individual or as required by law. Personal information shall be retained only as long as necessary for the fulfillment of those purposes.

6. Accuracy. Personal information shall be as accurate, complete, and up-to-date as is necessary for the purposes for which it is to be used.

7. Safeguards. Personal information shall be protected by security safeguards appropriate to the sensitivity of the information.

8. Openness. An organization shall make readily available to individuals specific information about its policies and practices relating to the management of personal information.

9. Individual Access. Upon request, an individual shall be informed of the existence, use, and disclosure of his or her personal information and shall be given access to that information. An individual shall be able to challenge the accuracy and completeness of the information and have it amended as appropriate.

10. Challenging Compliance. An individual shall be able to address a challenge concerning compliance with the above principles to the designated individual or individuals accountable for the organization's compliance. (Consumer Measures Committee 2011).

The legal framework in Canada includes the federal *Privacy Act* (1985) and provincial and territorial privacy acts such as the British Columbia *Freedom of Information and Protection of Privacy Act* (1996). The provincial and territorial legislation applies to municipal and regional governments (including local boards, agencies and commissions) except in Ontario, which has a separate *Municipal Freedom of Information and Protection of Privacy Act* (2007). There is also sector-specific privacy legislation, such as the Manitoba *Personal Health Information Act* (2011) and the federal *Statistics Act* (2005). Parallel protections are applicable to private sector organizations through the federal *Personal Information Protection and Electronic Documents Act* (2000) and similar provincial legislation in Quebec, Alberta and British Columbia. This private sector-oriented legislation is significant from the perspective of this discussion because it extends elements of the public sector privacy protection regime to the increasing number of private sector organizations that provide government services to the public.[6] The *Criminal Code* also contains provisions on invasion of privacy and the electronic interception of private communications (Department of Justice Canada 2102b).

At its best, privacy protection legislation in Canada specifies in some detail obligations placed on public servants to:

- stay within the limitations imposed in the legislation on the purposes for which information can be collected

- gain consent for collection from the individual from whom the information is being collected

- adhere to specific conditions under which information can be collected indirectly without the individual's knowledge

- explain to the individual why the information is being collected

- ensure the information is accurate and complete

- provide an opportunity to individuals to correct information that is incorrect

- ensure that information is stored safely

- abide by the conditions set out in the legislation under which it is appropriate to disclose personal information, share it with other agencies or use it in data-linking initiatives either inside or outside of the jurisdiction

- retain information that has been used for a specified period of time

- use information only for the purposes for which it was obtained.

Most governments provide public servants with further policy guidance designed to ensure compliance with the spirit and requirements of their privacy legislation. By way of example, the federal government issued a *Policy on Privacy Protection* (Treasury Board of Canada Secretariat 2008b) clarifying the obligations of various players with respect to the *Privacy Act* and reinforcing the duty to abide by its provisions. *The Directive on Privacy Practices* (Treasury Board of Canada Secretariat 2013b) provides direction with respect to the management of Personal

---

6. Some provinces have privacy acts which make it a civil offense to violate the privacy of an individual, but they are so limited in scope that they provide no useful direction to the public servant about the abuse of personal information. Despite its name, the federal Protection of Privacy Act of 1974 actually legalizes wiretapping in the course of criminal investigations.

Information Banks in line with the provisions of the *Privacy Act*. The *Directive on Privacy Impact Assessment* focuses on techniques for "assessing the privacy implications of new or substantially modified programs and activities involving personal information" (Treasury Board of Canada Secretariat 2010, n.p.).

Increasing Threats to Informational Privacy

Despite what looks like a comprehensive commitment to protect informational privacy at all levels of government in Canada, some of the existing legal and administrative regimes have been criticized as being inadequate to the task. In some cases, the provisions of the legislation are just not robust enough relative to international standards. For example, the federal *Privacy Act*, unrevised since it came into force, does not specify an obligation to obtain consent when collecting information on an individual. Provincial regimes that demand consent often don't insist on the provision of enough information for the individual to understand what he or she is consenting to. Other regimes don't specify clearly enough the manner or degree to which information collected is to be safeguarded. For example, the federal Act, written before the era of cloud computing, does not directly address the storage by federal government agencies of personal data on private servers, possibly even outside the country. Some laws fail to clearly establish who can have access to personal information and when proof of the need for such access is required. Other regimes do not deal specifically enough with the issue of data matching. Under most privacy legislation, the obligation to inform the public and those citizens specifically affected when security is breached and information is accessed or stolen is limited or non-existent. The enforcement powers of some privacy commissioners are restricted, with the result that public servants can ignore a commissioner's findings and recommendations if the publicity costs are not too high (Commission d'àccess à information du Québec 2007; Flaherty 2008; Roy 2013).

Even where the obligations to protect informational privacy are reasonably robust and well enforced, the defensibility and limits of those protections have been tested in recent years by government initiatives designed to enhance public security, safety and health, transform the delivery of public services, and ensure employee integrity. In the wake of 9/11, the desire to make intelligence systems more effective has led to more extensive international and domestic Internet and telephone data gathering, sharing and matching initiatives across agency, jurisdictional and national boundaries, raising serious questions about collection approval processes, collection limitations, consent, data reliability and oversight. As a result of the leaks by Edward Snowden, Communications Security Establishment Canada has been drawn into controversies about the extent of its electronic and voice communications surveillance programs and its cooperation with the activities of the U.S. National Security Agency and other national spy agencies. Questions have also been raised about the appropriate use of identifiers (e.g., social insurance, passport, driver's licence numbers and more comprehensive identity cards) and the security of linked data in initiatives such as the federal government's Advanced Passenger Information/Passenger Name Record program. This program collects information about travellers before they travel, links data provided by travellers with information in other government databases and, as required, shares the data with other law enforcement agencies and countries (Canada Border Service Agency 2008). The federal government has also made it easier for law enforcement agencies to obtain and continue a wiretap and delay informing individuals that they had been subject to a wiretap (Cavoukian 2003). Public health pandemics such as SARS and the spread of HIV/AIDS have led to demands for the naming of potential carriers, mandatory testing, contact tracing and information sharing.

On the service-delivery side, the integration of services generally requires substantial matching of data that previously was kept in separate data banks in different agencies. For efficiency, probity and safety reasons, there have also been a number of government initiatives designed to allow workplace surveillance, including telephone, e-mail and Internet usage monitoring, computer keystroke monitoring, video surveillance, badge-based location tracking of employees, drug and alcohol testing and satellite tracking of government vehicles. At the interface between privacy and confidentiality, governments and corporations are struggling to control employees' increasing use of blogs and other third-party social media tools to make substantive and sometimes negative observations about their employers, workplaces and clients. This is a particularly difficult question in circumstances in which employers have encouraged employees to develop their social media profiles.

The adequacy of direction provided by privacy legislation is also being tested by the development of new technology-driven opportunities for public servants to violate informational privacy. This problem is clearly accelerating as new surveillance tools come on stream. Under what conditions should law enforcement officials be allowed to use automated licence plate-recognition technology? How do we protect privacy in the face of the demand to use CCTV cameras and robotic devices to monitor public spaces? What safeguards have to be put in place to counter the potential privacy threats (e.g., identity theft, linkage to other databases, stigmatization as bad insurance risk) associated with the collection and use of facial biometric identification data and personal genetic testing data (Ontario Information and Privacy Commissioner 2012)? Under what conditions should law enforcement or security officials be allowed to use thermal sensing to observe heat patterns in your home, spyware to monitor and possibly disable your computer, chemical sensors to establish what substances you have contacted, full body scanners to see if you are hiding anything under your clothes, satellite tracking devices to follow your car, or a "communications interception device that can shut down cell phone service, act as a mobile cell tower and intercept phone messages, and build lists of all unique cell phone identifiers over a four block area" (British Columbia Civil Liberties Association 2012b, n.p.)? Will emerging government-wide identity management systems be robust enough to protect individual privacy while allowing citizens to access a wide spectrum of government services online and enabling government agencies to link and share information about citizens for research and service-delivery purposes (Roy 2013)? As governments increasingly create and tailor public services for mobile devices, what privacy safeguards need to be built into the design of the government service-delivery software and the operating systems of the devices themselves (Ontario Information and Privacy Commissioner 2010)? What privacy mitigation efforts should accompany the use of service-monitoring devices such as "smart" hydro meters? The emerging capacity of governments and corporations to mine "big data" also raises privacy concerns since almost everything an individual does in the digital age creates an electronic record that can be stored, combined and searched. The potential benefits in areas such as medical research, law enforcement and national security are significant, but so too is the potential for individual identification and tracking. How relevant are the existing rules governing consent, collection limitations and integration in the world of big data (Kuner et al. 2012)? The dilemmas seem endless, and it is often unclear whether existing Fair Information Practices are appropriate or effective in the context of new technologies for information gathering, integration, storage and sharing.

Security threats, public health concerns and technological advances aside, the annual reports of the privacy commissioners also make clear that the most basic and uncontested privacy protection rules are often flouted by public servants who do not appear to attach a particularly high level of priority to the protection of informational privacy. Flash drives containing unencrypted, sensitive government employee information are carelessly left on a bus. Individuals who provide data to government anonymously are identified publicly. Social media are accessed indiscriminately by employers for employee background checking. Sensitive health data are provided to law enforcement officers and private investigators. Information about clients is shared with politicians, police, and intelligence agencies without permission. Data sets are combined without authorization. "Extra" data are collected from recipients of social services without their consent.

What Do We Mean by Privacy?

In part, a duty to protect privacy may be given short shrift by public servants because they are reflecting a wider societal uncertainty about the importance of privacy. This uncertainty is rooted partly in confusion about what privacy means. Arthur Schafer (1980) summarized the problem of meaning in the following way:

> It is surprisingly difficult to give a straightforward definition of the concept of privacy. Despite innumerable attempts by contemporary philosophers and jurists to formulate a definition, the concept has remained elusive. One can discover no consensus in either the legal or philosophical literature. (p. 4)

More recently, Daniel Solove (2008) confirms that this problem has not gone away. He describes privacy as "a concept in disarray. Nobody can articulate what it means" (p. 1).

The traditional approach to privacy equates it with non-interference, the right to be left alone to live one's life with the minimum of interference; to limit access to one's personal space. Schafer argues that a non-interference approach to defining privacy is necessary because it covers situations where others are intrusively observing us. But it is inadequate for many critics because privacy is easily invaded without any interference (e.g., your photograph is taken from a distance, your movements are tracked through the GPS in your car), and interference can occur without any diminution of privacy (e.g., limitations placed on your freedom of expression). Moreover, the non-interference lens is insufficient because it doesn't deal easily with situations in which loss of control over personal information is the crux of the issue. To deal with the latter phenomenon, Alan Westin (1967) famously defined privacy as "the claim of individuals, groups or institutions to determine for themselves when, how, and to what extent information about them is communicated to others" (p. 7). While still subject to criticism

(Davis 2006), "non-interference" and "information control" approaches to defining privacy capture a considerable portion of what we are concerned about in this chapter.

The status and boundaries of the concept of privacy are up in the air as well. Some defenders of privacy protection refer to privacy as an important, stand-alone right (Onn et al. 2005) while others see it as a "widely shared taste" (Rosenberg 2000), an "interest" (Thomson 1975) or a "condition" (Parent 1983) which may enable more fundamental rights such as liberty or property, but often at the expense of other interests. Not surprisingly, in the circumstances, defensible boundary lines between personal information that should be protected as private and personal information that may be observed, collected, retained, shared and even disclosed by government are as unclear as the meaning and status of the concept of privacy itself. As Rule (2007) puts it:

> there is no natural line of separation between the realm of the private and personal matters of legitimate interest to others...The very information about ourselves that we experience as most intensely private often stands to affect others in the most direct and compelling ways. Indeed it is often the most "private" information about ourselves – our health, our political attitudes, or our feelings about those around us – that ultimately holds greatest interest for others. When and whether such interest should be considered legitimate is not somehow given in the nature of things. It is a matter of constant definition and redefinition in public sensibilities. (p. 2)

This is especially true in circumstances in which technological and attitudinal change presents new challenges to traditional boundaries between the public and the private. When there is so little clarity about the meaning of privacy, its conceptual status and the nature of the information which can defensibly be kept private, is it surprising that disagreements about privacy protection are so frequent and intense?

For and Against Privacy

Consequentialists only defend claims to informational privacy when the benefits or harm-mitigation effects of protecting it outweigh the costs. As Rule (2007) puts this position: "the best use of personal data is the 'highest use,' the one commanding the greatest reward for the largest number of people. Defense of privacy is thus not *inherently* more worthy than its invasion" (p. 10). Within our liberal democratic state, informational privacy is seen by many as an essential ingredient in the exercise of free political expression and choice, and the maintenance of family life (Solove 2008). Privacy is also argued to be necessary to enhance individual creativity and research, allow for emotional release, carry on self-evaluation and protect intimate personal communications (Gavison 1984; Gerstein 1984). It is similarly argued that privacy promotes individual and social relationships of love, trust and respect (Fried 1984). While such arguments are often associated with a duty ethics perspective (see below), such positive benefits of privacy for the society and individual citizens can also form the basis of a powerful consequential argument in its favour.

On a more practical level, consequentialists would also defend informational privacy when it protects individuals from intrusive and potentially harmful outcomes such as discrimination, ridicule, stigmatization, fraud, identity theft, misuse of trade secrets and misleading profiling. In this respect, we don't want to underestimate the ignorance and carelessness of officials who collect and integrate personal information. A now amusing illustration is the FBI Cold War-era investigation of the noted Harvard economist, John Kenneth Galbraith, who was described as "doctrinaire" by another economist. In the growing file on Dr. Galbraith, this was translated into the fact that he was a follower of "Dr. Ware" and the FBI spent considerable time over the next twenty years trying to clarify what dangers to the free world were associated with this relationship.

But there are also strong consequential arguments against attaching too much importance to the concept of privacy. Schafer (1980) observes that "[a] number of Western social scientists have argued that privacy has become an unhealthy obsession of contemporary liberal society" (p. 18). According to this view, privacy breeds alienation, discontent, family-based solitude, and an egoistic individual, engrossed in competitiveness and self-fulfillment and indifferent to his fellow man and the wider community. Some feminist ethicists attack privacy "as a shield to cover up domination, degradation and abuse of women and others" (DeCew 2012). Posner (1981) argues that privacy protection is too often used to suppress personal information such as tax, criminal and health records that are useful to the government and society. Such suppression interferes with the public right to know, can inhibit research and analysis, and can endanger the security and safety of citizens (Etzioni 1999).

The preferences of citizens come into any contemporary calculation of utility. Privacy skeptics make much of the disconcerting fact that while members of the public in Western democracies express support for privacy protection in the abstract, they seem almost infinitely willing in specific circumstances to consent to the sacrifice of personal privacy to other interests such as security, safety, economic gain, improved health and convenience. But in many instances the consent may not be "informed." That is to say, expressed preferences may not be well supported by clear understanding of the potential impacts of privacy reduction. Citizens have demonstrated little ability to assess the downstream harm that the gathering, aggregation, mining and sharing of individual sets of data might bring them. Thus they readily give up informational privacy bit by bit, not recognizing the potentially negative impact of the ability of governments and corporations to collect, integrate and analyse the many specific pieces of information on individuals. Cohen (2000) argues that a "comprehensive collection of data about an individual is vastly more than the sum of its parts (p. 1398).

Others take a more Kantian perspective, defending privacy as a right which creates duties of protection among those obligated to defend the right (Benn 1971, pp. 1-3; Schafer 1980, p. 16). In this view, "respect for individuals' right to control certain kinds of personal information forms part of a broader respect for personal dignity and autonomy that every social order must embody" (Rule 2007, p. 11). Privacy from this perspective is an end in itself.

> Even when no extrinsic harm comes to a person as a result of losing his or her privacy, that person has a prima facie ground for claiming the right not to be spied upon or watched without knowledge or consent. Humans are self-conscious beings. To monitor their conduct without authorization is to show a less-than-proper respect for their dignity. (Schafer 1980, p. 17)

Davis (2006) concludes that privacy can be thought of as a right based on its key supporting role relative to other rights:

> Given the importance of the values that privacy promotes, some of which themselves are moral rights, respect, and dignity for example, it would follow that privacy is a right in those societies in which it plays a role in fostering these important values. (p. 130)

Moore supports Westin's claim that privacy is a cultural universal despite the fact that the boundaries of what should be protected as private vary from society to society and over time (Moore 2003; Westin 1967, p. 12). Most advocates of a duty to protect the right of privacy do see the right as conditional in character – contextually determined – and one which can be waived by the right holder and overridden by other rights and interests identified by those tasked with protecting the right.

It may also be possible to look past the consequences of privacy violation and the obligation to protect privacy's conditional status as a right and, instead, construct a virtue ethics defence for privacy protection. To do this one would have to argue that respect for the privacy of individuals who relate to the state is a core value and character trait of a professional public servant entrusted with sensitive personal information. The existence of significant privacy protection legislation would buttress this contention to some degree, while the fact that we place so little emphasis on privacy protection in public service value statements, codes of conduct and ethical training programs would weigh against it.

Making Hard Privacy Choices

So governments and public servants potentially face a wide array of moral arguments from diverse interests for and against privacy protection. Existing Fair Information Practices and derivative omnibus privacy legislation provide checklists of issues related to practices (e.g., collecting, storing, aggregating, sharing, correcting and disclosing private information) which need to be attended to when evaluating a privacy protection regime. But both are less helpful in sorting out whether a change in practice itself (e.g., collecting genetic data or using a new surveillance or data-matching technique) is morally defensible.

The triad of ethical theories set out in chapter 2 may not be as instructive as we might hope in contemporary circumstances. In the face of rapid technological and attitudinal change, trying to establish universally defensible duties (e.g., drawing a sustainable, permanent line in the sand between the public and the private; or specifying a one-size-fits-all standard for consent) seems an anachronistic task. Potential violations of privacy now come in too many forms. Similarly, depending on a weakly established "protection of privacy" virtue to guide public servants to morally defensible decisions seems inadequate to the challenge. Consequential analysis – imperfectly done and on its own – might be inclined to discount the "soft" benefits of privacy (noted above) and overvalue the potentially more measurable cost-saving, health, safety or security benefits that new technologies might produce.

Helen Nissenbaum (2010) offers a more nuanced justificatory framework for making hard privacy protection decisions which respects societal norms and shares the consequentialist's focus on the public's preferences and specific circumstances in which privacy might be violated – while avoiding potentially crass cost-benefit calculations which privacy advocates fear. Her framework is based on the notion of "contextual integrity," which becomes a "benchmark for privacy" (p. 140). Contextual integrity requires that any existing or proposed system or practice affecting individual privacy be judged in relation to "context-relative informational norms"; that is, the expectations which citizens bring to the determination of their level of comfort with a particular "flow of personal information" in the context of the goals of the system or practice being analysed. Among many other examples, Nissenbaum uses the case of providing online access to court records to illustrate how the analysis might work. She notes that "although the consideration of harms and benefits are important, their significance must be understood in the light of ways entrenched and novel information flows contribute to the end, purposes and values of the justice system" (p. 220). On the one hand, online access might enhance transparency of the operations of the justice system, and thus increase accountability. On the other, creating the capacity for anyone to use a search engine without an audit trail to access information about jurors, abused spouses or witnesses might compromise the ability of the court system to achieve its fundamental goals.

> Concerns such as these illustrate ways in which harms and risks of harms could be assessed, not simply by putting them on a scale, but interpreted in light of their meaning and significance for the context of the justice system. Crucial considerations weighing in favour of constraints on access include a decrease in willing jurors and a justice system which does not adequately serve those who need it. (p. 221)

The interaction among the consequences of the proposed change, the goals of the program or activity being affected and the comfort levels of the participants with the change in information flows may call for "constraints on access to be introduced either by obfuscating some of the information in the records or by means of certain, limited access control or authorization mechanisms" (p. 221). The Ontario Privacy Commissioner argues that this kind of approach to ethical assessment is not so much a call for balance between privacy and other values, such as security or safety, as it is positive support for building "privacy by design" into the consideration or development of any new networked system or information communication technology which has the capacity to alter existing privacy protection practices. Maintaining or establishing a flow of personal information that users of a system or practice find acceptable need not be a zero-sum game if the approach to privacy impact assessment is proactive, up-front and sensitive to the specific context, rather than reactive, after-the-fact and ideologically driven (Cavoukian 2012).

Case 6.4 focuses on the increasing use of data matching to combat security and public health threats and crime.

CASE 6.4: FOCUS ON FRAUD

The following conversation takes place between Diane, a Director, and Stuart, an Assistant Director in the Provincial Treasury Board Secretariat. For purposes of this case, we will assume that fraud has been suspected in 7% of the Ministry of Human Resources' caseload (up from 4%) and there is concern that the real incidence might be higher.

Diane: The problem of welfare fraud is a serious one and the Ministry of Human Resources is becoming concerned that it might seriously undermine the legitimacy of income assistance and retraining programs. Have you come up with any suggestions on how to tackle it?

Stuart: Yes, I have. I propose a merger of several available government data sets including health and disability support records, vehicle ownership data and the files of the marriage, birth, personal assets and land registries. I am also proposing that we insist that applicants allow us to access their banking and personal financial records. We should also be able to link all of these data sets to parallel data banks in other jurisdictions to capture people who might be claiming from the federal government or in more than one province. Finally, we will be enhancing our approach to personal identification documentation and I am exploring the possibility of introducing biometric identification technology, including fingerprint imaging.

Diane: That sounds very comprehensive. But we've got to be careful here. I am particularly concerned about the data matching aspects of all of this. Are we going to be using the information in the various data banks for reasons other than those for which it was collected? How will we confirm the accuracy of all these data sets? Can we guarantee security? This proposal will raise questions about the individual's right to privacy.

Stuart: Diane, you told me yourself that welfare fraud is getting out of hand. We've got to do something to control it. If the program clients have told the truth in their applications, there won't be any problem. If they lied, don't we have a right to know? Anyway, if it's necessary, we can always get people to waive their rights when they apply for financial assistance. Hell, people looking for a car loan allow private financial institutions to match data much more extensively than this proposal contemplates. Is this any more intrusive than sending inspectors around to claimants' residences at 7am like the old days? Where's the beef?

Diane: I'm not so sure...

Would you subscribe to an action of this sort to cut down on welfare fraud? If so, what conditions, if any would you put on its implementation?

In the following scenario, we pose a dilemma about the limits of personal privacy for an employee who is seriously engaged in social networking.

CASE 6.5: BLOG ON, DUDE!

You manage the Environmental Protection Branch in the Forestry department. One of your new, younger employees, Anton, is a very active user of online social networks, especially Facebook, where he uses his profile page as a diary, which he updates daily. Anton has over 150 "friends" with access to his Facebook page.

Recently, in response to negative coverage of the ministry's approach to sustainability, Anton has started providing very personal and positive accounts of the work that he and his colleagues are doing every day to enhance the provincial forests. His online friends like this material. One of Anton's friends mentions his page to a journalist. As a result, Anton is interviewed on a couple of local TV public affairs shows, and there is a piece about him in the local newspaper. The coverage is positive – in marked contrast to the usually hostile reaction from the environmental community to the ministry's approach to forest management.

A couple of other employees bring this activity to your attention and ask if it is appropriate. You mention to Anton that it would be prudent if he did not deal with his work life on Facebook. He reacts very negatively to this suggestion, pointing out that he is creating a very positive image for the branch in his online diary, and he is doing it on his own time. The next day a colleague tells you that Anton has recounted his conversation with you in his most recent journal entry, describing your request as a violation of his privacy.

Is Anton doing anything wrong? Should you insist that he stop making reference to his work on his Facebook page?

The final privacy case provides an opportunity to examine the defensibility of increasing surveillance of public service employees.

CASE 6.6: TESTING, TESTING...

As the manager of the Public Works Department, you are being backed into a really tough corner. Three weeks ago one of your garbage trucks struck and badly injured a pedestrian. The subsequent investigation revealed that the driver of the truck was legally impaired. The ensuing uproar led the mayor to indicate during a council meeting that he favoured a program of random substance abuse testing of all employees handling heavy equipment. He also indicated his support for testing all applicants for municipal jobs for substance abuse.

You can see the mayor's point. The city has an obligation to reduce the risk to citizens. But you are bothered by his narrow view of the issue. While human error has resulted in accidents involving municipal equipment in the past, this is the first documented case of substance abuse. In fact, your works department has an exemplary safety record. The union is extremely upset by the mayor's position. It argues that existing substance abuse tests have proved to be unreliable, often condemning someone for using a painkiller or allergy medication. They also argue that the proposal is arbitrary and unfair since it would test existing employees randomly without their performance having been called into question and reject prospective employees without providing any opportunity for them to defend themselves or question the validity of the test.

The mayor has asked you to bring forward a testing plan for consideration by council. How should you respond?

Conclusion

In this chapter we have discussed how a public servant should deal with information. How much openness is enough? There is obviously a balance to be struck between a completely transparent process and the ability to function effectively. It is possible that openness may be a good policy to stop bad things from happening, but may be ill-conceived as a means to get good things to occur (Cleveland 1985b). The trick is to find the middle ground between the paralysis of government in a goldfish bowl and the over-concentration of power inherent in an information monopoly. How much privacy is enough? This seems to be a question that will not easily accommodate a one-size-fits-all answer. We will need to pay attention up front to the privacy expectations of those affected by new collection and management information technologies in order to responsibly meet the information needs of governments focused on the security, health and safety of their citizens.

References

Alberta Corporate Human Resources. (2011). *Code of conduct and ethics for the public service of Alberta*. Retrieved from http://www.chr.alberta.ca/Practitioners/?file=legreg/code/ee-respons-under-the-code&cf=819

Alberta Government. (2012). A*ccountability, transparency and transformation mandate*. Retrieved from http://alberta.ca/servicealbertamandate.cfm

Alberta Government Services. (2005). *Information security classification*. Edmonton: Government and Program Support Services Division. Retrieved from https://www.rimp.gov.ab.ca/publications/pdf/infosecurityclassification.pdf

Alberta Public Affairs Bureau. (2010). *Government of Alberta social media –Web 2.0 policy*. Retrieved from http://publicaffairs.alberta.ca/pab_documents/GOASocialMediaPolicyPlusAppendix-approved.pdf

Alford, F. (2001). *Whistleblowers: Broken lives and organizational power*. Ithaca, NY: Cornell University Press.

Australian Department of Finance and Deregulation. (2010). *Social media 101: A beginner's guide for finance employees*. Retrieved from http://agimo.govspace.gov.au/files/2010/04/social-media-101.pdf

Australian Public Service Commission. (2012). *Circular 2012/1: Revisions to the Commission's guidance on making public comment and participating online.* Retrieved from http://www.apsc.gov.au/publications-and-media/current-circulars-and-advices/2012/circular-20121

Barkat, H., Jaeggli, L., & Dorsaz, P. (2012). *Citizen 2.0: 17 examples of social media and government innovation.* Retrieved from http://citizen20.redcut.ch/Citizen%202.0%20(EN).pdf

Bayles, M. (1981). *Professional ethics.* Bemont, MA: Wadsworth Publishing.

Benn, S. (1971). Privacy, freedom and respect for persons. In J. R. Pennock & J. W. Chapman (Eds.), *Nomos 13: Privacy* (pp. 1-21). New York: Atherton Press.

Bok, S. (1978). *Lying: Moral choice in private and public life.* Toronto: Random House.

Bok, S. (1983). *Secrets: On the ethics of concealment and revelation.* New York: Random House.

British Columbia. (2012). *Open information.* Retrieved from http://www.openinfo.gov.bc.ca/

British Columbia Civil Liberties Association. (2012a). *Privacy handbook.* Retrieved from http://bccla.org/privacy-handbook/

British Columbia Civil Liberties Association. (2012b). *Police refuse to confirm major purchases are rights violating devices.* Retrieved from http://bccla.org/news/2012/11/police-refuse-to-confirm-major-purchases-are-rights-violating-devices/

British Columbia, Public Service Agency. (2008). *Policy statement - Standards of conduct.* Retrieved from http://www.bcpublicserviceagency.gov.bc.ca/policy/HR_policy/09_Standards_Conduct.htm

Canada, Government of. (2011). *Consulting with Canadians.* Retrieved from http://www.consultingcanadians.gc.ca/hm.jspx?lang=eng

Canada, Government of. (2013). *Canada's action plan on open government.* Retrieved from http://data.gc.ca/eng/canadas-action-plan-open-government

Canada Border Service Agency. (2008). *Advance passenger information/passenger name record program - ARCHIVED.* Retrieved from http://www.cbsa-asfc.gc.ca/media/facts-faits/004-eng.html

Cavoukian, A. (2003). *National security in a post-9/11 world: The rise of surveillance...the demise of privacy?* Toronto: Information and Privacy Commissioner of Ontario. Retrieved from http://www.ipc.on.ca/images/Resources/up-nat_sec.pdf

Cavoukian, A. (2012). *Operationalizing privacy by design: A guide to implementing strong privacy practices.* Toronto: Information and Privacy Commissioner of Ontario. Retrieved from http://www.ipc.on.ca/images/Resources/operationalizing-pbd-guide.pdf

CBC News. (2010, September 20). *Federal scientists face tighter media rules.* Retrieved from http://www.cbc.ca/news/technology/story/2010/09/20/federal-scientists-rules-media.html

City of Toronto. (2000). *Conflict of interest policy.* Retrieved from http://.www toronto.ca/calldocuments/conflict_of_interest_policy.htm

Cleveland, H. (1985a). The twilight of hierarchy: Speculations on the global information society. *Public Administration Review, 45*(1), 185-195.

Cleveland, H. (1985b, July/Aug). How much sunshine is too much? *Across the Board, 22*(7,8), 15-23.

Cohen, J. (2000). Examined lives: Informational privacy and the subject as object. *Stanford Law Review, 52*(5), 1373-1438.

Cohen, J. (2003). Deliberation and democratic legitimacy. In D. Matravers and J. Pike (Eds.), *Contemporary political philosophy: An anthology* (pp. 342-360). London: Routledge.

Commission d'accès à information du Québec. (2007). *Technology and society in a time of societal choices: Summary.* Retrieved from http://www.cai.gouv.qc.ca/documents/CAI_RQ_2011_res_eng.pdf

Conservative Party of Canada. (2006). *Stand up for Canada.* Retrieved from http://www.cbc.ca/canadavotes2006/leadersparties/pdf/conservative_platform20060113.pdf

Consumer Measures Committee. (2011). *Canadian Standards Association model code for the protection of personal information: CAN/CSA-Q830 - ARCHIVED.* Retrieved from http://cmcweb.ca/eic/site/cmc-cmc.nsf/eng/fe00076.html

Curzon, D. (1977). The generic secrets of government decision making. In I. Galnoor (Ed.), *Government secrecy in democracies* (pp. 93-109). New York: NY University Press.

Davis, S. (2006). Privacy, rights and moral value. University of Ottawa *Law and Technology Journal, 3*(1), 109-131.

DeCew, J. (2012). Privacy. In E. Zalta (Ed.), *The Stanford encyclopedia of philosophy.* Retrieved from http://plato.stanford.edu/archives/ fall2012/entries/privacy/

Department of Justice Canada. (1982). *Constitution Act, 1982,* Part I: *Canadian Charter of Rights and Freedoms.* Retrieved from http:// www.laws-lois.justice.gc.ca/eng/Const/page-15.html

Department of Justice Canada. (2012a). *Oaths of Office Regulations* (C.R.C., c. 1242). Retrieved from http://laws-lois.justice.gc.ca/eng/ regulations/C.R.C.,_c._1242/FullText.html

Department of Justice Canada. (2012b). *Criminal Code* (R.S.C., 1985, c. C-46). Retrieved from http://laws-lois.justice.gc.ca/eng/acts/C-46/ page-161.html#docCont

Dworkin, T., & Baucus, M. (1998). Internal and external whistleblowers: A comparison of whistleblowering processes. *Journal of Business Ethics, 17*(12), 1281-1298.

Edmonton, City of. (2013). *OpenGov.* Retrieved from http://www. edmonton.ca/city_government/initiatives_innovation/open-data.aspx

Etzioni, A. (1999). *The limits of privacy.* New York: Basic Books.

FAIR (Federal Accountability Initiative for Reform). (2013). *Sections: About Whistleblowers; Federal Legislation;* Provincial Legislation. Retrieved from http://fairwhistleblower.ca

Flaherty, D. (2008). *Reflections on reform of the federal Privacy Act.* Retrieved from http://www.priv.gc.ca/information/pub/pa_ref_ df_e.pdf

Florini, A. (2007a). Introduction: The battle over transparency. In A. Florini (Ed.),*The right to know* (pp. 1-16). New York: Columbia University Press.

Florini, A. (2007b). Conclusion: Whither Transparency. In A. Florini (Ed.), T*he right to know (*pp. 337-348). New York: Columbia University Press.

Forcese, C. (2009). Canada's national security "complex": Assessing the secrecy rules. *IRRP Choices, 15*(5), 3-38.

Fraser, L. (2012, October 20). Savage takes Halifax's mayor seat by huge margin. *Chronicle Herald.* Retrieved from http://thechronicleherald. ca/municipal2012/151706-savage-takes-halifaxs-mayor-seat-by-huge-margin

Freedom of Information and Protection of Privacy Act. (1996). In Statutes of British Columbia, R.S.B.C. 1996, c. 165. Retrieved from http://www.bclaws.ca/EPLibraries/bclaws_new/document/ID/freeside/96165_00

Fried, C. (1984). Privacy. In F. Schoemann (Ed.), *Philosophical dimensions of privacy: An anthology* (pp. 203-222). Cambridge, UK: Cambridge University Press.

Gavison, R. (1984). Privacy and the limits of the law. In F. Schoemann (Ed.), *Philosophical dimensions of privacy: An anthology* (pp. 346-402). Cambridge, UK: Cambridge University Press.

Gerstein, R. (1984). Intimacy and privacy. In F. Schoemann (Ed.), *Philosophical dimensions of privacy: An anthology* (pp. 265-271). Cambridge, UK: Cambridge University Press.

Greenwood, C. (2013). "Democracy Watch" letter of request to Ms. Suzanne Legault, Information Commissioner of Canada, regarding report: *Muzzling civil servants: A threat to democracy.* Victoria: Environmental Law Clinic, University of Victoria. Retrieved from http://www.elc.uvic.ca/press/documents/2012-03-04-Democracy-Watch_OIPLtr_Feb20.13-with-attachment.pdf

Information Commissioner of Canada. (1998). *Annual report: Information Commissioner 1997-1998.* Ottawa: Minister of Public Works and Government Services Canada.

Kuner, C., Cate, F., Millard, C., & Svantesson, D. (2012). The challenge of 'big data' for data protection. *International Data Privacy Law, 2*(2), 47-49.

Lewis, D. (2008). Ten years of public interest disclosure legislation in the UK: Are whistleblowers adequately protected? *Journal of Business Ethics, 82*(2), 497-507.

Moore, A. (2003). Privacy: Its meaning and value. *American Philosophical Quarterly, 40*(3), 215-237.

Morison, J. (2010). Gov 2.0: Towards a user generated state? *The Modern Law Review, 73*(4), 551-577.

Mulgan, R. (2007). Truth in government and the politicization of public service advice. *Public Administration, 85*(3), 569-86.

Municipal Freedom of Information and Protection of Privacy Act. (2007). In Statutes of Ontario, R.S.O. 1990, Chapter M.56. Retrieved from http://www.e-laws.gov.on.ca/html/statutes/english/elaws_statutes_90m56_e.htm

Newfoundland and Labrador. (2012). First Session, 47th General Assembly. Bill 29: *An Act to Amend the Information and Protection of Privacy Act.* Retrieved from http://www.assembly.nl.ca/business/bills/bill1229.htm

Nissenbaum, H. (2010). *Privacy in context: Technology, policy and the integrity of private life.* Stanford: Stanford University Press.

Nova Scotia Public Service Commission. (2009). *Values, ethics and conduct: A code of conduct for Nova Scotia's public servants.* Retrieved from http://novascotia.ca/psc/about/overview/publicationsPolicies/codeofconduct/

Onn, Y., et al. (2005). *Privacy in the digital environment.* Haifa: Haifa Center of Law and Technology. Retrieved from http://weblaw.haifa.ac.il/he/Research/ResearchCenters/techlaw/DocLib/Privacy_eng.pdf

Ontario. Commission on Freedom of Information and Individual Privacy. (1980). Public government for private people: The report of the Commission on Freedom of Information and Individual Privacy. Vol. 2, Freedom of information. Toronto: Ministry of Government Services.

Ontario Information and Privacy Commissioner. (2010). *The roadmap for privacy by design in mobile communications.* Retrieved from http://www.ipc.on.ca/images/Resources/pbd-asu-mobile.pdf

Ontario Information and Privacy Commissioner. (2012). *Positive-sum is paramount: Achieving public safety and privacy.* Retrieved from http://www.ipc.on.ca/images/Resources/pbd-ctc.pdf

Ontario Ministry of Government and Consumer Services. (2008). *Information security and classification: Frequently asked questions.* Retrieved from http://www.verney.ca/onapw2008/presentations/665.pdf

Ontario Ministry of Government Services. (2010). *Citizen engagement.* Retrieved from http://www.mgs.gov.on.ca/en/IAndIT/STEL02_046927.html

Organization for Economic Cooperation and Development (OECD). (2012). *Whistleblower protection*. Retrieved from http://www.oecd.org/cleangovbiz/toolkit/50042935.pdf

Organization for Economic Cooperation and Development (OECD). (2013). *Guidelines on the protection of privacy and transborder flows of personal data*. Retrieved from http://www.oecd.org/sti/ieconomy/privacy.htm#newguidelines

Parent, W. (1983). Privacy, morality and the law. *Philosophy and Public Affairs*, 12(5), 269-288.

The Personal Health Information Act (2011). In Statutes of Manitoba, C.C.S.M. c. P33.5. Retrieved from http://web2.gov.mb.ca/laws/statutes/ccsm/p033-5e.php

Personal Information Protection and Electronic Documents Act. (2000). In Statutes of Canada, S.C. 2000, c. 5. Retrieved from http://laws-lois.justice.gc.ca/eng/acts/P-8.6/index.html

Posner, R. (1981). *The economics of justice*. Cambridge, MA: Harvard University Press.

Privacy Act. (1985). In Statutes of Canada, R.S.C. 1985, c. P-21. Retrieved from http://laws-lois.justice.gc.ca/eng/acts/P-21/index.html

Privy Council Office. (1990). *Notes on the responsibilities of public servants in relation to parliamentary committees*. Retrieved from http://www.pco-bcp.gc.ca/index.asp?lang=eng&page=information&sub=publications&doc=notes/notes-eng.htm

Public Interest Disclosure of Wrongdoing Act. (2010). In Statutes of Nova Scotia, Chapter 42. Retrieved from http://www.nslegislature.ca/legc/bills/61st_2nd/3rd_read/b118.htm

Public Servants Disclosure Protection Act. (2005). In Statutes of Canada, c. 46, s. 8. Retrieved from http://laws-lois.justice.gc.ca/PDF/P-31.9.pdf

Quebec. (2013). Charter of Human Rights and Freedoms. Publication Quebec. Retrieved from http://www2.publicationsduquebec.gouv.qc.ca/dynamicSearch/telecharge.php?type=2&file=/C_12/C12_A.html

Ramirez, M. (2007). *Blowing the whistle on whistleblower protection: A tale of reform versus power.* Cincinnati Law Review, 76, 183-233.

Rees, A. (2012). Sustaining secrecy: Executive branch resistance to access to information in Canada. In M. Larsen & K. Walby (Eds.), *Brokering access: Power, politics, and freedom of information process in Canada* (pp. 35-67). Vancouver: University of British Columbia Press.

Reid, J. (2002). *Response to the report of the Access to Information Review Task Force*. Ottawa: Minister of Public Works and Government Services.

Roberts, A. (2001). Structural pluralism and the right to information. *University of Toronto Law Journal, 51*(3), 243-271.

Roberts, A. (2002). Administrative discretion and the *Access to Information Act*: An "internal law" on open government? *Canadian Public Administration, 45*(2), 175-194.

Roberts, A. (2005). Spin control and freedom of information: Lessons for the United Kingdom from Canada. *Public Administration, 83*(1), 1-23.

Roberts, A. (2006). *Blacked out: Government secrecy in the information age*. New York: Cambridge University Press.

Robertson, G. (1972). Official responsibility, private conscience and public information. *Optimum, 3*(3), 5-18.

Rosenberg, A. (2000). Privacy as a matter of taste and right. In P. Frankel, F. Miller Jr. & J. Paul (Eds.), *The right to privacy* (pp. 68-90). Cambridge, UK: Cambridge University Press.

Roy, J. (2013). *From machinery to mobility: Government and democracy in a participative age*. New York: Springer.

Rule, J. (2007). *Privacy in peril*. Oxford: Oxford University Press.

Schafer, A. (1980). Privacy: A philosophical overview. In D. Gibson (Ed.), *Aspects of privacy law* (pp. 1-20). Toronto: Butterworths.

Security of Information Act. (1985). In Statutes of Canada, R.S.C. 1985, c. O-5). Retrieved from http://laws-lois.justice.gc.ca/eng/acts/O-5/

Sheedy, A. (2008). *Handbook on citizen engagement: Beyond consultation*. Ottawa: Canadian Policy Research Networks. Retrieved from http://www.cprn.org/documents/49583_EN.pdf

Smiley, D. (1978). *The freedom of information issue: A political analysis*. Toronto: Commission on Freedom of Information and Individual Privacy.

Solove, D. (2008). *Understanding privacy.* Cambridge, MA: Harvard University Press.

Statistics Act. (2005). In Statutes of Canada, R.S.C. 1985, c. S-9. Retrieved from http://laws-lois.justice.gc.ca/eng/acts/S-19/

Thomas, P. G. (2011). Problems with Canada's Public Servants Disclosure Protection Act. Optimum Online, *41*(1), 1-14.

Thomas, P. G. (2013). Communications and prime ministerial power. In G. Peters & J. Bickerton (Eds.), *Governing: Essays in honour of Donald J. Savoie* (pp. 53-84). Kingston: McGill-Queen's University Press.

Thomson, J. (1975). The right to privacy. *Philosophy and Public Affairs,* 4(4), 295-314.

Treasury Board of Canada Secretariat. (2003a). *Operational standard for the Security of Information Act.* Retrieved from http://www.tbs-sct.gc.ca/pol/doc-eng.aspx?section=text&id=12323

Treasury Board of Canada Secretariat. (2003b). *Values and ethics code for the public service.* Retrieved from http://www.tbs-sct.gc.ca/pubs_pol/hrpubs/tb_851/vec-cve01-eng.asp

Treasury Board of Canada Secretariat. (2008a). *Policy on access to information.* Retrieved from http://www.tbs-sct.gc.ca/pol/doc-eng.aspx?id=12453&section=text#sec5.1

Treasury Board of Canada Secretariat. (2008b). *Policy on privacy protection.* Retrieved from http://www.tbs-sct.gc.ca/pol/doc-eng.aspx?id=12510

Treasury Board of Canada Secretariat. (2009). *Guideline for employees of the Government of Canada: Information management basics.* Retrieved from http://www.tbs-sct.gc.ca/pol/doc-eng.aspx?id=16557&section=text#cha8

Treasury Board of Canada Secretariat. (2010). *Directive on privacy impact assessments.* Retrieved from: http://www.tbs-sct.gc.ca/pol/doc-eng.aspx?id=18308&section=text

Treasury Board of Canada Secretariat. (2011). *Guidelines for external use of Web 2.0.* Retrieved from http://www.tbs-sct.gc.ca/pol/doc-eng.aspx?id=24835&section=text

Treasury Board of Canada Secretariat. (2012a). *Duty of loyalty.* Retrieved from http://www.tbs-sct.gc.ca/rp/icg02-eng.asp

Treasury Board of Canada Secretariat. (2012b). *Communications policy of the Government of Canada*. Retrieved from http://www.tbs-sct. gc.ca/pol/doc-eng.aspx?id=12316&section=text

Treasury Board of Canada Secretariat. (2012c). *Access to information and privacy*. Retrieved from http://www.tbs-sct.gc.ca/atip-aiprp/ index-eng.asp

Treasury Board of Canada Secretariat. (2012d). *Values and ethics code for the public sector*. Retrieved from http://www.tbs-sct.gc.ca/pol/ doc-eng.aspx?id=25049&section=text

Treasury Board of Canada Secretariat. (2013a). *Public Servants Disclosure Protection Act: Information for employees*. Retrieved from http://www.tbs-sct.gc.ca/faq/pda1-eng.asp

Treasury Board of Canada Secretariat. (2013b). *The directive on privacy practices*. Retrieved from http://www.tbs-sct.gc.ca/pol/doc-eng.aspx?id=18309&section=text

Tromp, S. (2008). *Fallen behind: Canada's Access to Information Act in the world context*. Retrieved from http://www3.telus.net/ index100/report

Turnbull, L., & Aucoin, P. (2006). *Fostering Canadians' role in public policy: A strategy for institutionalizing public involvement in policy*. Ottawa: Canadian Policy Research Networks.

Vancouver. (2011). *Code of conduct*. Retrieved from http://vancouver. ca/files/cov/boards-committees-code-of-conduct.pdf

Vancouver. (2012). *Greenest city: 2020 action plan*. Retrieved from http://vancouver.ca/files/cov/Greenest-city-action-plan.pdf

Westin, A. (1967). *Privacy and freedom*. New York: Atheneum.

Chapter 7

The Accountable Public Servant

> [I]n a democratic society there is a marked
> tendency for citizens to become disillusioned,
> even cynical, when there seems to be no
> effective way to connect their criticisms
> of governmental action (or inaction)
> with identifiable public servants who are
> responsible for correcting problems. (Schafer
> 1999, p. 11)

> Accountability is not, and cannot be made,
> simple. (Denhardt and Denhardt 2003, p. 137)

Public servants have a long-standing traditional duty to account for their decisions and actions or inactions to their immediate superiors up through the hierarchical chain of command to deputy ministers, city managers, etc. and finally, at the federal and provincial levels, to elected officials who in turn are accountable to the public. In recent years the perceived growth in the power and discretion of public servants has heightened public concern about their personal accountability (Aucoin and Jarvis 2005, p. 47). Politicians and the media increasingly play to this concern by "outing" previously anonymous public servants and blaming them individually for things that have gone wrong (Savoie 2008a, p. 269). Demands for more accountability have resulted in increases in the monitoring of public service organizations by internal auditors, treasury boards, public service commissions and auditors-general. In addition, public servants are increasingly obliged to explain their behaviour to courts, tribunals, a widening circle of guardian agencies (e.g., ombudspersons, privacy commissioners, integrity commissioners) and, occasionally, to more formal public inquiries (Michael 2005). Professionals (e.g., engineers, foresters, social workers) working within the public sector are also subject to accountability regimes of self-regulating professional associations. With the increased focus placed on service quality, cross-ministry and intergovernmental service integration, contracting out, public-private partnerships, and stakeholder and citizen engagement, many public servants have raised questions about the limits of individual accountability in circumstances in which responsibility is shared with others both inside and outside the public sector. Paradoxically, the development of new policy, service-delivery and regulatory networks has created for many public servants a strong sense of personal accountability to their clients, "customers," stakeholders and service partners – an accountability which these actors increasingly demand as an entitlement and also reinforce by monitoring (Savoie 2008b). Finally, some public servants will claim that they are accountable to their own conscience (Laframboise 1983).

But through all of this there has been little significant change in statements concerning the formal accountability obligations of public servants as articulated by the governments which employ them. This has created confusion about the meaning of accountability and opened up the traditional duty to considerable debate. This chapter is concerned with the growing uncertainties about what is meant by the duty of accountability. Our focus is on the personal accountability of middle- and lower-level public servants, rather than the role accountability of the most senior public servants, ministers and city councillors – those who are formally responsible for everything an organization does or fails to do (Mulgan 2003, pp. 206-207; Savoie 2008a).

We first explore the traditional messages that governments continue to send to public servants about the duty of accountability. We then look at the more recent efforts to tie performance reporting to traditional hierarchical accountability. We go on to examine the other forces which are challenging the traditional vision of personal accountability to a single supervisor, including – as noted – the demands of courts, tribunals and more powerful monitoring agencies within government; obligations as "professionals" to external, self-regulating professional bodies; the impact of shared responsibility arrangements; and the emergence of accountability relationships between public servants and the wider universe of people and organizations with whom they work. We ask how those challenges are reshaping the traditional duty of accountability. Finally, we look briefly at the notion that, ultimately, the public servant is accountable to his or her own conscience.

Our "take away" message on the duty of accountability is not as straightforward as the reader might want. While the traditional notion of the duty of individual accountability is inadequate in the face of the complex accountability demands now made of public servants, the path to a more meaningful, complex and widely embraced definition of this important duty is far from clear.

The Traditional Accountability Narrative

Accountability is one of the foundation principles of a Western democratic society "rooted in British history" (Dubnick 1998, p. 72). Discussions of public service accountability at the federal and provincial levels in Canada and other Westminster democracies usually start with references to the notion of responsible government and the obligation of public servants to account to their superiors for how they have managed human and financial resources and treated members of the public, and for the efficiency and effectiveness of their programs (Savoie 2008a). Traditionally, in our (Canada's) system of responsible cabinet government, a public servant would be said to be accountable to his or her supervisor or manager. A chain of individual accountability extends up through the department or ministry until, ultimately, the deputy minister is accountable to the minister for the overall administration of the department. Finally, the minister is then accountable to Parliament.

This traditional accountability narrative formed the foundation of the final report of the Royal Commission on Financial Management and Accountability (1979):

> Accountability relies on a system of connecting links – a two-way circuit involving a flow of information that is relevant and timely, not only for managers but for those who must scrutinize the decisions and deeds of managers. We gauge its presence when we observe that a certain discipline has been imposed upon those who are assigned roles and duties in the system. In simple terms, accountability is that quality of a system that obliges the participants to pay attention to their respective assigned and accepted responsibilities. (pp. 9-10)

Responsibility and accountability are closely linked, but they are not the same. People tend to talk interchangeably about "holding someone responsible" and "holding someone accountable," but in the traditional narrative, the term "responsibility" refers to the giving and accepting of power or discretion, while the term "accountability" reflects the demand for compliance with the direction of those who provide that discretion (Uhr 1992, September). In the Westminster model narrative, as we discussed in chapters 1 and 3, the public servant is an *anonymous* figure who is given responsibility for providing impartial, expert advice and faithfully carrying out the directions of a more senior official or minister. With responsibility comes the duty of accountability. Ideally, the program manager or service-delivery officer, for example, is given well-defined responsibilities by a clearly identified supervisor, receives adequate authority and resources to carry out these responsibilities, and provides an accounting of how those resources were used and the responsibilities discharged. All of this generally takes place internally without the glare of public attention. A similar narrative would create the foundation for the traditional, hierarchically based duty of accountability at the municipal level of government, the differences at the local government level being that there is less emphasis on the anonymity of the public servant, and the accountability chain ends with the most senior municipal manager.

Classic accountability is also portrayed as:

> enforcing or explaining responsibility...
> Accountability involves rendering an account
> to someone, such as Parliament or a superior,
> on how and how well one's responsibilities
> are being met. It also involves rendering an
> account to someone on actions that have
> been taken to correct problems, and actions
> that have been taken to ensure they do not
> happen again. It involves accepting personal
> consequences, such as discipline for problems
> that could have been avoided had the individual
> acted appropriately. (Canadian Centre for
> Management Development 1996, p. 9)

Mulgan (2003) argues that accountability must have an *external* dimension (in that you give an account to someone else), an *interactive* dimension (you are asked to provide an account or to rectify a situation and you respond) and, finally, an *authority* dimension (reflecting the fact that those demanding accountability have the right to ask for an account and to sanction you if you have done something blameworthy and reward you if you have done something praiseworthy). Thus, *information, dialogue, rectification* and *sanctions* are key features of the traditional accountability narrative (Mulgan 2003, pp. 29-30).

As noted, traditional accountability takes place generally within the boundaries of a public servant's department. A public servant's primary obligation is to account for his or her actions or inactions to an immediate superior, that is, the individual or individuals with the authority to demand a response and to punish or praise. This approach to accountability recalls the classic debate between Carl Friedrich and

Herbert Finer, which took place in the middle of the last century. In this debate, Finer focused on the responsibility of public servants to follow the directions of their political leader and framed the obligation of accountability in terms of the right by authority of the political leader or his or her surrogate lower in the hierarchy to demand an accounting of how the public servants had carried out their direction within the context of the authority and resources provided to them (Finer 1941). Friedrich's position, which we return to later in the chapter, was that accountability had a more subjective or independent character, focusing on a wider circle of actors to whom one *feels* accountable, including, potentially, fellow professionals, those likely to be affected by one's actions or inactions and, ultimately, one's own conscience (Friedrich 1940).

Accountability is one of the key "trending" values of the new millennium. Almost every government in Canada has initiatives designed to strengthen accountability. Prime Minister Harper campaigned for more accountability on the heels of the sponsorship scandal and, after the 2006 election, passed an extensive *Federal Accountability Act* (2006). Among its many provisions, this legislation made deputy ministers accountable directly to Parliament for the financial administration of their departments and institutionalized whistle blowing within the federal public service. Other governments have jumped on the accountability bandwagon in recent years. For example, Newfoundland proclaimed a *Transparency and Accountability Act* (2006), linking strategic planning, decision making, transparency and annual reporting as well as creating a system of performance-based contracts for senior public servants. Alberta's *Government Accountability Act* (2009) focused on establishing stronger business plans and annual reporting obligations for government entities. Ontario passed similar-sounding legislation – the *Broader Public Sector Accountability Act* (2010) – but it focused largely on increasing the transparency and reporting standards of semi-autonomous agencies of government such as hospitals, colleges, universities and school boards that receive public funding.

From a public service perspective, the focus of most of this activity is on improving outcomes and management practices at the department or agency level and on the accountability obligations of deputy ministers and agency heads. But what about public servants below the deputy minister level? Oddly enough, the fundamental duty to be accountable is emphasized in some but not all public service codes of conduct. *The Alberta Public Service Vision and Values Handbook* focuses on individual accountability as one of four core values, stating that, as public servants, "we are responsible for our actions and for contributing to the effectiveness of the public service" (Alberta 2012a, n.p.). At the individual level, the value is translated into recommended behaviours such as, "I take responsibility for my actions and admit when I am wrong"; "I am open to appraisal and evaluation by others"; "I learn from mistakes, problems and other situations"; "I avoid defensiveness and stubbornness" (Alberta 2012a, n.p.). The New Brunswick *Public Service Values and Conduct Guide* (2009) does not emphasize accountability as a core value, but it does state that "[p]ublic servants are accountable for their actions within the framework of individual and collective ministerial responsibility and of the law" (n.p.). Accountability is not a core value in Ontario either, but one line of the Ontario Public Service Mission states: "We are accountable for how we fulfill our public service roles" (Ontario 2012). During a public service-wide values consultation in British Columbia (British Columbia, Public Service Agency 2008), accountability emerged as a key corporate value with a focus on a public servant who "sets clear and measurable goals and measures success; stays focused on government's priorities; (and) takes responsibility for decisions and completing tasks" (British Columbia, Public Service Agency 2012). The 2012 *Values and Ethics Code for the Public Sector* (Treasury Board of Canada Secretariat 2012a) mentions accountability only in the context of supporting the accountability obligations of ministers. Accountability is not even referenced in passing in the standards of conduct of most other governments at all three levels in Canada, where the primary concern is with the regulation of conflict of interest. Thus, while governments at all levels pay regular lip service to the duty of accountability, most have done little to codify and define for government employees the contemporary nature of this duty.

CASE 7.1: ACCOUNTABILITY OR SCAPEGOATING

Bob, the director of the oil policy branch, Ministry of Energy, is pulled into a meeting with his boss, the Assistant Deputy Minister (ADM). A month earlier, at the direction of the ADM, Bob and his team wrote a "big picture" memo for the minister on the trend in oil prices. The ADM reviewed the memo and passed it on to the minister's office. The memo contained the sentence: "This time around we won't be depending on a tap that some mullah or sheik can suddenly turn off." The minister's office apparently liked the memo and provided it "off the record" to some journalists. Somehow, a copy found its way into the hands of a Canadian-Islamic relations advocacy group. The group complained to the minister that the memo "promoted stereotyping of Muslims and Arabs," and the minister's office passed the complaint on to Bob's ADM.

In the meeting with Bob, the ADM says the comment had a pejorative tone to it and that in everyday discourse, terms like "mullah" and "sheik" are often used to caricature the leadership of Arab and Muslim states as feudal, irrational and even fanatical. He wants Bob to write a memo to him apologizing for the remarks and indicating that he and the members of his unit will be taking cultural sensitivity training. The memo will be copied to the minister and shared with the advocacy group.

When this plan is revealed to Bob, he is really upset. He argues that "sheik" is a term commonly used to refer to a Muslim leader in the Arabian peninsula and that the Supreme Leader of Iran, a major oil producer, is a "mullah" – a Muslim religious figure. He argues that he and his staff are being turned into scapegoats. He insists that there was nothing biased or racist about his comment, that he is very aware of diversity issues and that neither he nor his staff needs sensitivity training. He says he won't accept being sanctioned for saying something that he considers to be true, using language that would be considered to be unexceptionable around the ministry.

Taking into consideration the key features of the traditional accountability narrative (information, dialogue, rectification and sanctions), is Bob appropriately interpreting his duty of accountability in this case?

Performance Reporting and Accountability

Market-oriented management reforms initiated over the last two decades of the 20th century challenged aspects of the traditional hierarchical approach to accountability. To allow public servants to be more responsive to their clients and "customers," efforts were made in many jurisdictions to shift authority and responsibility downwards in public service agencies to service deliverers and their immediate supervisors and managers, who were encouraged to use increased discretion to be more responsive, take risks and be flexible in their pursuit of effective services and efficient administration. For public servants affected by such reforms, this intrusion of business techniques into traditional public administration had the effect of shifting the balance of accountability regimes from "tick box" accounting for following established rules and procedures and managing financial resources to a stronger focus on performance improvement (Thomas 2003, p. 549). Accountability regimes in affected governments were increasingly designed not only to "control for the abuse and misuse of authority" and "provide assurance in respect of the effective use of public resources and adherence to public service values" but also to "encourage and promote learning in pursuit of continuous improvement in governance and public management" (Aucoin and Heintzman 2000, p. 245) and move the focus of accountability "from red tape to results" (Hood 2011, p. 94).

Performance-oriented public service accountability regimes focus primarily on the results produced by the most senior public servants (e.g., deputy ministers, municipal chief administrative officers), whole departments or an entire public service. For example, the federal government annually publishes Departmental Performance Reports designed to assess how each department and agency has performed relative to the objectives established in its respective Reports on Plans and Priorities at the beginning of the fiscal year (Treasury Board of Canada Secretariat 2012b). The Alberta government's "Measuring Up" performance reporting system is portrayed as a key component of the government's accountability regime, reporting on "whether the government actually did what it said it would do" and what it needs to do in the future to enhance performance (Alberta 2012b). At the municipal level, participants in the Ontario Municipal CAO's Benchmarking Initiative report annually on performance in 37 service areas, "informing readers about the services provided within their municipality and how they compare to others" (OMBI 2012).

The public servant's individual accountability obligations within such a system – if it is operationalized effectively – are enlarged by virtue of the stronger focus on his or her responsibility to contribute to the effective performance of the wider organization. Accountability in this context is achieved through formal individual performance appraisal, which has become a key part of the performance management system of most contemporary governments (Ingraham 1998, p. 174). The appraisal is intended to provide feedback to the employee with respect to his or her contribution to the achievement of the organization's mission and adherence to corporate values, to identify strengths and weaknesses, to deal with compensation and career path issues, and to establish a strategy for enhancing the employee's capacity to contribute to the performance of the organization over the next year (Selden 2003).

While formal individual performance appraisal has become the primary internal vehicle for establishing the personal accountability of many public servants, its application has raised questions. The main concerns have been the potential for the exercise of subjective judgment, the failure of supervisors to deliver to the employee the resources and authorities required to meet agreed-upon performance objectives, the blindness of such appraisals to the increased sharing of responsibility for policy advice and program outcomes with a wide range of government, for-profit and not-for-profit organizations, and the reluctance of supervisors in such increasingly complex circumstances to impose penalties on individuals for what performance indicators suggest may be poor performance. As a result, a performance management system applied at the individual level is often of limited value in achieving the purposes of hierarchical accountability. It tends to focus on organizational outcomes (things that can be counted) at the expense of accountability for other significant aspects of the exercise of bureaucratic power; it often fails to make a strong connection between the resources and authorities available to the employee and his or her success or failure in achieving objectives; it can demoralize the employee rather than mobilize his or her efforts on behalf of the organizational goals; and, because of its perceived shortcomings, performance appraisal is too often devoid of consequences for the employee. As Behn (2001) notes, "[a]ll too often, linear, hierarchical, unidirectional performance appraisal just doesn't work" (p. 198). In short, as a device to focus personal accountability on what a public servant achieved rather than on how he or she achieved it, personal performance appraisal has fallen well short of its goal.

Another critical point is that when the going gets rough, supervisors and other monitors often downplay the focus on performance and revert to an emphasis on following orders and adherence to rules and standard procedures (Romzeck and Ingraham 2000). In a crisis or in the midst of an investigation of a scandal, there is less interest in the fact that a public servant embraced contemporary corporate values such as innovation and risk-taking in support of organizational objectives and much more concern about whether everything was done by the book. In such circumstances, those who normally might be rewarded for creative use of discretionary power might easily become scapegoats for not following the rules precisely. In addition, despite the superficial enthusiasm for performance-oriented accountability in many jurisdictions, the reality for many public servants in high-risk service-delivery or regulatory areas (e.g., child protection, security, environmental protection) is that employee empowerment and results-oriented performance appraisal were never really embraced by their employers. Instead, many public servants have experienced in recent years an increased emphasis on control-oriented accountability with demands for more "tick box" paperwork demonstrating that they have closely followed centrally imposed rules and procedures. This tendency is not unrelated to the rise of auditing and oversight, to which we turn our attention after looking at the following case.

CASE 7.2: ACCOUNTABLE FOR RESULTS

The Assistant Deputy Minister for Service Delivery provides the following report to her Deputy Minister.

We are getting amazingly negative blowback from the regional managers about our new performance management proposal. We want to tie a percentage of their pay to their success in meeting outcome targets for their clients, such as successful completion of training programs, uninterrupted employment, length of drug- or alcohol-free status, recidivism, and other outcomes in our Strategic Plan. As you know, we are already doing this with contractors in other programs with good results – their performance has improved since we tied their payments to results.

The managers are really resisting this. Their argument is that they just don't have enough control over their clients through our various employment and social service programs to be held accountable for results. In their view, the client group is subject to too many health, social and economic forces beyond the influence of the ministry's programs. Their alternative proposal is to make regional managers accountable for outputs such as numbers enrolled in training and addiction programs, initial employment placements, etc. My reaction was that outputs are not enough; what we want are real results. We give them the resources and considerable discretion, and we want regional managers who can deliver the goods. We want them to be accountable for outcomes.

Is it reasonable for the regional managers to resist the duty to be accountability for performance?

Increased Auditing, Oversight and Investigation

One of the most fascinating developments in recent years has been the growth in the number of monitoring and oversight agencies provided with the power to hold the public servant to account. With the emergence of contemporary administrative law and the application of the Charter of Rights and Freedoms, administrative tribunals, boards and courts have increasingly used their capacity for judicial review of administrative action to force public servants to defend actions or inactions which citizens, foreign nationals or organizations have complained violate their rights or are unreasonable, procedurally unfair, biased or even outside the boundaries of the powers provided by legislation. Public servants working in areas as diverse as taxation, immigration, workers compensation, income assistance, pension administration, environmental protection and land use by-law enforcement have been affected by this development (Ellis 2013, p. 2).

But have courts and tribunals enhanced the accountability of individual public servants? There is no doubt that high-profile Charter-based cases have drawn attention to significant violations by public servants of the rights of women and First Nations, for instance, and led to historical changes in policies and procedures as well as costly forms of government restitution in some instances (Mullan 2001). But it is not as clear that lower-profile administrative law decisions have been as effective as vehicles of public service accountability. Such decisions are often handed down well after the action or omission has taken place. And while appeal tribunal or court cases have become more frequent, they still only affect a small number of administrative decision-making public servants. In many cases, an official other than the public servant who actually made the decision in question appears before an appeal tribunal or court on behalf of the decision-making unit. Individual judgments are often very narrow in their impact and can have limited "inhibitory" consequences for other public servants. Moreover, pursuing a court case can be expensive. Governments can appeal decisions which go against them to higher-level tribunals and courts, leading to further delays and costs as well as diminished accountability consequences for the individual public servants involved in the original action. Finally, public services provided by private or not-for-profit agencies are often outside the remit of administrative law.

Nevertheless, administrative law cases can occasionally lead to the actions or omissions of individual public servants being exposed to media comment and public scrutiny. An example is the 2012 decision of the Federal Court condemning public servants in the federal Aboriginal Affairs department for unreasonably appointing a third-party manager to take over the financial affairs of the Attawapiskat First Nation after it had complained publicly about the deplorable state of housing on its reserve (*Attawapiskat First Nation v. Canada* 2012).

The investigations and reports of other oversight and monitoring authorities may also vary in significance as vehicles of effective individual accountability. *Internal* evaluation and audit branches have become powerful vehicles of the executive control dimension of accountability within government departments. Their demands for information on the efficiency and effectiveness of operations, the reliability of financial reporting, as well as personnel, risk, technology, information, governance and even ethics management, are designed to establish the degree to which the organization is achieving its objectives and complying with law, regulations and centrally established policy. Internal audit reports usually focus on areas of perceived or potential problems, where the problem could create substantial risk for the organization. The auditors want to know what went wrong or could go wrong, what policies or laws apply to the situation and what should be done to fix the problem or reduce the risk that it will ever happen again. The increase in the scope of internal audit generates enormous reporting requirements and is often portrayed as the bane of a hard-working public servant's existence (Clark and Swain 2005).

While the results of internal audits are often invisible to legislators or the public, *external* audits have become a major force on the political scene at all three levels of government, with opposition politicians and the media eager to use auditors' reports to launch attacks on the government. Despite the increasing visibility of external auditing, however, it is arguable that external audits have become less significant vehicles of individual accountability as their focus (at least for senior governments) has shifted from close scrutiny of financial expenditures and rule compliance by public servants within individual departments or agencies to the examination of the processes and systems put in place by departments to assure efficient and effective management of government programs. Such reports rarely focus attention on specific individuals. Nonetheless, the reports of external auditors have on occasion sparked closer scrutiny of the activities of individual public servants in specific units. For example, the federal Auditor General's 2003 report on the management of government advertising expenditures led to the uncovering of the "sponsorship scandal," and the subsequent commission of inquiry and media coverage drew attention to the behaviour of individual public servants in a number of departments (Office of the Auditor General of Canada 2003). Similarly, the Auditor General's report on due diligence in the initial procurement process for the F-35 fighter aircraft started a train of internal departmental scrutiny, parliamentary committee inquiries and media investigations which focused in part on the role of individual public servants involved in both of these events (Office of the Auditor General of Canada 2012). But even in these cases, the focus was largely on senior public servants.

Individual accountability for the lower- and middle-level public servant becomes more meaningful when oversight agencies such as a provincial, territorial or municipal ombudsperson or one of the many more narrowly focused – often departmentally based – oversight agencies (e.g., taxpayers' ombudsperson, military ombudsperson, prison ombudsperson, privacy commissioner, police complaints commissions, integrity commissioner) receive a complaint and begin to investigate (Hyson 2009). Most of these organizations have strong investigative powers that obligate public servants to provide requested information and answer questions posed to them. While many such cases are resolved by mediation between the complainant and the representatives of the service-delivery or regulatory organization, investigations by oversight agencies often throw light on the abuse of power or the unfairness or inefficiency of individual public servants by forcing them to explain their conduct and then, in some cases, reporting publicly on how the complainant was treated and what changes need to be made to make the treatment fair and reasonable.

Interactions between courts, administrative tribunals and oversight agencies, on the one hand, and public servants, on the other, have some but not all of the features of a traditional accountability relationship which, as set out earlier, are *information, dialogue, rectification* and *sanctions.* As noted, they generally oblige individual public servants who exercise authority to provide information and answer questions about how they have conducted themselves. By way of example, the Fisheries and Oceans Canada Values and Ethics Code states:

> When called upon to testify in court proceedings or to provide information in the course of an investigation, judicial inquiry, fact finding, etc., we are required to do so in a full and forthright manner. We shall not knowingly provide false, misleading, or inaccurate information. We shall conduct ourselves honestly, ethically and with integrity. We will avoid speculation or personal opinions. (Fisheries and Oceans Canada 2012, part 2, s. 3)

However, this obligation is not universal. Some laws and policies setting out the powers of internal and external oversight agencies establish circumstances in which public servants may refuse requests for information or dialogue concerning an action or inaction in which they were involved. The National Defence and Canadian Forces Ombudsman, for instance, can for undefined legal, operational or security reasons, be deprived of information and access to public servants on a matter which the office is investigating (National Defence and Canadian Forces Ombudsman 2012). There are also occasions in which individual public servants are advised by government lawyers not to answer questions (or questions on some topics) or not to appear before the investigatory body seeking information. A classic case is the federal Department of Justice's successful efforts to block testimony by non-military public servants to the Military Police Complaints Commission during its investigation of the handover of Afghan detainees to Afghan security forces (Military Police Complaints Commission 2012).

Only the courts and administrative tribunals can enforce rectification. The rulings of ombudspersons and other "complaint" commissions may result in improvements in performance, but such improvements are at the discretion of the leadership of the agency employing the individual or individuals whose behaviour has been found wanting. Similarly, formal sanctions do not always flow from the judgments of courts, tribunals or oversight agencies because they have no direct managerial authority over the offending employees. Some observers argue that this is something less than full accountability "because it omits the implication that there are consequences for mistakes or non-performance" (Thomas 2008, p. 39).

What is most significantly deficient in these accountability relationships from the perspective of the traditional model is the role of the supervisor or manager. Action in such cases is usually provoked by a complaint from a citizen, outside organization or employee, or probing by an auditor, and initiated by the court or oversight agency, rather than being driven by the superior officer who provided the public servant with responsibilities, authorities and resources to do the job. Thus, from one perspective, the existence of these forums represents a failure of traditional hierarchical accountability. The complainant could not get the public servant or the supervisor to treat him or her in a manner considered fair or reasonable and as a result seeks assistance outside the organization. In other cases, the internal or external oversight agency identifies a real or potential problem that the line managers may be ignoring, investigates it and brings the results to the attention of the relevant managers. However, some observers argue that this truncated form of accountability is not accountability at all; rather, it is "answerability," a public servant's "duty to inform and explain" without a strong focus on either rectification or sanctions (Canadian Centre for Management Development 1996, p. 9). But as Thomas (2008) notes, "for the individuals involved a loss of reputation represents a significant cost so that the neat theoretical distinction between accountability and answerability is not so easily maintained in 'the real world'" (p. 39).

Loss of reputation can be a particularly damaging consequence when a public servant's activities attract the attention of a public inquiry. Inquiries into events such as the sponsorship scandal, the tainted blood scandal, the Walkerton water disaster and the tasering death of Robert Dziekanski by RCMP officers in the Vancouver Airport may be rare, but they often cast the actions or inactions of public servants in a grim light. The inquiry commissioner may not be permitted to assign personal blame, but relentless questioning by commission counsel, widely publicized final reports and pervasive coverage by traditional and social media can leave a public servant's reputation and career in tatters. But, of course, there are exceptions. During the Maher Arar inquiry, the Canadian ambassador to Syria was publicly pilloried for his claim that he was unaware of the well-documented human rights violations occurring in Syrian jails, but that had no apparent effect on his career, as he was subsequently posted to further ambassadorial positions (CBC News 2005, June 17).

The Confusion of Shared Accountability

In chapter 1 we discussed the challenges which the phenomenon of "many hands" presented to the acceptance by public servants of personal responsibility for actions or inactions of government in which they are involved. The collective nature of much contemporary government work makes public servants reluctant to take individual responsibility for what happened and how it was done. This syndrome confounds efforts to establish the nature and extent of their duty to account to superiors in circumstances in which they perform their tasks in a team setting or collaborate with other departments, governments and partners in the private and not-for-profit sectors.

Let's first clarify the kinds of circumstances in which collective action creates problems for a public servant's duty of accountability. The most common examples of diffused responsibility are teams made up of participants from several units within one or more agencies established to manage a multi-faceted project or policy problem (e.g., to integrate immigration and economic and social development policies). Such arrangements are often temporary. Increasingly, however, government organizations are "joining up" on a semi-permanent basis. On the service-delivery side, for instance, there is the situation in which public services of more than one branch or department are bundled or integrated around larger, user-defined problems or life events (e.g., exporting, finding employment). In such circumstances, the simple connection between the public servants in one unit and their service users is replaced by a more complex relationship among service users and a "joined up" group of agencies (represented in some cases by a "single window" service centre or a third-party bundling agency such as Service Canada), with the result that none of the public servants in the combined agencies is prepared to be held to account for either the failure to achieve the jointly sought outcome or how that outcome was accomplished. In fairly rare instances, the integration of service delivery or policy development can extend across jurisdictional lines, engaging public servants and agencies from two or more levels of government.

The shared accountability stakes are further raised when public servants involved in service delivery are participants in formal contracting or partnership arrangements with not-for-profit or for-profit organizations in which substantial service design and delivery responsibilities can end up in the hands of agents outside the public sector. For example, many governments partner with major information technology vendors (e.g., IBM, CGI Group, Sierra Systems) not just to provide back office support for the creation of integrated, multi-channel (in person, phone, Internet, etc.) service-delivery systems but also to share the actual service-delivery responsibilities with the vendors who might, for instance, end up running the call centre for the ministry or the city administration or processing payments to or from clients. Even more common is the shifting of social service-delivery functions to the wide array of not-for-profit agencies which now contract with governments at all levels. The policy-side equivalent of this development is the hollowing out of the policy analysis and advisory capacities of government in favour of a network model of policy development in which public servants act more as facilitators, gatekeepers or aggregators, identifying and engaging stakeholders, including individual citizens, community groups, industry associations, think tanks and foundations. In effect, these players have become partners rather than merely supplicants in a network-based policy development process.

The emergence of these diverse "joined up" arrangements raises difficult questions about the ultimate accountability of agency heads and ministers for activities over which they have even less control than they do over the actions of their own employees. But what do these arrangements mean for public servants at the operational level – the individuals who are creating and working within these joined-up arrangements? How can individual public servants clarify their accountability obligations in circumstances in which power, authority and risk are dispersed among the participants, rules and procedures of different agencies may not be aligned and financial resources may be drawn from multiple budgetary envelopes?

Behn (2001) puts forward the idealistic notion of a "compact of mutual, collective responsibility" as the fundamental building block of accountability in a world of network governance. He characterizes such compacts as "ethical commitments" to a "common purpose," involving "obligations willingly accepted," entailing a "personal sense of duty to others" entered into "as a team" and "abandoning the search for individual scapegoats" (pp. 125-126).

Central to the notion of such a compact is the clarification of objectives, responsibilities and business practices among the participants. As Mulgan (2003) pithily notes: "if neither ends nor means are clearly definable, accountability tends to be problematic" (pp. 235-236). If you are, for instance, a manager in a provincial children and families ministry working with a number of not-for-profit child protection agencies, this requirement can be very challenging. Do the agreements with service providers clarify the anticipated outcomes, and who is responsible for what? Are workplace values, normal work loads, funding arrangements, qualifications and training for case workers, rules and procedures for risk assessments, internal arrangements for supervision, monitoring and reporting agreed upon? Are acceptable conditions established for oversight and evaluation so that the various auditors and inspectors are clear on their respective mandates, their access rights to workers, case files and financial data, and the limitations placed on such access because of privacy protection? Are professional staff, supervisors and managers in both the delivery agencies and the ministry clear on their duty to report if they become aware of a child requiring protection? Are there mechanisms in place to deal with conflicts which emerge about any of the above conditions?

This kind of clarity of goals, operational responsibility and procedures can be very difficult to achieve in a joint enterprise. In some cases, in fact, such clarity is not even sought by one's employer. In shared-responsibility situations involving not-for-profit or private sector partners or contractors, there can be pressure to focus more on accountability for outcomes than procedure or means of delivery since an important rationale for outsourcing is to take advantage of the potentially more flexible, expert and innovative business practices of non-governmental organizations. But this may not improve the accountability situation from the public servant's perspective. First, it is notoriously difficult to attribute outcomes – good or bad – to the activities of individual organizations in a partnership. Second, it may not be possible for the government to free itself of all responsibility for how partner agencies go about their business. Who then is accountable and for what if clients or citizens are abused or treated unfairly by the contracted agency?

CASE 7.3: ASK THEM, NOT ME

I followed the policies and procedures laid down by the department when I contracted with Training For Life (TFL). I even raised some questions with my boss about problems with the agency's track record – there were some complaints from clients during an earlier contract with the ministry in the Central Region, which as far as I know were never investigated. But no one asked me to follow up mostly because TFL is the only agency offering leadership skills training for at-risk teens in the area. So I got the normal assurance from TFL that they had done criminal records checks on the staff and signed off on the contract.

Now there appear to be reliable reports that TFL staff members have sexually abused some young clients at their remote training camp. But surely that is their problem. I appreciate that I may not have pushed hard enough to get quarterly performance reports from them, but you and I both know that most of our contracted agencies are way behind on their reporting. In any case, how would the reports have helped with this problem? I just didn't have the time or resources to visit the camp. I may be the contract manager, but I won't be held to account for the way this contract has turned out. I did what I could in the circumstances.

For what (if anything) and to whom should this contract manager be held to account?

More problematic still, in some longer-term public-private partnership arrangements, is that anticipated outcomes, division of responsibilities and operating procedures are all purposely left "loose." Service-transformation partnerships between government and IT vendors can sometimes have this "loose-loose-loose" character to accommodate the possibility that rapid changes in technology over the course of the partnership may alter the nature of the service outcomes being sought, the allocation of responsibilities and authorities to each party and even the methods of delivering the service.

In some cases, institutional efforts are made to deal with the inevitable uncertainties surrounding accountability in such circumstances by creating joint information-sharing, decision-making, problem-solving, evaluation and reporting forums and processes which force the public and private or third-sector partners to share responsibility and which allow senior officials and government oversight agencies to question and seek information from both the public servants and the representatives of the contractor or partner agency. But more often than not such "mutual, collective responsibility" is a sham. Instead, to avoid "buck passing," a public servant manager is treated as the "senior responsible owner" and becomes solely accountable to supervisors and oversight agencies within the government for the actions and omissions of partners and contractors with whom the manager is working (Dutil et al. 2011; Langford and Harrison 2001).

The attempt to maintain the veneer of traditional hierarchical accountability in the context of dispersed and collective responsibility puts the public servant in the unenviable position of answering for performance and operating practices of partners and contractors for which he or she may have little direct responsibility and imperfect knowledge (Grimshaw et al. 2001, p. 426). In such circumstances, sanctions (deserved or not) are more easily levied, but rectification becomes more challenging as the public servant who is the "senior responsible owner" may have to depend on partners (with whom he or she is trying to build trust) to impose remedies (Mulgan 2003, pp. 201-202). All of this becomes particularly problematic in circumstances in which the government has entered into outsourcing or partnership arrangements at least partly with the intention of avoiding normal government accountability processes (Moe 2001).

Professional Accountability

To this point we have examined the duty of accountability to superiors and monitoring agencies within government. But some public servants – those in recognized professions – also have a well-established duty of accountability to self-regulating professional societies. This obligation has proved problematic in some instances and led to the proposal of more informal accountability relationships among professionals in the workplace.

Large numbers of public servants are members of professions (e.g., social worker, pharmacist, engineer, doctor, accountant, lawyer) which, defined by their expertise, have been given the power by provincial governments to certify or license members, regulate their behaviour and enforce standards of conduct by limiting their right to practice – up to and including revocation of a licence. Most professional societies with these powers have established elaborate processes designed to resolve complaints about members from other members of the profession or the public (Brockman 1998). These processes generally provide the regulator with the prerogative to request information about individual performance, ask questions, demand rectification and level sanctions – all the components of what we describe earlier in this chapter as a full accountability relationship.

Critics have raised a number of concerns over the years about the accountability functions of professional associations (Pue 1996-97). They see many of these associations as little more than lobbying organizations that protect members' narrow interests and deal seriously with only the most egregious forms of unprofessional behaviour or incompetence – and then usually with modest sanctions and little regard for transparency. Further, this form of accountability often depends on concerns about poor conduct or professional incompetence being reported to the disciplinary body of the association by professional colleagues, because lapses in expert judgment or skill may not be visible to clients and members of the public. Unfortunately, many professionals are reluctant to report colleagues to regulators (Association of BC Forest Professionals 2011).

Thus, professional associations, accused of having lost sight of their obligation to protect the wider public interest, are not at first glance the most likely candidates for the role of holding public service professionals to account for the same offence. To get around the shortcomings in this complaint-driven form of professional accountability and forestall further government intrusion into professional self-regulation, there has been a more recent movement to establish less formal, peer-to-peer accountability among professionals in the workplace.

In the classic Friedrich-Finer debate on accountability noted earlier, Friedrich criticized the limitations of Finer's control-oriented, hierarchical accountability. While acknowledging the need for external control and upward accountability, Friedrich also wanted to open up the public servant to accountability to the standards of his or her profession in the form of scrutiny by fellow professionals (Friedrich 1940, p. 12). Friedrich's approach would seem to favour a more informal accountability relationship among professionals within the workplace than the complaint-driven, adversarial processes characteristic of traditional professional self-regulation. Nonetheless, we can hear echoes of his recommendations in the evolving regimes of professional self-regulation as well as in the concepts of participatory accountability and accountability to personal conscience, which we will examine shortly.

Taking a line from Friedrich, Dubnick (1998) argues that:

> [f]idelity (an internalized sense of honour and loyalty to the peer or professional reference group) is critical to the success of responsible accountability. It might seem strange to associate

> such emotional commitments as "fidelity" and
> loyalty with technical expertise and professionalism
> but these subjective ties are in fact critical to the
> professional endeavor. (pp. 78-79)

Peer-to-peer accountability attempts to take advantage of such professional fidelity to solve problems among colleagues. The process might start with a professional questioning the practice of a colleague, or alternatively, a professional taking the initiative to seek the advice of colleagues about his or her own professional practices. In either case, the voluntary accountability process might include efforts to clarify facts, define the nature of the concern or problem, discuss ways in which professional practice might be improved, provide continued assistance from colleagues to improve the quality of professional practice and, finally, establish a follow-up process allowing a third-party colleague to monitor performance. Such a peer-to-peer accountability process features the provision of information, dialogue, and rectification, all the elements of a traditional hierarchical accountability relationship with the exception – at least at the outset – of the involvement of a supervisor and the leveling of formal sanctions. Where a peer-to-peer accountability process revealed a potential serious violation of professional standards, the informal process could be abandoned and both the supervisor and the professional regulatory body become more formally engaged.

The limited effectiveness of formal professional self-regulation is further threatened by increasing collaboration among professionals in the public sector. Health and social service professionals, in particular, regularly work in teams or networks made up of members of different self-regulating professions. On the social service side, for instance, governments may form teams made up of police officers, social workers, child care workers, addiction counsellors, etc. to deal with a cross-jurisdictional issue such as family violence. Each one of these professionals is accountable to a different self-regulatory body and subject to different standards of professional practice. In these circumstances, it is commonplace for complaints about the behaviour of the team to fall between jurisdictional cracks in professional self-regulation. This has led to proposals for collaborative inter-professional investigation by cooperating self-regulatory bodies and, more importantly from our perspective, efforts to develop a culture of collaborative accountability within working teams. The latter would see team members taking collective responsibility for the team's actions or omissions and working cooperatively with joint adjudication bodies representing two or more professions to clarify what went wrong and what needs to be done to avoid the problem in the future (Working Group on Collaborative Regulation of the Nova Scotia Health Professionals Regulatory Network 2009). Like the efforts to adapt the duty of accountability to a world of outsourcing and public-private partnerships examined in the previous section, reform initiatives in this area are largely experimental, and there is little sign that we are moving in some predictable manner towards a clearly articulated collaborative duty of professional accountability which easily accommodates the increasingly "joined up" nature of professional work or contemporary public service.

Participatory Accountability

As we have seen, for most public servants the fundamental obligation of accountability is upward, focused on the hierarchical superior who delegates the power which he or she exercises as a public servant and on other entities (courts, watchdog agencies, professional associations, etc.) with the legal power to establish standards, request information, ask questions and, in some cases, demand rectification and level sanctions. But in the view of many public servants, accountability can also be "participatory" (Hupe and Hill 2007) based on the principle "that those whose rights or interests are adversely affected by the actions of someone else have a right to hold that person to account for the manner in which they have been treated" (Mulgan 2003, p. 13). This approach owes much to Friedrich's notion of what has become known as "subjective" or "independent" accountability: the obligation felt by many public servants to account "outward" and "downward" to an array of political and administrative actors. Accountability becomes in this conception a "social relationship in which an actor feels an obligation to explain and to justify his conduct to some significant other" (Bovens 1998, p. 172).

Dubnick (1998) argues that the obligation which emerges from viewing accountability as a social relationship has an ethical dimension which is as important as (and complementary to) traditional accountability's roots in the political theory of responsible government. He draws on Robert Nozick's conception of ethical theory to portray the obligation to account in social relationships as an expression of the "moral push" to be virtuous and enhance one's self worth by valuing others and the "moral pull" of others demanding "to be treated as valued individuals" (Dubnick 1998, p. 76). The "others" can be employees supervised by a public servant, colleagues, clients and their families, interest groups, or representatives of other public, private and not-for-profit organizations with whom he or she is collaborating.

We have already seen hints of this in the accountability relationship of a public servant with the courts. In that case, the public servant is answering questions posed in court, but those questions are often being posed in the name of an individual or organization affected by the public servant's decision or action.

In the workplace, the most prominent manifestation of participatory accountability would be innovations such as the 360-degree performance appraisal, which engages the public servant in accountability relationships not only with his or her supervisor but also with employees, team members and colleagues. Accountability in these circumstances takes the form of explaining what you are trying to achieve and why you are exercising your authority in a certain way, answering questions posed and listening to feedback about the positive and negative impacts of the way you conduct yourself. There are strong connections here to developments in the area of professional accountability, the efforts to graft personal performance measurement on to hierarchically oriented accountability and – as we shall see – ideas for solving the dilemma of joint accountability. If accountability is in significant part about improving performance (rectification) then it makes sense to expand the accountability relationship beyond superiors to embrace the widest circle of individuals and groups affected by one's work. Robert Behn (2001), a strong advocate of 360-degree accountability, argues that:

> [m]ultiple perspectives provide a richer understanding of how an individual is performing and of how he or she can improve. Moreover, when people get the same feedback from multiple sources, they are less able to dismiss it as the outgrowth of some minor misunderstanding or personal vendetta. (p. 198)

Beyond the workplace, there have been three significant drivers of participatory accountability. The first has been the New Public Management emphasis on treating the government service recipient as a "customer." The key features of this inherently business-like relationship are that the service provider respects customers, answers their questions, responds effectively to their complaints and accounts to them directly. Devices such as the citizen service charters and service satisfaction surveys are concrete symbols of this effort to build a culture committed to service standards and direct accountability to the service recipient (Mulgan 2003, pp. 172-173).

The second driver has been the introduction of a wide variety of new players to the service delivery and regulatory mix that public servants have to manage. Outsourcing to private sector and not-for-profit organizations and partnering with other government units and large private sector companies have increased the pressure on public servants to account to these new players. The success of joint service-delivery models depends on building trust relationships, which, in turn, depend on high levels of information sharing. In relationships of mutual dependency, information sharing inevitably takes on the character of reciprocal accountability. Public servants need information from contractors and partners to fulfill their responsibilities, but, equally, the contractors and partners will want the public servants they deal with to provide information, answer questions and rectify problems that present barriers to their mutual success.

The third driver has been the demand for more deliberative democracy, legitimizing governing processes through more open, informed and equal engagement of citizens and affected stakeholders in decision making at all levels. As discussed in chapter 6, this has led public servants to engage citizens and stakeholder groups in policy-making, program implementation and even program evaluation. Increasingly, such interactions have become electronic, migrating from traditional consultation vehicles such as surveys, town hall meetings, focus groups, etc., to network-oriented tools and techniques developed or adapted for the Internet, mobile communication devices and social media (e.g., issue forums, deliberative polls and representative survey panels). In the course of this ongoing evolution from e-Gov through Gov 2.0 to Citizen 2.0, access to government data has also exploded (either willingly on the part of government or through illegal "data dumps" by organizations such as WikiLeaks), providing citizens and non-governmental organizations with more of the information required to constructively consider policy and implementation options, monitor and evaluate government activities and recommend course corrections (Dunleavy et al. 2006; Roy 2013).

All of these developments tend to fuel demands for more direct accountability by public servants, who, more than politicians, have become the government face of service transformation and citizen engagement. The logic is simple: if a public servant provides more information and engages partners, contractors, citizens and stakeholders in the design, development and delivery of government services, then these different actors are going to exercise "moral pull," demanding ongoing involvement in these activities, and, specifically, more information on how well their specific interests are being served. The public servant, for his or her part, is going to feel the "moral push" to accommodate those demands by engaging in reciprocal feedback and rectification exercises.

We don't want to forget that traditionalists reject this expansion of the concept of accountability, and no Canadian government recognizes participatory accountability as a formal duty – although Ontario comes close in its statement of public service values when it lists "responsiveness" as a core value and explains: "We engage with clients, stakeholders, bargaining agents, the general public, and our staff to find out how we can do better" (Ontario 2012). The traditionalists draw attention to the watering down of the concept, the lack of the elements of rectification and sanctions in these diverse relationships and the potential for this expanded form of accountability to undermine loyalty to the employer.

CASE 7.4: FEELING ACCOUNTABLE TO STAKEHOLDERS

A government negotiator is explaining to an old friend a frustrating problem that has come up at one of his treaty tables.

The treaty process, at least in its early years, was advertised by federal and provincial governments as "open," which meant that negotiators made serious efforts to engage the public and stakeholder groups (fishers, environmentalists, chambers of commerce, etc.) likely to be affected by a treaty settlement in their area. As the negotiations evolved, the emphasis of stakeholders and the public shifted from demands for more information about our vision, agenda, policies and negotiation strategies, etc. to demands for reports on what exactly the government negotiators were putting on the table and explanations for any divergence between the advice they had given to the negotiators and the results the negotiators were actually prepared to accept. There was strong pressure on the negotiators to continue to be open and meet the demands for downstream accountability.

Unfortunately, this imperative to maintain a trust relationship with the public and stakeholder groups by meeting their accountability demands was often hamstrung by pressure from superiors and other parties to the negotiations to keep secret the details of what was actually transpiring at the treaty table. I felt an obligation to report back to the concerned groups what was actually happening and they expected it. But there was also a strong pressure to keep the compromises we were making secret until a deal was made. It put me as a negotiator in a hard place. I had stressed our openness, sought their advice and now couldn't tell them what was happening.

In these circumstances, does the treaty negotiator have a duty of accountability to stakeholders?

Accountability to One's Conscience

In this chapter we have been examining a spectrum of accountability relationships to which contemporary public servants are exposed, ranging from hierarchical accountability to superiors and their agents (e.g., internal auditors), legal accountability (to tribunals, courts and commissions of inquiry), accountability to oversight agencies (e.g., the auditor general, ombudsperson), professional accountability to standard-setting bodies (e.g., the Law Society) and participatory accountability to peers, employees, stakeholders and the public. This almost – but not quite – completes the spectrum of potential accountability relationships. Many public servants at all levels also talk about their accountability to themselves or their conscience.

Like participatory accountability, this is a notion of accountability which traces its lineage back to Friedrich's distinction between objective and subjective responsibility. Channeling Friedrich, Laframboise refers to independent accountability, which he says "is subjective in character. Its base is personal integrity – the quality or state of sound moral principle – uprightness, honesty and sincerity coupled with a sense of wholeness derived from truth to one's inner self. One in effect calls one's self to account for one's actions" (Laframboise 1983, p. 326). Terry Cooper (2006) insists on the importance of independent accountability: "As an expression of our beliefs, personal and professional values, and character traits," independent accountability "is just as real as the more tangible manifestations" of its objective counterpart (p. 81).

Following the line of arguments suggested by Laframboise and Cooper, conscience has been described as "an amalgam of personal and other values" which emerge from "a life-long socialization process" influenced by "family, peer groups and educators" as well as "political superiors and administrative colleagues" (Kernaghan 1984, p. 578). Thus conscience becomes a value-based form of moral reasoning, "the faculty by which an individual distinguishes between what is right and wrong" (p. 577) and a well-recognized approach to making ethical decisions, which we reference in our discussions of intuitionism and virtue theory in chapter 2. Using the method for reaching reflective equilibrium set out in that chapter, a public servant, faced with a difficult ethical choice, might see evidence of his or her conscience at work at the very outset if one of the options being proposed by a superior or stakeholder provokes an immediate personal and intuitive negative reaction (i.e., "this just feels wrong to me"). As the process of ethical decision making proceeds, the public servant is faced with conflicting rules or principles emerging from applicable laws, regulations, court decisions, policies, codes of conduct, positions of stakeholders, etc. At this point, he or she will see conscience come into play again as various ethical theories are brought to bear in an attempt to establish which rule or principle (and the action which would result from following it) is most ethically defensible.

As a public servant struggles to establish what rule to follow or option to adopt, the issue of personal conscience can become problematic. If a public servant's conscience is dominated by values that are in line with his or her official role, then following Polonius's advice, "to thine own self be true," should result in a decision which is legitimately in the public interest and not "false" to oneself in the role of a public servant. If, by contrast, a public servant's conscience is dominated by personal interests or political, ideological and religious beliefs, then the attempt to reach reflective equilibrium is far less likely to be in the wider public interest. For example, accountability to one's conscience does not, *in extremis*, permit a "rogue" public servant to ignore the orders of superiors simply because these orders offend some element of his or her personal moral code. An example of indefensible conduct here would be the actions of provincial marriage commissioners refusing to marry same-sex couples because same-sex marriage offends their personal religious values.

We also have to ask at this point whether talking in terms of "accountability to conscience" is helpful in the context of the focus of this chapter. Throughout we have been discussing accountability in terms of an *ex post facto* obligation to produce *information*, enter into *dialogue*, provide *rectification* for harm caused and accept *sanctions*. It is an obligation which a public servant enters into as a result of taking on official responsibilities and making decisions and taking actions with a view to fulfilling those responsibilities. As outlined above, personal conscience is likely to be a more significant feature of making hard choices in the exercise of discretion than it is of answering for those choices after they have been made, unless – improbably we hope – an official's conscience does not recognize accountability as a core value of a responsible public servant.

Final Thoughts on the Duty of Accountability

So where does all of this leave the duty of accountability for the average public servant? Clarifying responsibilities and objectives with one's immediate supervisor, securing resources necessary to the task, reporting regularly to that supervisor, answering his or her questions, discussing and fixing problems related to resourcing, procedures and performance, and receiving personal evaluations (including rewards and sanctions) related to these activities from the supervisor – all of these represent legitimate accountability obligations of every public servant working in a hierarchical setting. Similarly, responding to the information requests of internal and external auditors and, if things go wrong, providing information and answers to courts, tribunals, oversight agencies and commissions of inquiry legally empowered to deal with complaints or launch investigations without the provocation of a complaint also represent equally compelling accountability obligations in a democratic system. As noted, this is not to turn a blind eye to the warnings found on ancient maps and charts: "here be dragons." The extensive literature on accountability clearly illustrates the manner in which all of these hierarchical accountability processes can be transformed from opportunities for procedural correction and performance improvement into oppressive forums for scapegoating and blame-shifting (Hood 2011).

From this point, the duty of accountability becomes less clear. First, we have the accountability confusion engendered when public servants engage colleagues in other departments or governments or private and not-for-profit organizations as partners or agents in regulatory and service-provision functions. There is no question that public servants retain upward accountability obligations when responsibilities are shared with others, but the dilemma is our capacity to clarify who is responsible for what and create forums for joint accountability, bringing the diverse set of players together with more senior public officials, auditors, oversight agencies and legislative bodies to share information, answer questions, assess progress and agree upon solutions to problems of procedure or performance. There have been some interesting efforts to create such institutional arrangements, but they seem plagued by disputes – too often legal ones – about jurisdiction, information sharing and scapegoating. The duty of accountability of individual public servants involved in such activities is far from clear, and until we work out how to handle joint accountability, potentially fraught with danger.

We also examined the notion of professional accountability. While legally endorsed professional regulatory bodies have established accountability obligations for some public servants, the effectiveness of these complaint-driven processes is often questioned. Less formal peer-to-peer accountability represents an appeal to the fidelity of professionals in the public service to the core values of their profession but needs to be handled with caution. Proposals to establish a duty of collaborative accountability for public servants from different professions working in integrated teams are commendable but largely untested. Thus both the nature of the duty of accountability of public servants as professionals and the priority that should be attached to this form of accountability remain in flux.

There is equal uncertainty about the nature or even the defensibility of the participatory accountability obligations of public servants to employees, citizens, clients, and other stakeholders to whom a public servant may "feel" accountable. As we have seen, provocative developments in areas such as deliberative democracy, citizen and employee empowerment, partnering, etc., have created demands for an accountability component to close the loop of processes that involve a wider circle of players in the agenda-setting, planning, deciding and implementing functions of public servants. At this point, despite considerable pressure from stakeholders and others, there is little agreement on how a public servant should respond to the accountability demands of other players outside the traditional hierarchical setting within which an individual public servant operates. However, whether we call this phenomenon accountability or something else, in the real world of government, responding to these demands – at least informally – has become a significant fact of life for many public servants.

Finally, we recognize the importance of conscience as a filter for ethical decision making, but raise concerns about the notion of accountability to conscience. In the end, public servants look to be stuck with the "paradox of accountability" for some time to come (Gregory 2003; Harmon 1995). In this paradox, the traditional duty of accountability to one's superior, the courts and oversight agencies (internal and external) is important and defensible, but by its very nature it identifies the public servant as a solitary, robotic character whose simple responsibility is to follow the directions of a superior, report to that superior and oversight agencies on performance, rectify problems and accept sanctions or rewards as appropriate. There is no room in this vision for the need for professionally credentialed public servants to respond to complaints leveled against them through standard-setting regulatory agencies. This traditional vision is also largely indifferent to the accountability plight of a public servant working with others over whom he or she may have only limited effective control. Finally, and even more significantly, this accountability vision is blind to the reality of a public servant working in a complex collective and collegial setting with many others to whom he or she may feel a real duty of accountability.

References

Alberta. (2012a). *Alberta public service vision and values handbook.* Retrieved from http://www.chr.alberta.ca/apsvisionandvalues/documents/manager-supervisor-handbook.pdf

Alberta. (2012b). M*easuring up: Progress report on the government of Alberta strategic plan, 2011-12.* Alberta Ministry of Finance. Retrieved from http://www.finance.alberta.ca/publications/measuring/measup12/measuring-up-2012.pdf

Association of BC Forest Professionals. (2011). *Professional accountability processes.* Retrieved from http://www.abcfp.ca/regulating_the_profession/documents/Pro_accountability_process_for_review_May_2011.pdf

Attawapiskat First Nation v. Canada. (2012). FC 948. Retrieved from http://canlii. ca/en/ca/fct/doc/2012/2012fc948/2012fc948.html

Aucoin, P., & Heintzman, R. (2000). The dialectics of accountability for performance in public management reform. In G. Peters & D. Savoie (Eds.), *Governance in the twenty-first century: Revitalizing the public sector* (pp. 244-280). Montreal: McGill-Queen's University Press.

Aucoin, P. & Jarvis, M. (2005). *Modernizing government accountability: A framework for reform.* Ottawa: Canada School of Public Service. Retrieved from http://publications.gc.ca/collections/collection_2008/csps-efpc/SC103-15-2005E.pdf

Behn, R. (2001). *Rethinking democratic accountability.* Washington: Brookings Institution Press.

Bovens, M. (1998*). The quest for responsibility, accountability and citizenship in complex organizations.* Cambridge, UK: Cambridge University Press.

British Columbia, Public Service Agency. (2008). *BC public service values consultations: Summary results.* Retrieved from http://www2.gov.bc.ca/local/myhr/documents/jobs_hiring/bc_public_service_values_consultations_summary_results.pdf

British Columbia, Public Service Agency. (2012). *Corporate values of the B.C. public service.* Retrieved from http://www2.gov.bc.ca/myhr/article.page?ContentID=cc65a73a-2b2f-3bce-8057-b132b0c07fa6

Broader Public Sector Accountability Act. (2010). In Statutes of Ontario, S.O. 2010, Chapter 25. Retrieved from http://www.e-laws.gov. on.ca/html/statutes/english/elaws_statutes_10b25_e.htm

Brockman, J. (1998). "Fortunate enough to obtain and keep the title of profession": Self-regulating organizations and the enforcement of professional monopolies. *Canadian Public Administration, 41*(4), 587-621.

Canadian Centre for Management Development. (1996). *A strong foundation: Report of the task force on public service values and ethics.* Ottawa: CCMD.

CBC News. (2005, June 17). S*harp rebuke for ambassador over Arar comments.* Retrieved from http://www.cbc.ca/news/canada/ story/2005/06/16/arar050616.html

Clark, I., & Swain, H. (2005). Distinguishing the real from the surreal in management reform: Suggestions for beleaguered administrators in the government of Canada. *Canadian Public Administration, 48*(1), 453-476.

Cooper, T. L. (2006). *The responsible administrator: An approach to ethics for the administrative role* (5th ed.). San Francisco: Jossey-Bass.

Denhardt, J., & Denhardt, R. (2003). *The new public service: Serving, not steering.* Armonk, NY: M.E. Sharpe.

Dubnick, M. (1998). Clarifying accountability: An ethical theory framework. In C. Sampford & N. Preston (Eds.), *Public sector ethics: Finding and implementing values* (pp. 68-81). London: Routledge/ Leichhardt.

Dunleavy, P., Margetts, H., Bastow, S. & Tinkler, J. (2006). New public management is dead—Long live digital-era governance. *Journal of Public Administration Research and Theory, 16*(3), 467-494.

Dutil, P., Howard, C., Langford, J., & Roy, J. (2010). *The service state: Rhetoric, reality and promise.* Ottawa: University of Ottawa Press.

Ellis, R. (2013). *Unjust by design.* Vancouver: UBC Press.

Federal Accountability Act. (2006). In Statutes of Canada, S.C. 2006, c.9. Retrieved from http://laws-lois.justice.gc.ca/eng/acts/F-5.5/

Finer, H. (1941). Administrative responsibility and democratic government. *Public Administration Review, 1*(4), 335-350.

Fisheries and Oceans Canada. (2012). *Values and ethics code.* Retrieved from http://www.dfo-mpo.gc.ca/reports-rapports/vicr-virc/vicr-virc2012-eng.htm#pro

Friedrich, C. (1940). Public policy and the nature of administrative responsibility. In C. Friedrich (Ed.), *Public Policy* (pp. 3-24). Cambridge, MA: Harvard University Press.

Government Accountability Act. (2009). In Statutes of Alberta, RSA 2000, c. G-7. Retrieved from http://www.canlii.org/en/ab/laws/stat/rsa-2000-c-g-7/latest/rsa-2000-c-g-7.html

Gregory, R. (2003). Accountability in modern government. In G. Peters & J. Pierre (Eds.), *Handbook of public administration* (pp. 557-568). London: Sage.

Grimshaw, D., Vincent, S., & Willmott, H. (2001). New control modes and emergent organizational forms: Public-private contracting in public administration. *Administrative Theory & Praxis*, 23(3), 407-430.

Harmon, M. (1995). *Responsibility as paradox: A critique of rational discourse on government.* London: Sage.

Hood, C. (2011). *The blame game.* Princeton: Princeton University Press.

Hupe, P., & Hill, M. (2007). Street level bureaucracy and public accountability. *Public Administration, 85*(2), 279-299.

Hyson, S. (Ed.). (2009). *Provincial and territorial ombudsman offices in Canada.* Toronto: University of Toronto Press.

Ingraham, P. W. (1998). Making public policy: The changing role of the higher public service. In B. G. Peters & D. Savoie (Eds.), *Taking stock: Assessing public sector reforms* (pp. 164-186). Montreal: McGill-Queen's University Press.

Kernaghan, K. (1984). The conscience of the bureaucrat: Accomplice or constraint? *Canadian Public Administration, 27*(4), 576-591.

Laframboise, H. (1983). Conscience and conformity: The uncomfortable bedfellows of accountability. *Canadian Public Administration, 26*(3), 325-343.

Langford, J., & Harrison, Y. (2001). Partnering for e-government: Challenges for public administrators. *Canadian Public Administration, 44*(3), 393-416.

Michael, B. (2005). Questioning public sector accountability. *Public Integrity, 7*(2), 95-109.

Military Police Complaints Commission. (2012). *Commission's final report –MPCC 2008-042 - Concerning a complaint by Amnesty International and the BC Civil Liberties Association in June 2008.* Retrieved from http://www.mpcc-cppm.gc.ca/03/afghan/2012-06-27/index-eng.aspx

Moe, R. (2001). The emerging quasi-federal government: Issues of management and accountability. *Public Administration Review, 61*(1), 290-312.

Mulgan, R. (2003). *Holding power to account: Accountability in modern democracies.* Basingstoke, UK: Palgrave Macmillan.

Mullan, D. (2001). Administrative law. Toronto: Irwin Law.

National Defence and Canadian Forces Ombudsman. (2012). *Mandate: Ministerial directives.* Retrieved from http://www.ombudsman.forces.gc.ca/en/ombudsman-about-us/ministerial-directives.page#ombudsmanmandategeneralduties

New Brunswick. (2009). *Public service values and conduct guide.* Retrieved from http://www2.gnb.ca/content/dam/gnb/Departments/ohr-brh/pdf/other/values_conduct_guide.pdf

Office of the Auditor General of Canada. (2003). *November Report. Chapter 3 – The sponsorship program.* Retrieved from http://www.oag-bvg.gc.ca/internet/English/parl_oag_200311_03_e_12925.html

Office of the Auditor General of Canada. (2012). *Spring Report. Chapter 2 – Replacing Canada's fighter jets.* Retrieved from http://www.oag-bvg.gc.ca/internet/English/parl_oag_201204_02_e_36466.html

OMBI. (2012). Ontario Municipal CAO's Benchmarking Initiative: *Partnering for service excellence.* Retrieved from http://www.ombi.ca/

Ontario. (2012). *The Ontario public service careers: Who we are.* Retrieved from http://www.gojobs.gov.on.ca/WhoWeAre.asp

Pue, W. (1996-97). Foxes, henhouses, unfathomable mysteries, and the sufferance of the people: A review of regulating professions and occupations. *Manitoba Law Journal, 24*(2), 283-300.

Romzeck, B., & Ingraham, P. (2000). Cross pressures of accountability: Initiative, command and failure in the Ron Brown plane crash. *Public Administration Review, 47*(3), 227-238.

Roy, J. (2013). *From machinery to mobility: Government and democracy in a participative age.* New York: Springer.

Royal Commission on Financial Management and Accountability. (1979). *Final Report.* Ottawa: Supply and Services Canada.

Savoie, D. (2008a). *Court government and the collapse of accountability.* Toronto: University of Toronto Press.

Savoie, D. (2008b). Searching for accountability in a government without boundaries. *Canadian Public Administration, 47*(1), 1-26.

Schafer, A. (1999). A wink and a nod: A conceptual map of responsibility and accountability in bureaucratic organizations. *Canadian Public Administration, 42*(1), 5-25.

Selden, S. (2003). Innovations and trends in HRM practices. In G. Peters & J. Pierre (Eds.), *Handbook of public administration* (pp. 62-71). London: Sage.

Thomas, P. G. (2003). Accountability. In G. Peters & J. Pierre (Eds.), *Handbook of public administration* (pp. 549-556). London: Sage.

Thomas, P. G. (2008). The swirling meaning and practices of accountability in Canadian government. In D. Siegel & K. Rasmussen (Eds.), *Professionalism and public service: Essays in honour of Kenneth Kernaghan* (pp. 34-62). Toronto: University of Toronto Press.

Transparency and Accountability Act. (2006). In Statutes of Newfoundland, SNL2004, Chapter T-8.1. Retrieved from http://assembly.nl.ca/Legislation/sr/statutes/t08-1.htm

Treasury Board of Canada Secretariat. (2012a). *Values and ethics code for the public sector.* Retrieved from http://www.tbs-sct.gc.ca/pol/doc-eng.aspx?id=25049&section=text#cha5

Treasury Board of Canada Secretariat. (2012b). *Overview of government spending and performance.* Retrieved from http://www.tbs-sct.gc.ca/ppg-cpr/dpr-rmr-eng.aspx

Uhr, J. (1992, September). *Public accountabilities and private responsibilities: The Westminster world at the crossroads.* Paper presented at the American Political Science Association annual meeting, Chicago.

Working Group on Collaborative Regulation of the Nova Scotia Health Professionals Regulatory Network. (2009). *Collaborative self-regulation and professional accountability in Nova Scotia's health care system.* Retrieved from http://hli.law.dal.ca/Files/WG_Document_Nov_4_2009.pdf

Chapter 8

Managing Ethical Behaviour

[T]he ultimate purpose of codes is to get
members to internalize the spirit of their
provisions. (Grundstein-Amado 2001, p. 468)

In the preceding chapters, we examined commandments or rules
governing the behaviour of public servants in regard to the public
interest, political neutrality, conflict of interest, confidentiality, the
protection of privacy and accountability. We found considerable
uncertainty and debate among governments, public servants and ethics
"experts" about the meaning of these rules, the legitimacy of traditional
interpretations and how to make choices among rules when they clash
in complex ethical dilemmas.

Even if public sector organizations could achieve clarity and
agreement on what good behaviour looked like, we would still be faced
with the challenge of encouraging and enforcing that behaviour. This
chapter focuses on how public sector organizations can build institutions
that foster a culture in which public servants manifest a sense of
personal moral responsibility. How can we create a hospitable climate
for responsible behaviour within public sector organizations? How can
we foster good behaviour, enforce rules and sanction offenders? In
these tasks, we are faced with significant policy choices. Should we
adopt a code of conduct? What form should this take? Should it for
instance place relatively more emphasis on values compared to rules?
Is legislation necessary? How effective is ethics education and training?
Do we need ethics counsellors and/or commissioners? Are criminal
sanctions likely to be effective deterrents? In short, what regime
should we use to guide and regulate the behaviour of public servants
and encourage responsible public service? How important is ethical
leadership to responsible conduct?

There is no easy answer to the question of what kind of ethics
regime works – and solid empirical evidence on the comparative
benefits of various measures to encourage ethical behaviour is scarce.
While some measures may be more effective than others, building a
more responsible public service is a complicated challenge requiring a
multi-dimensional solution. It is, however, easy to compile a long list of
measures that governments can use to build and sustain an effective
values and ethics regime. Several of these measures can be grouped

into four main categories: codes of conduct, values and ethics education and training, enforcement and sanctions, and ethical leadership. Each of these categories is discussed below.

Starting with a Code of Conduct

A popular and relatively inexpensive means of fostering responsible behaviour is a document (or documents) setting out values, ethics rules and/or ethics guidelines for the public service as a whole or for individual departments and agencies. Such a document is usually described as a code of conduct or a code of ethics and it often includes, or is complemented by, a statement of values.

Some governments have both a values statement and a code, either in the same document or in separate ones. New Brunswick's (2009) *Public Service Values and Conduct Guide* contains a values statement followed by guidelines elaborating on each value. The Ontario government has a brief statement of values to guide public servants' behaviour and relationships, but the 2006 *Public Service of Ontario Act* covers such ethics issues as conflict of interest, political activity rights and whistle blower protection.

In Canada, legislation ensures a modicum of commonality in governments' ethics rules. For example, all governments can call on the "Offences Against the Administration of Law and Justice" sections of the *Criminal Code* to deal with the bribery of public officials, fraud, the sale or purchase of office, and influence peddling (Department of Justice Canada 2013). Similarly, virtually all governments have an oath of office establishing secrecy obligations, and, in very special circumstances, they can use the provisions of the *Security of Information Act* (1985) to try to ensure confidentiality. But after that, the various regimes diverge in a multitude of directions.

For most Canadian governments, the traditional approach to promoting responsible public service has been to create new policies, rules and, occasionally, laws in response to widely visible instances of irresponsible behaviour and then to enforce them in a desultory manner until the onset of the next crisis. By the late 1960s, this stop-and-go approach had resulted in a patchwork of rules at all levels of government in Canada, which some governments gradually began to transform into more integrated codes of conduct. While many governments have continued to improve and update their codes, many others have done little, so there is considerable variation in the nature and quality of codes from one government to another. Moreover, there is still substantial resort to the stop-and-go approach and a consequent persistence of patchwork rules and regimes.

Rather than resort to legislation, most Canadian governments have been inclined to write down rules for responsible administrative behaviour in the form of guidelines, policy directives or codes of conduct. The tendency to make rules in reaction to problems means that it is unusual to find all the rules governing ethical issues in one place. In addition to codes of conduct, rules may be found in letters from the prime minister, premier or city manager to senior officials and in minutes, bulletins or policy directives from management boards, public service commissions or government-wide purchasing agencies. Rules may also appear at the departmental or branch level in the form of supplementary codes of conduct and directives from senior managers to more junior employees. Most of the recent rules dealing with public servants' use of the Internet in the workplace are found in policy statements rather than in codes of conduct.

Even codes of conduct, which would appear to be tailor-made for one agency or a whole government to gather together its key rules, sometimes focus on a single issue – frequently conflict of interest – leaving the rest of the rules in relative obscurity. When to this hodgepodge of written rules is added the large number of behavioural norms that remain at the level of unwritten conventions, the result is a considerable amount of employee confusion and cynicism. Often, the rules are not only ill-defined, dispersed and inaccessible but also generally unenforced and frequently unenforceable. In many jurisdictions, senior managers turn a blind eye to inappropriate political activity, conflict of interest violations and unwarranted intrusions into the personal privacy of citizens because the effort involved in pursing these offences is too great. When the offences are pursued, criminal charges or internal disciplinary actions are often thwarted by the burden of proof required. Criminal sanctions (jail terms or fines) are rare, and internal sanctions generally tend toward the lenient end of the scale (letters of reprimand as opposed to demotions, suspensions or dismissals).

These negative factors are exacerbated by the attitude of those senior managers who take a paternalistic approach toward employees in ethical matters, dictating legalistically worded codes of conduct or new rules from on high with little or no consultation. Once the rules are in place and the crisis that gave rise to them has abated, managers often lose interest in them and so do little to foster their acceptance within the organization. In this context, because individual employees do not see responsible behaviour as a key component of the organizational culture, they often cut ethical corners and ignore the rules to get things done.

Benefits and Deficiencies of Codes of Conduct

A code of conduct for public servants can rescue the key values of the organization from the confusion and obscurity of unwritten convention and unread policy manuals and display them prominently for public servants and the public to see.[7]   In a sense, a written code is the obvious antidote to the failure of traditional regimes to provide an acceptable starting point from which to launch a comprehensive offensive against unethical behaviour in the public service. A carefully crafted code of conduct can be the centrepiece of a broad values and ethics regime. It can serve to establish a consensus within the organization concerning both values to be pursued and behaviours to be avoided. Jeremy Plant (2001) asserts that the enduring significance of · all codes is "how they can lift public servants above the 'do's and don'ts' of ordinary organizational life to give meaning and reality to the highest values of a democratic society" (p. 328).

A code can sensitize employees to the ethical dimension of their decisions, and it can assist them in resolving ethical dilemmas by becoming the focal point for consultation among colleagues and superiors about difficult issues that arise in the work place. It sets out criteria against which public servants can evaluate their own behaviour as well as that of their administrative superiors, peers and subordinates. A code provides a useful mechanism for training new staff on the values and rules to which they are expected to adhere. Ideally, over time, most public servants will internalize the code's provisions as an integral part of their decision-making process. As explained below, a code can also serve as a means of administrative control and a basis for disciplinary action for those public servants who are not influenced by the code's hortatory provisions.

A code can be a viable vehicle for communicating these values and unacceptable practices not only to employees but to the public as well. It can enhance trust and confidence in public servants by reducing the public's uncertainty as to what kinds of behaviour are ethical or unethical.

A code of conduct also has limitations. Some codes are lengthy and difficult to understand, involve too little consultation with those to whom they apply and/or take a heavily negative tone. Codes that focus on what public servants should not do pay little or no attention to the positive values and behaviours that the organization is trying to foster.

---

7. An examination of the benefits and deficiencies of codes of ethics can be found in Chandler (1983), Kernaghan (1974; 1980) and Plant (2001).

Even codes that are succinct, simply written and positive receive their share of criticism. It is argued that they tend to be too general and, therefore, too vague to be helpful in resolving ethical dilemmas. It is also difficult for a code of this kind to serve as a reference point for public servants from across a wide range of government departments and agencies. Moreover, such a code cannot be easily used for disciplinary purposes. Indeed, many codes have no enforcement provisions. Some codes, in dealing in detail with such matters as conflict of interest, may negatively affect the individual rights and private lives of public servants who are not engaged in any wrongdoing. A good example is conflict of interest rules that require public servants to disclose not only their own financial interests but those of their spouses and dependent children as well.

Seeking Compatible Codes

Questions are frequently raised about the compatibility of public sector codes of conduct with other codes, notably those guiding political staff, those adopted by professional associations to which public servants belong and those for lobbyists. In chapter 4, we noted the need for guidance for political staff to ensure that they respect the political neutrality that is required of public servants.

Professional Codes

Professions like engineering, law and planning have a code of conduct for their members, but these codes do not distinguish between public and private sector members. Some professional and semi-professional groups that are composed solely of government employees (e.g., the International Public Personnel Association of Canada) also provide a code of conduct for their members. These professional codes usually complement government-wide codes and deal with many of the same matters (e.g., conflict of interest, confidentiality), but the two types of codes are sometimes in tension – as, for example, when the environmental standards provisions of a professional planner's code conflicts with the accountability provisions of a public sector code.

Social contract ethical theory offers some advice in dealing with such conflicts when the public service code is deemed to be "a law of the state." David McGraw (2004), relying on social contract theory, describes a professional code as "an agreement made by members of a social group, who agree to obey the rules of the contract because of a perceived mutual benefit" (p. 242). Thus the laws of the state should take precedence when there is a clash with a professional code because the general public has consented to the laws but only the members of the profession have agreed to the provisions of their code. McGraw argues that "professional codes of ethics should not be understood as moral absolutes, but merely as agreements existing in a domain that is subordinate to the legal system...[W]here a mere rule in a professional code of ethics conflicts with a law of the state, the professional code of ethics should be pre-empted. Both are social agreements, thus in almost all cases the more global should prevail" (p. 242).

Codes on Lobbying

As noted in chapter 5, lobbying has significant implications for the post-employment variation of conflict of interest that is routinely covered in public sector codes. The federal *Policy on Conflict of Interest and Post-Employment* (Treasury Board of Canada Secretariat 2012a) provides that "[a]ll public servants have a responsibility to minimize the possibility of real, apparent or potential conflict of interest between their most recent responsibilities within the federal public service and their subsequent employment outside the public service" (s. 3). After they leave government, senior and certain other officials are, among other limitations, required to observe a "limitation" or "cooling off" period in respect of such matters as those with which they had official dealings while in government.

In addition to such measures, some governments have statutes or codes dedicated to regulating the ethical conduct of lobbyists, including their relations with public servants. The federal Lobbyists' *Code of Conduct* under Canada's *Lobbying Act* (1985) aims to ensure that lobbyists act ethically "with the highest standards and with a view to conserving and enhancing public confidence and trust in the integrity, objectivity and impartiality of government decision-making" (Office of the Commissioner of Lobbying in Canada 2012, n.p.). The Improper Influence section of the Code provides that "[l]obbyists shall not place public office holders in a conflict of interest by proposing or undertaking any action that would constitute an improper influence on a public office holder" (n.p.). A similar clause in Ontario's *Lobbyists Registration Act* (1998) stipulates a fine of up to $25,000 for breaches of the Act. The City of Toronto has a Lobbying By-Law that includes a Lobbyists' Code of Conduct providing, for example, that "[l]obbyists shall not place public office holders in a conflict of interest or in breach of the public office holders' codes of conduct or standards of behaviour" (City of Toronto 2009, c. 140:31-33). This by-law was a response to the Bellamy Inquiry's findings regarding the undue influence of lobbyists in the Toronto computer scandal (Bellamy 2005). To this point, no Canadian code of conduct for public servants places any obligations on them to report contacts with lobbyists or misbehaviour on the lobbyists' part.

Values and Rules

Since the mid-1980s, in response to the increased emphasis on values in the study and practice of public administration (Kernaghan 1997; 2003; 2007; Van Wart 1998), codes of conduct have increasingly included references to core public service values. In the best of these efforts, statements of core values are closely linked to the more detailed rules that follow. New Brunswick's (2009) *Public Service Values and Conduct Guide* describes five fundamental values – integrity, respect, impartiality, service and competence – that "are central to [public servants'] relationships with elected officials, the public and other public servants" (n.p.). These values are the foundation for the more detailed provisions contained in a Conduct Guide that elaborates on each of the values. For example, the value of integrity involves public servants acting "honestly, fairly and openly; they honour their commitments; and they do not use public office for private or personal gain." This is followed by such provisions as:

> Public servants do not, without due authority,
> disclose or make known any matter that
> comes to their knowledge by virtue of their
> public service employment.
>
> Public servants disclose any real or apparent
> conflicts between their personal or private
> interests and their official duties. (n.p.)

An appendix to the Conduct Guide includes reference to statutes and other official documents related to the Values Statement and the Guide.

A Charter of Public Service

A proposal with a persistent presence in Canada's public sector values and ethics discourse calls for the adoption of a Charter of Public Service.[8] The Charter would go beyond a conventional statement of values and/or a code of conduct for public servants. It is envisaged as a moral contract that would "commit and bind ministers, MPs and public servants alike, in support of a professional public service, dedicated to the public interest" (Canada 2004, p. 30). It would be endorsed by both ministers and Parliament. The Charter idea first appeared in the report

---

8. For a full discussion of the Charter idea, see Heintzman (2013, pp. 116-123).

of the Tait Task Force on Public Service Values and Ethics (Canadian Centre for Management Development 1996) and has subsequently been recommended by such other bodies as the Working Group on the Disclosure of Wrongdoing (Canada 2004) and the Gomery Commission of Inquiry into the Sponsorship Program (Canada 2006).

In designing codes of conduct, governments must decide what balance to strike between the use of values and rules as means of promoting responsible administrative behaviour. Ralph Heintzman (2007) suggests that codes of conduct should set out not only rules but also a vision of the good in the form of values (p. 594). However, there is a difference of opinion in the public administration community on the effectiveness of values compared to rules for fostering responsible behaviour.

For example, John Langford (2004) describes the values approach as proposing that a framework of core values reflecting "the shared beliefs of the members of the organization is an essential tool for public servants to work out appropriate ethical behaviour in specific instances and can also be used to justify the establishment of rules designed to deal with specific ethical dilemmas" (p. 434). Among his concerns about this approach is that values advocates, by including such a variety of entities under the rubric of values, do not make clear what a value is and how core values can be determined. Thus public servants receive little guidance as to the appropriate course of action in challenging circumstances. In addition, values advocates often recognize such a substantial number of values, many of which are poorly defined, that public servants cannot easily resolve the resulting value conflicts and they can, moreover, "value shop." He concludes that "[e]xcept for sending the vague message that a serious public service can't exist without adhering to certain values, [one] can find no guidance that would assist a public servant in understanding how some values might have a higher priority than others" (p. 439).

Langford rejects the distinction that values advocates make between ethical and non-ethical values and, in particular, he questions the classification of values into "clusters" such as ethical, democratic, professional and people values. He argues that public servants can't discern the practical difference between ethical values and other categories of values, and they become confused when reference is made to so-called non-ethical values in the context of making ethical choices. He notes that a rule-based ethics regime "is mechanistic, paternalistic and often reactive, and the results can be legalistic, burdensome and dull. But rules have the advantage of clearly setting out what the employer will accept as responsible behaviour" (p. 433).

Langford suggests that the real world of public service ethical choice is one in which public servants are "intuitively consequentialists [explained in chapter 1] and pragmatic in their everyday ethical reasoning" (p. 443). Rather than trying to balance values as a way of defending or attacking an action or rule, they analyse the negative and positive consequences of the action or rule for a range of stakeholders.

Ralph Heintzman (2007) responds to these considerations by denying that there is a dichotomy between attention to public service values and a consequentialist approach to public sector ethics: "due attention to public-service values...requires public servants to pay attention to the concrete impact of decisions on the full range of interests affected by them" (p. 577). He argues that public servants cannot assess consequences without reference to values like fairness and efficiency. Moreover, since rules do not exist to cover every decision, there is always a need to refer to values to fill in "the discretionary space between the rules" (p. 578). In his view, the real world of decision making is one in which most everyday decisions are *not* made on the basis of rules alone or after a rational exhaustive consideration of consequences.

On the issue of too many values, Heintzman contends that reducing the values universe to a small number cannot capture the full range of values or the complexity of public administration. A solution with the virtue of simplicity is to organize the values universe into such clusters as ethical, democratic, professional and people values – and to recognize that the values universe is small and simple compared to the rules universe. "No wonder most public servants do not function, day-by-day, with a rule-book in their hand...they rely on a very general sense of what the rules require, on their experience and common sense, and on what is right and proper in a public service, that is to say, on their public-service values" (pp. 584-585).

Heintzman argues that it is not attention to values that creates conflicts; rather it is attention to values that helps public servants resolve the conflicts that already exist in the concrete world where they have to act. He also argues that values are currently viewed as expressing a community's aspirations, whereas ethics is viewed as a subset of values that stresses the value of compliance with rules and laws (e.g., conflict of interest). He concludes by asserting that values express a vision of the good and thereby "nourish in us the feelings that make us want to uphold the good – to obey a rule, for example, when no one would know the difference, or to speak truth to power, when it is risky to do so" (p. 595).

Iain Gow (2008), in seeking "a practical basis for public service ethics," concludes that "neither a values-based approach nor a disciplinary [rules-based] one alone will solve all of the problems raised by public service ethics" (p. 115). Most codes, at all levels of government, include both values and rules (Langford and Tupper 2006, p. 132). Gregory Levine (2009), in his examination of codes of conduct for municipal staff in Canada, recommends that "codes should contain a statement of purpose that includes an outline of core values; a set of prohibitions, coupled with positive affirmations; a statement of penalties; and a reference to other policies and by-laws that deal with enforcement" (p. 15). The enduring challenge is to strike an optimum balance between values and rules as drivers of responsible behaviour.

What Does a Good Code Look Like?

Carefully crafted codes of conduct involving widespread consultation can ameliorate the limitations of codes so that a system for enhancing and controlling administrative behaviour can be built around them. A code should emerge from the group to which it is going to apply. This is not to suggest that a successful code must totally reflect the values of employees, thereby leaving no room for leadership in its construction. Rather it suggests that any significant departure from prevailing group norms must be discussed with the affected employees and carefully justified. If, for example, governments want new rules on post-employment practices to "take," they should consult the public servants who have to live with these rules.

If a code is to become a living part of an organizational culture it must be realistic. While it is counter-productive for a code to dwell exclusively or largely on the negative, it is equally dangerous to its credibility to burden it with lofty principles. Codes that exhort employees to seek sainthood if not martyrdom in the name of public service will soon be gathering dust. However, lofty language in a code's preamble can provide an uplifting beginning to a code composed of specific values, guidelines and/or rules. For example, the preamble to New Brunswick's (2009) *Public Service Values and Conduct Guide* asserts that public servants:

> commit to the highest ideals of public service
> and take pride in their work. They strive to
> ensure that citizens have trust and confidence
> in government. By advising the government
> of the day, managing programs, and serving
> citizens, public servants play a vital role
> in sustaining the province's democratic

institutions and fostering economic prosperity
and social wellbeing. (n.p.)

It is easier to understand and remember a code's content if it is
written in plain, non-legal language rather than written as a piece of
legislation. Legislated codes have a higher public profile, but they lack
flexibility, are hard to amend, do not make attractive socialization tools
because of their stilted and negative language, and have proved difficult
to enforce. They can also generate morale problems. "The machinery
required for more effective administration of these laws may be so
enormous and pervasive that an oppressive atmosphere of suspicion
and 'big brotherism' might result. Creativity and legitimate risk taking
might be diminished even further in bureaucratic organizations already
burdened with in-fighting, self-protection and fear" (Cooper 2006, pp.
169-170).

A good code cannot, however, ignore the law. Even a code that
is a clearly written and explicit statement of what constitutes good
conduct will fail if its provisions are in any way at odds with those found
in existing regulations or laws to which a public servant is subject. A
government cannot, for instance, support a code that endorses the
principle of sharing relevant information with clients if, at the same
time, there are confidentiality provisions in existing laws or regulations
suggesting that such sharing might be illegal.

Probably the most highly contested issue confronting code-builders
is that of optimal length. The challenge is to craft a comprehensive code
covering all of the major value dilemmas confronting public servants while
avoiding a lengthy code that has the virtue of clarity but is an unwieldy,
lifeless bureaucratic document. Case 8.1 illustrates the need to avoid the
disadvantages of both the economical "Ten Commandments" approach
and the detailed "Justinian Code" approach.

At one extreme, a code may be phrased in such vague and
nebulous language that it amounts to little more than a declaration
of pious hopes. At the other extreme, a code may be so specific and
detailed that it amounts to a lengthy and elaborate document in which
an attempt is made to incorporate all existing statutes, regulations
and guidelines relating to ethical conduct and covering every possible
contingency.

Neither approach seems to offer a workable solution. The "Ten
Commandments" approach is useful in informing public employees of
the kind of conduct expected of them. As noted above, however, it tends
to be so general that it is very difficult to apply to specific cases, and no
provision is made for penalties. The "Justinian Code" approach may be

equally unacceptable. A bulky, complex document to which few persons refer and which cannot be circulated easily may be less desirable than a very general statement of ethical standards (Kernaghan 1975, p. 11).

CASE 8.1: WHAT USE IS A CODE?

The following conversation takes place between two public servants, Steve and Tanya, during a coffee break.

Steve: I think the introduction of a code of ethics is a good way to improve the standard of conduct among public servants.

Tanya: I think codes are useless. It's totally unrealistic to assume that you can change people's behaviour by writing down a set of values and rules. General guidelines are too vague and don't help people in specific situations, and a detailed code encourages people to become too legalistic – to try and get around the rules somehow.

Steve: I don't agree. I think a code is useful as a guideline to encourage administrative responsibility. Codes have a symbolic function.

Tanya: Rules that are imposed on people from above will never effectively alter their behaviour. Ethical behaviour must be internalized – it must form part of the value system of the individual. We need to create an administrative culture in which people behave ethically because they really believe in a certain set of values.

Whose position would you defend in this case, Steve's or Tanya's? Why? If codes are used, should they be general guidelines (Ten Commandments approach), or should they be detailed enough to deal with a wide variety of circumstances (Justinian Code approach)?

One way of avoiding these two extremes is to construct a code in two parts: the individual value and rule statements that represent the "message" are interspersed with commentaries on these statements. A commentary can be no more than an explanation of the value statement or rule, or it can be made more illustrative of the behaviour being encouraged or discouraged by the inclusion of examples and even cases in which the statements or commentaries have been interpreted. The International City/Country Management Association's Code of Ethics with Guidelines (2004) supplements several major tenets with an elaborative guideline. For example:

Tenet 11

Handle all matters of personnel on the basis of merit so that fairness and impartiality govern a member's decisions, pertaining to appointments, pay adjustments, promotions, and discipline.

GUIDELINE

Equal Opportunity. All decisions pertaining to appointments, pay adjustments, promotions, and discipline should prohibit discrimination because of race, color, religion, sex, national origin, sexual orientation, political affiliation, disability, age, or marital status. It should be the members' personal and professional responsibility to actively recruit and hire a diverse staff throughout their organizations. (n.p.)

An advantage of such annotated codes is that the meaning of the value statements and rules in the code is clearer. Such codes are also excellent teaching tools, and they are flexible because the commentaries can be revised and the cases updated. This two-part approach to a code of conduct helps to get around the concern that a comprehensive code designed to apply to the whole government is likely to be too general to deal with the narrower needs of a particular department or agency. While creating more specific, supplementary codes for individual agencies with special needs is still a viable option, it is also possible to make the general code more relevant to such circumstances by tailoring the commentaries to fit the kinds of ethical challenges faced by particular agencies.

Making a Code Part of Day-to-Day Management

The best code of conduct in the world won't raise the ethical tone of a public service if the code is rooted in a hostile or indifferent organizational environment. Note that the Toronto Computer Leasing Inquiry found that the City had "an institutional culture that overlook[ed] code of conduct violations, including conflict-of-interest violations, without fear of repercussion" (Fernando 2007, p. 438).

Several of the steps that can be taken to make public sector organizations a hospitable setting for codes and, more generally, for the responsible public servant, are discussed below – with primary attention paid to values and ethics training, enforcement of ethics rules and ethical leadership.

Values and Ethics Training

The traditional rise and fall of concern about public service values and ethics has given way to more sustained concern, in part because of heightened media and public attention to governments' ethical performance. One result has been greater investment in ethics education and training, both within government and in post-secondary public administration programs. Many commentators argue that values and ethics leadership must be supplemented by more specific efforts to ensure that employees understand the values and rules contained in the code of conduct. Senior officials can demonstrate their commitment to high ethical performance by ensuring that employees at all levels of the organization are sensitized to ethical issues – and to the means of dealing with them – through formal training.[9] The long-standing practice of announcing a new code and then ignoring its existence should be replaced by a comprehensive and continuing program of ethics training, including reference to a code of conduct.

Codes can serve a useful purpose in ethics training by articulating the rules of appropriate behaviour and providing a framework for discussion of ethical issues. Ethics courses provide opportunities for applying a code to the resolution of specific issues and for consulting those affected by a code on its appropriate content and form. In addition, these courses can provide an intellectual basis and stimulus for a continuing dialogue on ethical issues.

While public servants are unlikely to "learn morality" in brief training courses, these courses can improve ethical behaviour by sensitizing participants to the ethical dimensions of their recommendations and decisions, and can help them develop skills for analysing the application of values and rules to particular issues. As noted earlier, there are many rules of varying degrees of clarity and specificity as to what constitutes ethical behaviour. Ethics training can foster understanding of what these rules mean in practice and stimulate formal changes to rules that are unrealistic or outdated.

A good way to start is to provide new employees with a thorough orientation to the values and rules contained in the code. In effect, an understanding and acknowledgment of the way the organization does business can be made a condition of employment. The process of reviewing and renewing the code can be incorporated into the normal pattern of employee training and management development. Case

---

9. For an examination of approaches to the content and conduct of ethics training, see Kernaghan and Mancino (1991).

study material can be developed from problems that have emerged inside the organization. Employees can, where appropriate, be given specialized training designed to reinforce specific values contained in the code (e.g., responsiveness and empathy toward clients). It is important that the organization recognize its responsibility for ongoing ethical sensitization. Without it, a code of conduct will have little impact on employees' behaviour.

There are substantial differences in the two major approaches to values and ethics training. The *compliance* approach focuses on the law and rules. At the extreme, it is "a largely prescriptive, coercive, punitive, and even threatening route" that is designed "to spur obedience to minimum standards and legal prohibitions" (Lewis 1991, p. 9). In contrast, the *integrity* approach tries "to create an awareness of a public service ethos, ethical standards and values, plus a process of moral reasoning to inspire exemplary actions or ethical conduct" (Hejka-Elkins 2001, p. 83). These two approaches can be effectively combined in a *fusion* approach that strives to ensure that public servants are knowledgeable about both the values and the rules of the organization (Lewis 1991, p. 11).

Values and ethics training is often one of the first programs to be sacrificed in the event of budget cuts. When this happens, the clear message to employees is that training designed to enhance the ethical culture of the organization is less important than other aspects of management. "The allocation of time, money and personnel for training in administrative ethics can be an indicator of the importance you as a leader attach to ethical conduct" (Cooper 2006, p. 209). However, technological advances promise to help offset the cost of ethics training. The federal government, for example, developed an online ethics course entitled, "Paving the Way; Values and Ethics Foundations for Employees." The course covers a broad range of values and ethics issues and uses realistic and interactive scenarios to foster understanding of approaches to resolving these issues.

Enforcement and Sanctions

Since some public servants will be unaffected by efforts to foster values and ethics-based behaviour, governments must have effective processes for preventing violations of the rules and for investigating, charging, and punishing public servants who break them. Bowman and Williams (1997) found that effective codes of ethics meet two conditions – acceptability and enforceability. Acceptability "refers to the act of getting people to conform to the ideal identified in the code of ethics," and enforceability "refers to processes whereby disciplinary actions are taken against members who are found guilty of code violations" or "to a system of rewards granted for members who exhibit a proper behaviour. There is no point in formulating a code if it does not contain a consistent and vigorous enforcement process" (Grundstein-Amado 2001, p 467-468).

There are differing views on how an effective system of enforcement and sanctions should be structured. Moreover, many governments have gradually developed a complicated ethics regime characterized by a diffusion of responsibilities and, therefore, of sanctions. Langford and Tupper (2006) have described how the "ethics program" permeates the management of the federal public service:

> Several important policy documents establish ethics as a major management responsibility. Senior officials have particularly important duties. The ethics program involves many government agencies, all senior managers and important administrative processes. It is institutionalized in new government units whose mandate is ethics management, by the designation of senior officers in departments and agencies with responsibility for ethics, by the creation of "values and ethics support networks," and by an emphasis on ethics training. (p. 126)

The various ethical problem areas in the public sector are often handled by different government agencies and under different statutes and policies. In the federal sphere, for example, the Public Service Commission manages political partisanship under the *Public Service Employment Act* (2003); the Privacy Commissioner safeguards privacy under the *Privacy Act;* and a Treasury Board policy governs workplace harassment.

Assigning responsibility for enforcing ethics codes and rules presents governments with a difficult challenge. The traditional approach is to allow senior management to administer ethical standards internally – subject, usually, to appeal to some form of staff relations board and, eventually, the courts. The downsides of this approach are that the level of enforcement can vary considerably from agency to agency, procedural rights can be violated, those doing the enforcing are often too close to the actions being questioned, and the whole process is complicated.

There is considerable controversy about the type of enforcement procedures and sanctions that should be adopted to support a code of conduct. The traditional techniques for keeping ethical order have come in for a lot of criticism. For example, because moonlighting has become more acceptable, it is now difficult to "cleanse" public servants of conflict of interest temptations by having them resign from all outside posts and divest themselves of potentially conflictual assets or place them in some form of trust. In any case, trust arrangements have often been found technically wanting: as one wag put it, "every blind trust seems to have a seeing-eye dog."

Moreover, such external "guardians" as auditors, privacy commissioners and access to information commissioners have had limited success in eradicating violations of the rules they are there to police. Part of the problem is that these guardians have insufficient authority to enforce the rules, so they are obliged to try to exercise influence by such means as filing reports on wasteful or unfair behaviour and on violations of privacy or information access rights. Where authority does exist (e.g., in relevant sections of the *Criminal Code* or *Income Tax Act*), it has often proved difficult to use for procedural reasons. Moreover, criminal sanctions are viewed by many as overkill in conflict of interest and breach of confidentiality situations. Even job-related sanctions (suspension, dismissal, etc.) are often ineffective.

The federal government supports its 2012 Values and Ethics Code by making it a condition of employment for public servants, and failure to comply with it is subject to appropriate disciplinary action, up to and including termination of employment. Alberta's Code of Conduct and Ethics (2005) provides that employees who don't comply with the Code's provisions "may be subject to disciplinary action, up to and including dismissal" (n.p.). Similarly, the City of Calgary's Code of Conduct stipulates in respect of conflicts of interest that "[t]he City will take corrective action in response to any infraction or transgression of the *Conflict of Interest Policy*. Misconduct...may result in disciplinary action being taken against the employee, up to and including dismissal from employment, seeking restitution, commencement of civil action, criminal prosecution, instructing the employee to divest [himself or herself] of the outside interest, transferring the employee to another position or any combination thereof" (Calgary 2004, p. 2).

CASE 8.2: LET THE PUBLIC HAVE A CLOSER LOOK

The following conversation takes place between Lorne and Sandy, two middle managers in a provincial public service.

Lorne: I don't think codes or legal actions are worth a damn. The only way to improve the ethical behaviour of public servants is more publicity. Why not just leave the problem up to auditing mechanisms? Publish any evidence of wrongdoing dug up by the auditor general, the ombudsperson or the information commissioner. Maybe we could even have a specialized ethics commissioner. If public servants know that their actions are being scrutinized and brought to the attention of the public, they'll be more careful.

Sandy: Is that fair? You're not giving them any guidelines to work from, but then you're saying if they misbehave they will be held up to public ridicule.

Lorne: It should be obvious to public servants how they should behave in most circumstances. The basic rule is simple – don't do anything you'd be ashamed to explain to randomly chosen members of the public. The various auditors simply become proxies for the public. Ethical behaviour wouldn't be a problem if the auditors had the power required to investigate the action of public servants and the publicity vehicles necessary to bring questionable behaviour to the attention of the public.

Would increased scrutiny and publicity ensure responsible administrative behaviour, as Lorne suggests? Would a specialized ethics commissioner add an effective capacity for scrutiny to the existing auditing mechanism?

What measures can be considered to remedy the deficiencies of the traditional approach? One option is the creation of a separate, government-wide ethics office, commission, or board – a common practice in state and municipal governments in the United States. Canada's (1984, ch. 13) federal Task Force on Conflict of Interest called on the government to establish an Office of Public Sector Ethics to administer an enforcement regime. More recently, the 2005 Bellamy inquiry on the Toronto computer scandal recommended that an integrity commissioner should have the power to recommend to City Council an appropriate range of sanctions for the misdeeds of municipal staff. Moreover, to "emphasize the importance of ethics within the organization, ethical misconduct should be regarded as among the most serious misconduct, and the sanctions should include the most serious penalties" (Bellamy 2005, p. 88).

While the adoption of this mechanism in the Canadian context should be seriously considered, there are concerns about the "big brother" connotations of a centralized enforcement bureaucracy and its impact on the effectiveness of ethical leadership by departmental managers. Questions have also been raised about the precise powers that should be granted to an ethics office. Can it work without independent investigative authority? Should it have the power to apply sanctions, or should it merely pass on its findings to the superiors of those under investigation? Can the scope of its authority be reconciled with the powers of the existing scrutiny and oversight officers (e.g., the auditor general, ombudsperson, and information and privacy commissioners)?

Another option is the disclosure – more particularly, the public disclosure – of all relevant assets and potentially conflictual outside activities as an alternative to such traditional anti-conflict of interest mechanisms as divestment, withdrawal and trusts. The theory is that if public officials' assets and outside activities are an open book, then they will be reluctant to involve themselves in decisions that might give rise to charges of conflict of interest. If charges do arise, demonstrating guilt or innocence should be relatively straightforward. According to Justice Parker (Canada. Commission of Inquiry into the Facts of Allegations of Conflict of Interest Concerning the Honourable Sinclair M. Stevens 1987):

> If modern conflict of interest codes are to
> ensure that public confidence and trust in
> the integrity, objectivity, and impartiality of
> government are conserved and enhanced, they
> must be premised on a philosophy of public
> disclosure. (p. 348)

Full public disclosure presents certain problems when applied to public servants. First, there is the sheer enormity of the numbers and the difficulties associated with managing the database, keeping it current and making it available to the public. Second, there are privacy concerns implicit in any scheme to make personal financial data available to the public and, therefore, the media. Finally, there is the matter of effectiveness. Knowing all about the outside activities and personal assets of public servants will not help to combat conflict of interest if confidentiality and anonymity combine to keep hidden the exact nature of their official duties.

Still another option is imposing hefty criminal sentences on public servants caught breaking the rules. The existence of these stiff sanctions would be the foundation of a substantial and continuing campaign designed to scare public servants into being good. From a Canadian perspective, two years in jail and fines as high as $100,000 look like powerful medicine. But would they be any more effective than the existing, underemployed criminal sanctions?

There is no easy answer to the questions that have been raised about effective enforcement procedures and sanctions. One approach may be to give up the search for "miracle" cures and concentrate first on locating the authority to employ traditional remedies in one special-purpose ethics office. The shadow cast by an ethics office dedicated exclusively to publicizing, administering and enforcing a realistic and comprehensive code of conduct might do a great deal to reduce the incidence of violations. Enforcement procedures and sanctions, while they are important, are only part of a complex mix of tools to encourage ethical conduct.

Values and Ethics Leadership

Leadership has a critical influence on public servants' values and ethics performance. Public service leaders can foster high ethical performance in two main ways – by encouraging and facilitating values and ethics-based behaviour throughout the organization, and by providing an exemplary ethical role model. The Management Accountability Framework (Public Works and Government Services Canada 2006) of the federal public service recognizes the importance of these two aspects in its leadership indicators:

> *Leadership recognized internally and externally as demonstrating strong ethics and values behaviour, as evidenced by:*
>
> * Leadership communication with employees about expected ethical behaviour and public service values;
>
> * Selection, evaluation, promotion and discharge of leaders based on their conduct with respect to PS values and ethics. (n.p.)

In addition, the federal Values and Ethics Code asserts that "Deputy Heads and senior managers have a particular responsibility to exemplify, in their actions and behaviours, the values of public service. They have a duty to infuse these values into all aspects of the work of their organizations" (Treasury Board of Canada Secretariat 2012b, n.p.).

A major determinant of an effective code of conduct is the clear and continuing commitment of senior management to the code's values and rules. As noted earlier, employee cynicism about ethical behaviour flows most directly from the perception that senior managers are paying only lip service to "good" conduct, when what they really want is "successful" conduct. To change this perception, senior managers have to demonstrate early and often their determination to see the organization pursue its goals within the behavioural boundaries laid down by the code. "Each manager must know that every one of his/her colleagues in the hierarchy has been required to adhere to the same standards as he/she must. With the leadership of the highest echelons of management, this will bring about a climate of integrity and ethical practice that all personnel will support" (Bowman 1981, p. 62).

The key to the success of this demonstration effect is getting senior managers to act as ethical role models. The evidence suggests that employees draw their inspiration from the behaviour they see, not the speeches they hear. They have to sense a consistency of behaviour that starts at the top of the organization and is reflected not only in the formal communications of their superiors but also in the "back channel" or informal information that flows through the organization. They will not place much premium on fairness, accountability, political neutrality or any other value featured in a code of conduct if they see their superiors abandoning these values in difficult circumstances. In addition, one of the singular afflictions of governmental organizations is the limited control that senior public servants have over the ethical demonstration effect of ministers. It is more difficult to persuade employees to avoid waste or conflicts of interest if ministers are spending public funds without regard for agreed-upon objectives or have a hand deep in the cookie jar.

Values and ethics-based leadership can be formalized by appointing values and ethics "champions" from among the senior public service, either on a service-wide basis or for a single department. Additional measures include the creation of a senior-level management committee on values and ethics matters and regular discussion of these matters in both senior and middle management meetings.

Although ethical leadership from both political and public service executives is essential, such leadership should not be confined to the top government officials. Mid- and junior-level employees can also serve as ethical role models, not only for their peers and subordinates but for those up the line as well. Thus a central consideration in values and ethics management is determining the best means of encouraging exemplary ethical conduct at all levels of the public service. For example, the strategies that a middle manager can use to change the ethical culture of a government organization include:

1. Remember that new rules won't help you alter peoples' attitudes and beliefs. Your approach should be more modest, but persistent and ongoing.

2. Try to build a comprehensive picture of the real beliefs and attitudes underlying your employees' behaviour...[W]ithout an accurate portrait of the existing ethical culture, you can't hope to effect change.

3. Discussions of specific ethical issues can often liberate employees from what they thought was a widely held belief or attitude.

4. Be prepared to rebuild the ethical culture incrementally. The long-term strategy is to build a consensus around small positive changes in attitudes and beliefs. (Langford 1991, pp. 54-55)

Other Values and Ethics Initiatives

In addition to the four major approaches discussed above, a wide range of other measures can foster responsible administrative behaviour.

In terms of formal structure, an increasingly popular measure is the creation of values and ethics offices (or just officers) for the public service as a whole or for individual departments. In 1999, the federal government established the Office of Public Service Values and Ethics within the Treasury Board Secretariat as a centre of expertise and leadership responsible for furthering values-based management within the public service. The Office, which made substantial progress in improving the values and ethics regime, was later downgraded to become part of a unit on Values and Ethics, Awards and Recognition in the Office of the Chief Human Resources Officer.

Some federal departments have their own values and ethics offices. For example, the Ethics Directorate of Public Works and Government Services Canada (PWGSC) manages the department's Ethics Program, which seeks to "support ethical leadership and improve the ethical climate " (Canada 2009, n.p.). Many federal departments have appointed ethics officers, advisors or counsellors to foster high ethical standards. In PWGSC, a Director of Ethics oversees the implementation of the Ethics Program, which has five main activities:

- Develops policies and practices that clarify or integrate values and ethics-related issues. This includes integrating values and ethics in strategic frameworks and core business lines and processes.

- Provides values and ethics advice and guidance to PWGSC employees...

- Educates PWGSC employees about values and ethics. This includes the delivery of mandatory and optional ethics training sessions, as well as the development of tailored workshops and dialogue sessions.

- Engages values and ethics leaders through the establishment of partnerships with the branches/regions/agencies, identifies "values champions" within PWGSC and educates senior leaders on values and ethics messages.

- Conducts research and development within the ethics field. This includes conducting research on best practices, developing a values and ethics learning strategy and building partnerships with other government departments. (Canada 2009, n.p.).

Note also that virtually every federal department has a senior official for public service values to support values-based leadership, and a senior officer for disclosure of wrongdoing who is responsible for implementing the *Public Servants Disclosure Protection Act* in the department (Treasury Board of Canada Secretariat 2013). In the municipal sphere, the report of the Toronto Computer Leasing Inquiry (the Bellamy Inquiry) suggested that, in addition to a City-wide integrity commission, "ethics coordinators" could be appointed for each City department to whom staff could turn for department-specific and confidential ethical advice (Bellamy 2005, p. 86).

The foregoing discussion makes clear that values and ethics considerations are a pervasive element in human resources management, including staffing processes. For instance, hiring procedures should involve questions that probe the values and ethical standards of applicants, and performance evaluation and incentive systems should reward behaviour that is in line with the key values in a code of conduct. Another important spur to ethical conduct is open government. Commitment to openness, transparency and public participation includes effective access to information laws and open data systems that enable the public and the media to better assess government's ethical performance.

Still other measures for fostering values- and ethics-based behaviour are:

- Developing a multi-year plan for integrating values and ethics

- Developing policies and guidelines for high-risk areas

- Ensuring that business plans have a values and ethics component

- Developing values and ethics learning materials

- Making values and ethics dialogue an integral part of staff meetings

- Conducting exit interviews with departing employees regarding their values and ethics experience

- Encouraging the formation of a values and ethics community across the public service

- Developing a checklist for managers to assess their organization's ethical regime (e.g., code of conduct, ethics training)

- Adopting an ethics hotline through which public servants can anonymously report allegations of wrongdoing (a controversial measure).

A small number of non-governmental organizations are devoted to promoting ethics in the public service or in the political realm, or both. The Federal Accountability Initiative for Reform (FAIR 2013) is the leading whistle blower advocacy organization in Canada. Its aim is to promote "integrity and accountability within government by empowering employees to speak out without fear of reprisal when they encounter wrongdoing" (n.p.). FAIR provides a lengthy and informative list of current whistle-blowing stories on its website http://fairwhistleblower. ca. Democracy Watch (2013) also monitors public service ethics but has much broader terms of reference. It is "a national non-profit, non-partisan organization, and Canada's leading citizen group advocating democratic reform, government accountability and corporate responsibility" (n.p.). Notable also is Transparency International Canada (2013), which is affiliated with 90 other National Chapters around the world. Its mission is to be "an informed voice that promotes anti-corruption practices and transparency in Canada's governments, businesses and society at large" (p. 1).

Measuring Values and Ethics Performance

The success of the mechanisms discussed above will depend to a large extent on the information that public servants – and especially their leaders – have about the state of values and ethics in their organizations. Are employees knowledgeable about the existence and content of the organization's code of conduct? Is there sufficient values and ethics training? Is the training perceived as effective? Do managers act as appropriate ethical role models? Is there fair and consistent enforcement of ethical standards?

Among the means by which values and ethics performance can be assessed are ethics reviews or audits, employee surveys, case studies and focus groups. The measures of performance can include *implementation* – to ensure that policies are in place and initiatives taken; *activities and outputs* – to ensure that established systems are operating; *institutional effectiveness* – to assess the overall performance of an ethics agency or system such as an Ethics Office; and *outcomes/results* – to ensure that ethics activities produce the intended results (OECD 2008, September 22, p. 5).

An especially strong argument can be made for a values and ethics review or audit. The possible benefits identified by Kaptein et al. (2005) are:

- First, by involving employees, the organization shows, not only that ethics receives managerial attention, but also that employee opinions count.

- Second, consulting employees stimulates their awareness of ethical issues in their own functions.

- Third, conducting an ethics review fosters support among employees for tackling ethical issues.

- [Fourth], employees may be aware of types of unethical conduct that their managers know nothing about.

- [Fifth],...the ethics of an organization is strongly influenced by how employees experience the organizational context. (p. 307).

Employee surveys can effectively inform a review or audit and can occur at a service-wide or an organizational level. The 2008 report on the federal government employee survey asserted that values were a pervasive influence in the public service. "Values are also a fundamental component of leadership itself, a place where 'walking the talk' has particular significance. It is also important that leaders work to create the right organizational environment where employees feel empowered to do the right thing" (Treasury Board of Canada Secretariat 2008, n.p.). The very brief values section of the federal survey found that the majority of employees believed they could disagree with their immediate supervisor on work-related issues without fear of reprisal and that supervisors could be counted on to keep promises. Kaptein et al. (2005) argue for the use of employee surveys to enhance the leadership's appreciation of the impact of organizational climate on ethical conduct and to inform leaders of the extent of unethical conduct in the organization.

CASE 8.3: PUT THEM IN THE SLAMMER

Nadiya and Tom, two federal public servants, are talking after a staff meeting at which a serious conflict of interest case was on the agenda.

Nadiya: I don't think I like the idea of using jail terms and fines to ensure ethical conduct.

Tom: You've got to force people to behave.

Nadiya: It seems to me to be awfully severe punishment. Take the example of a public official who accepts a bottle of liquor from one of his clients at Christmas. Turning something like this into a crime is like swatting a fly with a sledgehammer.

Tom: Yes, but maybe that official would never have accepted the bottle in the first place if he had known he might face the prospect of a court case and criminal charges. As it stands, suspensions and even job loss don't represent sufficient discouragement. Sanctions like this just don't seem to stop people from acting irresponsibly.

Nadiya: Maybe so, but I think jail terms and fines are a bit much. I know I would certainly be hesitant to come forward and accuse one of my employees if I knew he or she might go to jail or face a major fine.

Are criminal sanctions appropriate antidotes to unethical behaviour? Would they be more effective than the prospect of suspension or job loss? Would managers be more reluctant to take on cases of unethical conduct if criminal sanctions were involved? Would the existence of stronger sanctions encourage public confidence and trust in the public sector?

Conclusion

The focus in this chapter has been on the problem of designing a regime of institutions, mechanisms, procedures and sanctions that will foster and sustain responsible administrative behaviour among public servants. We have argued for the development of realistic and accessible codes of conduct. Since rules alone cannot be successful in promoting ethical behaviour, we have also emphasized the need for more attention to training to promote personal moral development and behaviour. We have stressed the importance of moving away from "top down" systems of rules, sanctions and scrutiny in favour of more participative and supportive mechanisms. Involving employees in discussions about codes of conduct will help make them part of the rule-making process and supporters of an ethical administrative culture. Instead of constructing more elaborate enforcement and control mechanisms, we recommend instruments such as ethics counsellors to promote agency-level discussion and resolution of value conflicts. There is still a place for fair enforcement and reasonable sanctions, but training, counseling, "bottom up" development of a code of conduct and good role models are more significant building blocks of a responsible public service. Finally, we note that a values and ethics regime will be much more successful if its content and impact are formally reviewed on a regular basis.

The challenge is to create an environment in which public servants respect the values and rules established within their respective governments and, over time, internalize them as habitual considerations in their decision making. "[I]f the codes' provisions are accepted and internalized, then the enforcement process is less needed. Instead of focusing on sanctioning or rewarding members for their actions, efforts should be directed toward transforming individuals' values system to reach the point when employees...have taken the accepted norms and rules as their own" (Grundstein-Amado 2001, p. 468). As long as these norms and rules are ethically defensible, this is a critically important means of fostering the personal moral responsibility of public servants emphasized throughout this book.

References

Alberta, Personnel Administration Office. (2005). *Code of conduct and ethics for the public service of Alberta*. Retrieved from http://www.assembly.ab.ca/lao/library/egovdocs/2005/alpe/158311.pdf

Bellamy, D. (2005). *Toronto computer leasing inquiry.* Vol. 4. Toronto: City of Toronto. Retrieved from http://www.toronto.ca/inquiry/ inquiry_site/report/pdf/TCLI_TECI_Report_Executive_Summary.pdf

Bowman, J. B. (1981). The management of ethics: Codes of conduct in organizations. *Public Personnel Management Journal*, 10(1), 59-66.

Bowman, J. B., & Williams, R. L. (1997). Ethics in government: From a winter of despair to a spring of hope. *Public Administration Review*, 57(6), 517-526.

Calgary, Corporate Administration. (2004, September 21). *Administration policy: Code of conduct*, HR-LR-005.

Canada. (1987). Commission of Inquiry into the Facts of Allegations of Conflict of Interest Concerning the Honourable Sinclair M. Stevens. *Report.* Ottawa: Supply and Services Canada. Chaired by the Honourable W. D. Parker.

Canada. (2006). Commission of Inquiry into the Sponsorship Program and Advertising Activities. *Restoring accountability: Recommendations [Phase 2 Report].* Ottawa: Public Works and Government Services Canada. Chaired by Justice J. H. Gomery. Retrieved from http://www.hrsdc.gc.ca/eng/publications_ resources/audit/2008/0060309/page02.shtml

Canada, Public Service Human Resources Management Agency. (2004). *Working group on the disclosure of wrongdoing.* Report. Ottawa: Public Works and Government Services Canada.

Canada, Public Works and Government Services Canada. (2006). *2005-2006 PWGSC Management Accountability Framework self-assessment.* Retrieved from http://www.tpsgc-pwgsc.gc.ca/ apropos-about/crg-maf/2005-2006-eng.html

Canada, Public Works and Government Services Canada. (2009). *Evaluation of the PWGSC Ethics Program (2008-610)*: Final Report. Retrieved from http://www.tpsgc-pwgsc.gc.ca/bve-oae/rapports-reports/.../2008-610-eng.pdf

Canada, Task Force on Conflict of Interest. (1984). *Ethical conduct in the public sector.* Ottawa: Supply and Services Canada.

Canadian Centre for Management Development. (1996). *A strong foundation: Report of the Task Force on Public Service Values and Ethics.* Ottawa: CCMD. Retrieved from http://publications.gc.ca/ collections/Collection/SC94-72-1996E.pdf

Chandler, R. C. (1983). The problem of moral reasoning in public administration. *Public Administration Review, 43*(1), 32-39.

City of Toronto. (2009). Toronto Municipal Code Lobbying By-Law, c. 140. *City of Toronto Act*, S.O. 2006, c. 11. Retrieved from http://www.toronto.ca/legdocs/municode/1184_140.pdf

Cooper, T. (2006). *The responsible administrator: An approach to ethics for the administrative role* (5th ed.). San Francisco: Jossey-Bass.

Democracy Watch. (2013). *About Democracy Watch*. Retrieved from http://democracywatch.ca/about/

Department of Justice Canada. (2013). *Criminal Code* (R.S.C., 1985, c. C-46, ss. 119-121). Retrieved from http://laws-lois.justice.gc.ca/eng/acts/C-46/FullText.html

FAIR (Federal Accountability Initiative for Reform). (2013). *Our mission*. Retrieved from http://fairwhistleblower.ca

Fernando, S. (2007). Ethics and good urban governance in Toronto. *Canadian Public Administration, 50*(3), 437-448.

Gow, J. I. (2008). Between ideals and obedience: Seeking a practical basis for public service ethics. In D. Siegel & K. Rasmussen (Eds.), *Professionalism and public service: Essays in honour of Kenneth Kernaghan* (pp. 99-126). Toronto: University of Toronto Press.

Grundstein-Amado, R. (2001). A strategy for formulation and implementation of codes of ethics in public service organizations. *International Journal of Public Administration, 24*(5), 461-478.

Heintzman, R. (2007). Public service values and ethics: Dead end or strong foundation? *Canadian Public Administration, 50*(4), 573-602.

Heintzman, R. (2013). Establishing the boundaries of the public service: Toward a new moral contract. In J. Bickerton and B. G. Peters (Eds.), *Governing: Essays in honour of Donald J. Savoie* (pp. 85-138). Kingston: McGill-Queen's University Press.

Hejka-Elkins, A. (2001). Ethics in in-service training. In T. L. Cooper (Ed.), *Handbook of administrative ethics* (2nd ed., pp. 79-103). New York: Marcel Dekker.

International City/Country Management Association. (2004). *The ICMA code of ethics with guidelines.* Washington, DC. Retrieved from http://icma.org/en/Page/72/The_ICMA_Code_of_Ethics_with_Guidelines

Kaptein, M., Huberts, L., Avelino, S., & Lasthuizen, K. (2005). Demonstrating ethical leadership by measuring ethics: A survey of U.S. public servants. *Public Integrity, 7*(4), 299-311.

Kernaghan, K. (1974). Codes of ethics and administrative responsibility. *Canadian Public Administration, 17*(4), 527-541.

Kernaghan, K. (1975). *Ethical conduct: Guidelines for government employees.* Toronto: Institute of Public Administration of Canada.

Kernaghan, K. (1980). Codes of ethics and public administration: Progress, problems and prospects. *Public Administration, 58*(2), 207-224.

Kernaghan, K. (1997). Shaking the foundation: New versus traditional public-service values. In M. Charih & A. Daniels (Eds.), *New public management and public administration in Canada* (pp. 47-65). Toronto: Institute of Public Administration of Canada.

Kernaghan, K. (2003). Integrating values into public service: The values statement as centerpiece. *Public Administration Review, 63*(6), 711-719.

Kernaghan, K. (2007). *A special calling: Values, ethics and professional public service.* Ottawa: Public Service Human Resources Management Agency of Canada.

Kernaghan, K., & Mancino, S. (1991). Approaches to ethics education. *Canadian Public Administration, 34*(1), 184-191.

Langford, J. W. (1991). Building an ethical government organization: A micro approach for middle managers. *Optimum: Journal of Public Sector Management, 21*(2), 49-55.

Langford, J. W. (2004). Acting on values: An ethical dead end for public servants. *Canadian Public Administration, 47*(4), 429-450.

Langford, J. W., & Tupper, A. (2006). How Ottawa does business: Ethics as a government program. In G. B. Doern (Ed.), *How Ottawa spends, 2006-2007* (pp. 116-137). Kingston: McGill-Queen's University Press.

Levine, G. J. (2009). *Municipal ethics regimes.* St. Thomas, ON: Municipal World.

Lewis, C. (1991). *The ethics challenge in public service: A problem solving guide.* San Francisco: Jossey-Bass.

Lobbying Act. (1985). In Statutes of Canada, R.S.C. 1985, c. 44 (4th Supp.).Retrieved from http://laws.justice.gc.ca/eng/acts/L-12.4/

Lobbyists Registration Act. (1998). In Statutes of Ontario, S.O. 1998, Chapter 27. Retrieved from http://www.e-laws.gov.on.ca/html/statutes/english/elaws_statutes_98I27_e.htm

McGraw, D. K. (2004). A social contract theory critique of professional codes of ethics. *Journal of Information, Communication and Ethics in Society, 2(*4), 235-243.

New Brunswick. (2009). *Public service values and conduct guide.* Retrieved from http://www2.gnb.ca/content/dam/gnb/Departments/ohr-brh/pdf/other/values_conduct_guide.pdf

Office of the Commissioner of Lobbying in Canada. (2012). *The lobbyists' code of conduct.* Retrieved from https://www.ic.gc.ca/eic/site/012.nsf/eng/h_00014.html

Organization for Economic Cooperation and Development (OECD). (2008, September 22). *Current Practices in Measuring Values and Ethics Performance.* GOV/PGC/ETH/RD(2008)2. Paris: OECD.

Plant, J. F. (2001). Codes of ethics. In T. Cooper (Ed.), *Handbook of administrative ethics* (pp. 309-333). New York: Marcel Dekker.

Public Servants Disclosure Protection Act. (2005). In Statutes of Canada, c. 46, s. 8. Retrieved from http://laws-lois.justice.gc.ca/PDF/P-31.9.pdf

Public Service Employment Act. (2003). In Statutes of Canada, c. 22, s. 112.

Public Service of Ontario Act. (2006). In Statutes of Ontario, c. 35, Part V, p. 85, s. 2.

Security of Information Act. (1985). In Statutes of Canada, R.S.C. 1985, c. O-5). Retrieved from http://laws-lois.justice.gc.ca/eng/acts/O-5/

Transparency International Canada. (2013). *Overview.* Retrieved from http://www.transparency.ca

Treasury Board of Canada Secretariat. (2008). *Public servants on the public service of Canada: Summary of the results of the 2008 public service employee survey.* Retrieved from http://www.tbs-sct.gc.ca/pses-saff/2008/report-rapport-eng.asp

Treasury Board of Canada Secretariat. (2012a). *Policy on conflict of interest and post-employment.* Retrieved from http://www.tbs-sct.gc.ca/pol/doc-eng.aspx?section=text&id=25178

Treasury Board of Canada Secretariat. (2012b). *Values and ethics code for the public sector.* Retrieved from http://www.tbs-sct.gc.ca/pol/doc-eng.aspx?id=25049&section=text#cha5

Treasury Board of Canada Secretariat. (2013). *Resources on the public servants disclosure protection act.* Retrieved from http://www.tbs-sct.gc.ca/ve/pda-eng.asp

Van Wart, M. (1998). *Changing public sector values.* New York: Garland.

INDEX

360-degree accountability, 235
9/11, 190
Abella I. & Troper H., 15
abolitionists, 73
Aboriginal rights, 43
abuse, 155
abuse of power, 225
    examples in Canada, 16
Acceptable Use of City Technology
    Resources Policy, City of Calgary, 146
accepting benefits
    category of conflict of interest, 144
    historical rule of thumb, 144
access to information legislation. *See*
    freedom of information legislation
accountability. *see also* personal
    responsibility
    360-degree, 235
    case study, 218
    cases in law, 223
    chain of, 215
    collective, 227–31
    complaint-driven, 232
    control-oriented, 221
    defined, 215
    difficulties assigning, 240
    dimensions of, 216
    Friedrich versus Finer debate, 217, 232
    in legislation, 218
    increased oversight, 222–27
    of supervisors, 226
    outward versus upward, 234
    oversight agencies, 224
    paradox of, 241
    participatory, 234–37
    peer-to-peer, 232, 233
    performance-based, 219–22
    preconditions for ensuring, 229
    professional, 231–34
    questions examined, 214
    senior responsible owner, 231
    to conscience, 238–39
    traditional narrative, 214–19
    versus answerability, 226
Accountable Government: A Guide for
    Ministers and Ministers of State, 104,
    112
act utilitarians, 55

Adams G. & Balfour D., 15
addiction, 155
administrative evil, 15
Advanced Passenger Information/Passenger
    Name Record, 191
Afghan detainees, 176, 225
Afghanistan, 21, 84
agent-neutral decision making, 54
Air Transport Association of Canada, 152
Alberta, 22, 52, 59, 115, 124, 144, 168,
    172, 188, 217, 218, 220, 263
Alberta Corporate Human Resources, 166
Alberta Government, 172
Alberta Public Affairs Bureau, 168
Alberta Public Service, 61
Alberta Public Service Vision and Values
    Handbook, 59, 217
Alberta Securities Commission, 16
Alberta, Personnel Administration Office, 131,
    145
Alford F., 171
Alliance for Climate Protection, 174
Alonso P. & Lewis G. B., 75
Amy D. J., 19, 82
Anglican prayer book, 120
anonymity of public servants, 106–9, 215
    erosion of, 107
answerability
    versus accountability, 226
Anti-Terrorism Act, 166
apparent conflict of interest, 136
    example of, 138
    test for, 136
Appiah K. A., 41
Applbaum A., 28
applied ethics, 1, *see also* ethical behaviour
Aquinas, Thomas, 50
Arar, Maher, 16, 227
art of voice, 30
asbestos, 17
Association of BC Forest Professionals, 232
Atmospheric Environment Service, 138
Atomic Energy of Canada, 20
Attawapiskat First Nation v. Canada, 223
Aucoin P., 61, 101, 109
Aucoin P. & Heintzman R., 220
Aucoin P. & Jarvis M., 213
Auditor General of Ontario, 16

audits
external, 224
internal, 223
of ethical behaviour, 271–72
Australia, 1, 20, 173
Australian Department of Finance and
Deregulation, 173
Australian Public Service Commission, 173
awareness of wrongdoing, 26
Bardach E., 21
Barkat H. et al., 172
Barnard, Chester, 19
Bayles M., 180
BC Liberals
ethnic vote scandal, 113
Begin, Monique, 25
Behn R., 221, 228, 235
beliefs, 42
cultural differences, 42
versus moral judgments, 44
Bell S., 132, 146
Bellamy D., 16, 132, 265, 269
Belluz J., 17
Benn S., 196
Bennett C., 42
Benoit L., 112, 113
Bentham, Jeremy, 55
Bentley, Arthur F., 73
bias
in decision making, 89
big brotherism, 257, 265
Bishop v. Trochu (Town), 124
blame avoidance, 18
blame shifting, 23, 240
Bok S., 174, 176, 180, 181
Boston J. et al., 81
Bovens M., 234
Bowman J. B., 267
Bowman J. B. & Williams R. L., 261
Brady F. N., 58
Braidwood Commission, 16
Brandt B., 42
Brewer G. A. et al., 75
British Columbia, 17, 22, 86, 113, 123, 134,
152, 169, 173, 188
British Columbia Civil Liberties Association,
186, 192
British Columbia, Deputy Minister to the
Premier, 113
British Columbia, Public Service Agency,
123, 134, 142, 167, 218
British subjects, 17

Broader Public Sector Accountability Act, 217
Brockman J., 231
Brown P., 63
Buchanan J. M. & Tullock G., 73
Business Development Bank, 145
CAC. See Consulting and Audit Canada
Calgary, 80, 146, 263
City of, 124, 132
Calgary, Corporate Administration, 146
Calgary, Corporate Services, 124
Canada, 20, 49, 80, 103, 105, 109, 116,
136, 137, 139, 157, 169, 170, 172,
173, 175, 188, 190, 215, 248, 253,
264, 268
Canada Border Service Agency, 191
Canada Revenue Agency, 139, 150
Canada, Privy Council Office, 104, 112
Canada, Public Service Commission, 105,
119, 120
Canada, Public Service Labour Relations
Board, 137, 143
Canada, Public Service Staff Relations
Board, 121, 122, 137, 150, 157
Canada, Task Force on Conflict of Interest,
139, 141
Canadian Air Transportation Administration,
151
Canadian Centre for Management
Development, 59, 61, 71, 74, 79, 216, 226,
254
Canadian Constitution, 48, 50, 64
Canadian Food Inspection Agency, 137
Canadian Human Rights Museum, 17
Canadian Nuclear Safety Commission, 20
Canadian Red Cross Society, 25
Canadian Security Intelligence Service, 16,
122
Canadian Standards Association Model
Code for the Protection of Personal
Information, 187
candour, 180
case studies
accountability, 218
codes of conduct, 258
collective accountability, 230
confidentiality, 183
conflict of interest, 143, 147
deception, 184
dirty hands, 34
fraud, 199
loyalty, 111
many hands, 33

outside employment, 149
participatory accountability, 237
performance reporting, 222
personal responsibility, 32
political rights, 117
political staff, 113
post-employment, 154
public comment, 123
public interest, 74, 88
public scrutiny, 264
relativism, 46
risk assessment, 84
sanctions, 272
social media, 200
superior's hands, 31
surveillance, 201
whistle blower, 185
Cassinelli W., 74
categorical imperative, 51, 126, 141
Cavoukian D., 199
CBC Fifth Estate, 17
CBC News, 20, 168, 227
censorship, 180
in wartime, 182
census
controversy over, 21, 124
centralized control of public service, 15, 221
CFIA. *See* Canadian Food Inspection Agency
CGI Group, 228
chain of accountability, 215
champions. *See* leadership
Chandler R. C., 250
Charbonneau Commission, 13
Charter of Human Rights and Freedoms, 187
Charter of Public Service, 253
Charter of Rights and Freedoms, 15, 21, 43, 50, 114, 123, 187, 222
Chase S. & Grant T., 21
Chinese National Offshore Oil Corporation, 80
Citizen 172, 236
citizen engagement, 172, 177
example of, 172
limited effect of, 173
Citizenship and Immigration Canada, 146
civil servants. *See* public servants
Civil Service Values and Ethics Guide, 94
Clark I. & Swain H., 224
Cleveland H., 178, 202
Cochran C. E., 73, 74
Code of Conduct, 174
Code of Conduct and Ethics for the Public

Service of Alberta, 131, 144, 166, 263
Code of Conduct, City of Calgary, 263
Code of Conduct, New Brunswick, 104
Code of Ethics, Parks Canada, 104
codes of conduct, 248–53
achieving credibility, 256
balancing length and detail, 257
benefits of, 250
case study, 258
commentary in, 258
conflicts between, 251
consultation in creating, 256
difficulty enforcing, 249
hospitable setting for, 259
limitations of, 250
lobbying, 252
of professions, 251
subject to law, 257
values and rules in, 253-56
variations across jurisdictions, 248
writing successful, 256–59
coercive state power, 15
Cohen J., 177, 196
Cold War, 15
collective accountability, 227-31
and professional associations, 233
case study, 230
complications of, 227
failure of, 231
collective responsibility, 26, 214
Colvin, Richard, 21
command and control model, 15
commandments
and intuitionism, 50
defined, 7
divine, 53
relevance today, 10
commentary
to illustrate codes of conduct, 258
Commission d'accès à information du Québec, 190
Commission on Freedom of Information and Individual Privacy, 177, 178
Commissions of Inquiry
Bellamy, 132, 259, 264, 269
Braidwood, 16
Charbonneau, 13
Gomery, 113, 254
Maher Arar, 16, 227
Oliphant, 151
Parker, 136, 137, 265
sponsorship scandal, 16

tainted blood scandal, 16
Walkerton, 16
common good. *See* public interest
Communications Security Establishment Canada, 191
communities of belief, 45
compatibility of interests, 141
competing values, 61, 92, 115, 254
compliance approach
    to ethics training, 261
computer leasing scandal, 16, 259, 264, 269
Confederation, 101
confidentiality, 164–68
    case study, 183
    questions examined, 163
    required by oaths and laws, 165
    versus disclosure, 182
    vulnerability to abuse of power, 179
conflict of interest
    case study, 143, 147
    categories of, 142
        accepting benefits, 144
        influence peddling, 146
        outside employment, 148
        personal conduct, 155
        post-employment, 151
        self-dealing, 142
        using confidential information, 147
        using government property, 146
    changing focus of concern, 134
    consequences to society, 138–42
    continuum of severity, 142
    defining duty with respect to, 131–36
    disclosure, 265
    examples of, 132, 154
    failed attempts, 138
    financial gain, 132
    insider trading, 148
    lobbying, 151
    non-financial gain, 132
    questions examined, 131
    types of, 136-38
        apparent, 136
        potential, 137
        real, 136, 137
Conflict of Interest Code, Canada Revenue
    Agency, 150
Conflict of Interest Policy, 135, 145, 166
conflicting interests, 90
Confucian rule of reciprocity, 53
consensualist approach

to making policy decisions, 91
consensus, 91
    on ethical behaviour, 47
consequentialism, 48, 58
    challenges to, 57
    cost-benefit analysis, 89
    suitability in the public service, 58
consequentialist approach
    in defence of secrecy, 174
    in defence of transparency, 179
    in defence of whistle blowing, 179
    to balancing political neutrality and
        political rights, 126
    to conflicts of interest, 141
    to privacy, 194
consequentialists, 27
Conservative Party of Canada, 110, 115, 172
Consulting and Audit Canada, 143
Consulting with Canadians, 173
Consumer Measures Committee, 187, 188
Consumer Packaging and Labelling Act, 72
contextual integrity, 198
contractarianism, 49
cooling off period
    leaving public service, 153, 252
Cooper T., 261
Cooper T. & Bryer T., 18
Cooper T. & Wright D., 18
Cooper T. L., 59, 61, 62, 131, 238
Correctional Service of Canada, 18
corruption, 3, 138, 141
cost-benefit analysis, 83
    in making policy decisions, 89
Council of Forest Industries, 152
Cousineau S., 80
Crewson P. E., 75
Criminal Code, 3, 25, 135, 142, 144, 146, 164, 165, 189, 205, 248, 263, 275
criteria for moral responsibility, 29
critical comment. *see also* dissent
    resignation as a form of, 123
    versus public comment, 121
Crotty M., 42
CSA. *See* Canadian Standards Association
cultural practices
    examples of relativism, 42, 43
culture of transparency, 182
Curzon D., 179
Davis S., 194, 196
De George R., 45
deception, 24, 161, *see also* propaganda
    case study, 184

to fight crime or terror, 181
DeCew J., 186, 195
decision making
"veil of ignorance", 53
agent-neutral, 54
analyzing risk in the public interest, 82–86
bias, 89
consequentialist approach to, 48
complexity of, 56
consulting stakeholders, 94
effect of public perception on, 47
example using reflective equilibrium, 64
fully informed, 179
identifying stakeholders' interests, 56, 94
influence of ideology on, 89, 239
influence of political staff on, 112
justifying, 47–62
power of public servants, 5, 14
pragmatic approach to, 54
privacy considerations, 201
public participation in, 107
public policy, 80–82
reconciling conflicting interests, 90
reconciling public opinion and technical analysis, 93
reflective equilibrium approach to, 63
relativism in, 41–44
requirement to justify, 48
risk assessment in, 83
role of beliefs in, 42
role of conscience in, 238
secrecy during, 175
examples of, 176
transparency, 174
using public interest as a guideline, 91
using virtue ethics, 58–62
defending decisions. See justifying decisions
democracy. see also Westminster model
importance of privacy protection in, 195
participatory accountability in, 236
role of information in, 176
secrecy as an obstacle to, 178
Democracy Watch, 270
demonstration effect. See leadership
Denhardt J. V. & Denhardt R. B., 72, 74, 213
Denhardt K., 59
deontologists. See duty theorists
Department of Aboriginal Affairs, 223
Department of Agriculture, 148
Department of Employment and Immigration, 150

Department of Energy, Mines and Resources, 152
Department of External Affairs, 17
Department of Fisheries and Oceans, 17
Department of Foreign Affairs and International Trade, 120, 121, 145
Department of Justice Canada, 18, 21, 165, 187, 189, 225, 248
Department of the Environment, 138
Department of the Secretary of State, 143
Departmental Performance Reports, 220
digital age, 192
Dilulio J. D., 75
Directive on Privacy Impact Assessment, 190
dirty hands, 13, 84
case study, 34
excuse for rejecting personal responsibility, 26
disclosure
of interests by public servants, 265
discretion, 121–25, 171
discrimination, 3, 80, 195
disinformation. See deception
dissent
attempts by federal Government to stifle, 124
formal and informal options, 30
moral obligation to, 30
whistle blowing as an act of, 179
divine
commandments, 53
revelation, 48
right of kings, 174
standard for ethical behaviour, 50
Dobel J. P., 131
Dobell A. R., 93
dominant principle approach
to making policy decisions, 86
Donahue A. K., 82
double standards, 43
Downs A., 92
Drucker P., 47
drug and alcohol testing, 191
Dubnick M., 215, 232, 234
Dunleavy P. et al., 236
Dunn W. N., 81
Dutil P., 112
Dutil P. et al., 231
duty ethics, 48
approach to accountability, 234
approach to conflicts of interest, 141
flaws of, 54

right versus good, 50
to privacy, 196
duty theorists, 48, 126
duty to report, 22, 126, 227
Dworkin T. & Baucus M., 171
Dziekanski, Robert, 226
Edmonton, 172
Egger, Rowland, 61
e-Gov, 236
E-Health Ontario contracting scandal, 16
Ellis R., 51, 62, 222
Ellis R. D., 83
end-point ethics, 57
enforcement
of ethical behaviour, 261-66
challenges, 262
entrapment, 181
equal opportunity, 259
equality, 89
Eshleman A., 13
ethic of neutrality, 19, 72
flaws of, 22, 25
ethic of structure, 24
ethical behaviour
commandments defining, 7
competing edicts, 10
divine or natural standard, 50
increased attention towards, 3
intention versus outcome, 90
justifying, 47–62
legislating, 257
managing effectiveness of values
versus rules, 254
other methods for, 268
questions examined, 247
through codes of conduct, 248–53
through enforcement and sanctions,
261–66
through leadership, 266–68
through training, 260–61
measuring, 271–72
media coverage of, 4
modelled by senior management, 267
moral dilemmas, 3
pluralism, 47
precautionary principle, 84
principles, 50
public interest as a guide to, 86–91
relativism, 41–44
rules governing, 1
spirit versus letter of law, 119
strategies for encouraging, 268

ethical relativism. See relativism
ethical theories, 2
feminist, 49
integrating conflicting, 62, 66
public choice, 73
social contract, 251
ethics "champions", 267
Ethics Directorate of Public Works and
Government Services Canada, 268
ethics of care, 49
ethics of prudence, 47
ethics office, 266, 268
Etzioni A., 195
exempt staff. See political staff
exit option, 30
external audits, 224
F-35 military aircraft scandal, 224
Facebook, 120
FAIR, 21, 170, 171, 270
Fair Information Practices, 187, 192, 197
FBI, 195
Federal Accountability Act, 217
Federal Accountability Initiative for Reform.
See FAIR
federal communications policy, 85, 167
Federal Court of Canada, 136
feminist ethics, 49
Ferguson J. & King D., 144
Fernando S., 259
financial gain, 132
Finer H., 16, 217
Fisheries Act, 17
Fisheries and Oceans Canada, 225
Flaherty D., 187, 190
Florini A., 177
FOI. See freedom of information
Forcese C., 165, 170
Ford, Toronto Mayor Rob, 20
Foreign Affairs, 21
Fraser L., 172
Fraser v. Canada, 109, 115, 122
fraud, 165, 195, 248
case study, 199
freedom of expression, 182
Freedom of Information and Protection of
Privacy Act, 86, 188
freedom of information legislation, 164
anonymity concerns, 107
exemptions and exclusions, 175
limitations of, 165, 170
reduced record-keeping as a result of,
170

uptake in all jurisdictions, 169
Fried C., 52, 195
Friedrich C., 217, 232, 238
fusion approach
    to ethics training, 261
future employment. *See* post-employment
Galbraith, John Kenneth, 195
Garofalo C. & Geuras D., 59, 62
Gauthier D., 49
Gavison R., 195
Gergin M., 124
Gerstein R., 195
gifts. *See* accepting benefits
Globe and Mail, 13, 80
golden rule, 53
Gomery Commission, 113, 254
Good D. A., 103
Goodin R., 58
Goodsell C. T., 91
Gortner H., 33
Gov 2.0, 236
Government Accountability Act, 217
Government of Canada, 165
Gow J. I., 256
Gowans C., 44
Greenwood C., 168
Gregory R., 241
Grimshaw D. et al., 231
group norms, 256
Grundstein-Amado R., 247, 262, 273
guardian moral syndrome, 27
Guidelines for External Use of Web 2.0, 168
Halifax, 172
Hamilton M. R., 72
harassment, 3, 262
Harmon M., 241
Harper Government, 108
Harper, Prime Minister Stephen, 172, 217
Harrison J., 44
Hart D. L., 59
Harvard, 195
Health Canada, 17, 25, 42, 86
Heintzman R., 61, 62,76, 78, 79, 86, 254, 255
Hejka-Elkins A., 261
Held V., 49
Heritage Canada, 121
Hersh S., 21
Hillel, Rabbi, 53
hiring
    considering applicants' values, 269
    equal opportunity, 259

Hirschman A., 30
HIV/AIDS, 191
Hobbes T., 27
Hodge G., 77
Hodgetts J. E., 91
homosexuals
    treatment by Security Panel, 15
Hondeghem A. & Perry J. L., 75
Hood C., 18, 24, 220, 240
Hubbard R., 79
Hubbard R. & Paquet G., 78
Human Rights Watch, 174
Hume M., 17
Hupe P. & Hill M., 234
Hursthouse R., 60
Hyson S., 224
Iacobucci F., 16
IBM, 228
identity theft, 192, 195
ideology, 89
Immigration and Refugee Board, 132
impartiality. *See* political neutrality
Income Tax Act, 263
Industry Canada, 15
influence peddling, 248
    category of conflict of interest, 146
information. *see also* freedom of
        information legislation, *see*
        also privacy protection, *see also*
        confidentiality, *see also* secrecy, *see*
        also transparency
    "overclaiming" sensitivity of, 170
    access to personal, 187
    candour in sharing, 180
    censorship, 167
    classification, 180
    deception, 192
    in the digital age, 132
    insider, 118
    internal versus public disclosure, 170,
        180
    leaks, 180, 236
    managing ethically
        questions examined, 163
    non-disclosure, 165
    proactive versus reactive disclosure, 169
    propaganda, 180
    public's right to, 176
    restrictions on requests for, 165
    sharing
        and accountability, 236

technological advances for, 168
shifting control over, 168
surveillance, 191
Information Commissioner of Canada, 163
informed consent, 196
Ingraham P. W., 220
insider information, 132
insider trading, 148
Institute of Public Administration of Canada, 148
integrity approach
to ethics training, 261
intelligence systems, 190
interests. *see also* conflict of interest
compatible, 141
of all stakeholders, 94
private, 131, 133
public versus private, 92-93
special, 94
internal audits, 223
International City/Country Management Association, 258
International Public Personnel Association of Canada, 251
intuitionism. *See* virtue ethics
IPAC. *See* Institute of Public Administration of Canada
Iran, 21
Iraq, 21
Jackson M. & Stewart G., 18
Jacobs J., 21, 27, 50
Japanese Canadians
internment and deportation of, 15, 17
Jefferson J., 143
Jewish immigration
blocking of, 15
Judeo-Christian morality, 53
Juillet L. & Rassmussen K., 101
justice as fairness, 87
justifying decisions, 47-62
limitations of rules-based approach, 54
requirements for, 48
Kant, Immanuel, 51, 52, 141, 196
Kaptein M. et al., 271, 272
Keenleyside, Hugh, 17
Kernaghan K., 89, 102, 114, 135, 153, 238, 250, 253, 258
King, Prime Minister Mackenzie, 17
Kinsman G. & Gentile P., 15
Kluge E-H. W., 94
Kroeger A., 101, 119
Kuner C. et al., 192

Kymlicka W., 55, 56
Laframboise H., 214, 238
Lambert S., 121
Lang, Patrick, 21
Langford J. & Harrison Y., 231
Langford J. W., 61, 62, 133, 135, 148, 156, 254, 268
Langford J. W. & Tupper A., 5, 256, 262
Law Society, 238
Le Grand J., 15
leadership
ethics "champions", 267
in promoting ethical behaviour, 266-68
leaking information, 180
Leblanc D., 139
legislation
accountability, 218
freedom of information, 107, 164, 165, 169, 170, 175
of ethical conduct
effect on morale, 257
privacy protection, 187, 188, 189, 190, 191, 197
whistle blower, 14, 30, 170-71, 172, 217
Les Mains Sales, 26
lesser evil
argument for unethical behaviour, 26
Levine G. J., 72, 256
Lewis C., 91, 261
Lewis D., 171
Lexchin J., 17
liberty, 89
lobbying, 151
treatment in codes of conduct, 252
Lobbying Act, 252
Lobbyists Registration Act, 252
Lobbyists' Code of Conduct, 252
local government. See municipal government
Locke, John, 50
Lombardo T., 59
loyal administration, 14
loyalty, 109-12
case study, 111
of political staff, 112-14
to employer versus accountability to public, 237
to one's conscience, 238
Lynch T. D., 59
MacDermott K., 20
Machiavelli N., 27
MacIntyre A., 53

MacNair M. D., 72
mad cow disease, 86
Mahoney, Federal Court of Canada Justice, 136
Makin K., 21
Management Accountability Framework, 266
Manitoba, 22, 94, 188
    many hands
    case study, 33
    collective accountability, 227
    excuse for rejecting personal
        responsibility, 24
May K., 110
McArthur D., 24
McGraw D. K., 251
measuring
    ethical behaviour, 271–72, see also
        performance reporting
        through surveys, 271
Measuring Up performance reporting system,
    220
media attention
    on administrative law cases, 223
    on allegations of conflict of interest, 139
    on auditors' reports, 224
    on governments' ethical performance,
        260
    on politicians versus public servants,
        140
    on post-employment, 151
merit, 105–6
Michael B., 213
Miki R., 17
Military Police Complaints Commission, 21,
    225
military secrecy, 176
Milloy J., 15
Mining Association of Canada, 152
ministerial responsibility, 106–9, 215
    conflicting views of, 106
    for anonymity of public servants, 175
ministers
    criticism of public servants by, 108
    duty to hear truth from public servants,
        79
    example of conflict of interest, 140
    public comment, 122
    setting example for public servants, 267
minority government, 110
Mitchell J., 78, 79
moderate relativists, 46
Moe R., 231
moonlighting. See outside employment

Moore A., 197
Moore M. H., 91
moral agent, 14
moral courage, 14, 29
    creativity, 79
    evidence of, 18
    of whistle blowers, 180
moral dilemmas, 3
    confidentiality versus openness, 183
    defining serious, 63
    justifying decisions, 47–62
    limitations of codes of conduct in
        resolving, 251
    process for handling, 63
moral imagination, 64
moral relativism. See relativism
moral responsibility. See personal
    responsibility
morale, 78, 108, 140
    effects of moonlighting on, 149
    effects of performance reporting on, 221
Morgenthau H., 27
Morison J., 172
Mosher F., 13
Mrozek A., 16
Mulgan R., 21, 181, 214, 216, 229, 231, 234,
    235
Mullan D., 223
Mulroney, Right Honorable Brian, 151
Municipal Freedom of Information and
    Protection of Privacy Act, 188
    municipal government
    citizen engagement in, 172
    differences from parliamentary
        government, 104
    neutrality model in, 103, 106, 120
    public comment, 124
    public interest, 79
    security of tenure, 111
mutilation, 42
Nagel T., 28, 58
National Defence and Canadian Forces
    Ombudsman, 225
National Intelligence Estimate, 21
natural law theory, 50
negative responsibility, 26
neo-conservativism, 6
neutral service, 92–93
neutrality model, 19, 78, see also political
    neutrality at different levels of
    government, 103
    roles of ministers vs public servants, 96

tenets of, 102
New Brunswick, 72, 104, 218, 248, 253, 256
New Public Management, 235
Newfoundland and Labrador, 165, 217
Nexen Inc., 80
Nielsen K., 27
Nissenbaum H., 163, 198
Noddings N., 49
non-disclosure, 165
    policies defining, 167
Nova Scotia, 22, 169, 171, 173
Nova Scotia Public Service Commission, 173
Nozick R., 54
Nozick, Robert, 234
Oakley J. & Cocking D., 60
oath of office, 165
obligations of public servants. See personal
    responsibility
OECD. See Organization for Economic
Cooperation and Development
Office of Public Sector Ethics, 264
Office of Public Service Values and Ethics, 268
Office of the Auditor General of Canada, 224
Office of the Chief Human Resources Officer,
    268
Office of the Commissioner of Lobbying in
    Canada, 252
Official Languages Support Program, 121
Official Secrets Act, 165
Oliphant Commission, 151
OMBI. See Ontario Municipal CAO'S
Benchmarking Initiative
Onn Y. et al., 194
Ontario, 22, 119, 120, 173, 177, 178, 188,
    217, 218, 237, 248,252
Ontario Information and Privacy
    Commissioner, 192, 198
Ontario Ministry of Government Services, 173
Ontario Municipal CAO's Benchmarking
    Initiative, 220
Ontario Statutory Powers Procedure Act, 72
open government, 163, 172
    enabling ethical behaviour, 269
Open Government Strategy, Canada, 172
operational guidelines
    "loose", 230
    using public interest as, 86–91
OPSEU v. Ontario (A.G.), 101
Organization for Economic Cooperation and
    Development, 180, 187, 271
Osborne v. Canada, 104, 118
Ostry B., 141

Ottawa, 169
outside employment, 135, 140, 263
    case study, 149
    category of conflict of interest, 148
outsourcing, 231, 236
pandemics, 191
Parent W., 194
Parfit D., 13
Parker Commission, 136, 137, 265
Parks Canada, 104
Parrish J., 3
Parsons W., 19
participatory accountability, 234–37
    case study, 237
    drivers of, 235
    moral push and pull, 236
partisanship, 105–6, 116–21
    "promiscuous", 109
    and political rights, 114
    of political staff, 106, 112–14
    versus political neutrality, 116–21
    versus political sensitivity, 109
partnerships
    "loose", 230
    public and private, 228, 236
patronage, 105-6
    negative outcomes of, 115
peer-to-peer accountability, 232, 233
Pennock J. R., 74, 91
performance reporting, 219–22
    case study, 222
    limitations of, 221
    participatory accountability in, 235
    rewards for ethical conduct, 269
Perry J. L., 75
Perry J. L. & Hondeghem A., 75
Perry J. L. & Wise L. R., 75
personal conduct
    category of conflict of interest, 155
    questions examined, 156
Personal Health Information Act, 188
Personal Information Protection and
    Electronic Documents Act, 188
personal responsibility
    awareness of wrongdoing, 26
    blame shifting, 23
    case studies, 30–34
    case study, 32
    criteria for, 29
    defined, 215
    diffusing, 24
    excuses for rejecting, 19–29

in the neutrality model, 19
questions examined, 1
to advance the public interest, 71
to justify decisions, 47–62
versus legal responsibility, 3, 25
virtue ethics approach to, 49
Pettit P., 61
pharmaceutical industry, 17
Picard A., 25
Plant J. F., 250
pluralism, 46
policy. See public policy
Policy on Access to Information, 169
Policy on Conflict of Interest and Post-Employment, 132, 136, 145, 151, 252
Policy on Privacy Protection, 189
political neutrality
defining the duty, 101–4
questions examined, 101
versus political partisanship, 116–21
versus public comment, 121–25
political rights, 103, 114-16
case study, 117
example, 121
expanding versus restricting, 114
political staff, 106, 112–14, 251
case study, 113
role defined, 112
politicians
public interest, 75–77
relationships with public servants, 102
polygamy, 43
Posner R., 195
post-employment, 140
"cooling-off" period, 153
case study, 154
category of conflict of interest, 151
examples, 151
lobbying, 151
Post-Employment Good Practices Framework, 153
potential conflict of interest, 137
power
abuse of, 16, 225
in the name of confidentiality, 179
coercive state, 15
conferred on secret holders, 176
dispersed, 228
misused by public servants, 14
of public servants, 14, 72
speaking truth to, 78–79
pragmatism

in ethical decision making, 54
precautionary principle, 84
preservationists, 73, 86
Preston N., 59
Preston N. et al., 59
principles. *see also* commandments
competing versus dominant, 89
of ethical behaviour, 50, 74
of justice, 87
protecting personal information, 187
utilitarian, 50
privacy, 186–201
"by design", 199
consequentialist approach to, 194
defined, 193–94
duty ethics approach to, 196
increasing threats to, 190
non-interference versus information control, 194
of government. See secrecy
protection. See privacy protection
types of, 186
use of identifiers, 191
virtue ethics approach to, 197
Privacy Act, 188, 189, 190, 262
Privacy Commissioner, 262
privacy protection
arguments against, 195
challenges of new technologies, 191, 194
contextual integrity of, 198
erosion of without informed consent, 196
examples of disregard for, 192
legislation, 187, 188, 189, 191, 197
limitations of, 190, 191
making decisions about, 201
questions examined, 164, 186, 192
private morality
versus public morality, 28, 58, 174
Privy Council Office, 120, 167
procedural approach
to making policy decisions, 90
professional accountability, 231–34
professional associations, 251
codes of conduct, 251
criticism of self-regulation in, 232
propaganda, 180
in wartime, 182
PSC. See Public Service Commission
PSEA. See *Public Service Employment Act*
PSIC. See Public Service Integrity

Commissioner
PSM. See public service motivation
public choice theory, 73
public comment, 121
    case study, 123
public confidence. See public trust
public interest
    abolitionists, 73
    analyzing risk, 82–86
    as an operational guide, 86–91
    case study, 74, 88
    determined by elected officials, 72
    difficulty defining, 73
    duty to advance, 71, 72
    justice-as-fairness principle, 87
    municipal government, 79
    neutral service and avoiding self-
        interest, 92–93
    policy making, 82
    politicians, 75–77
    preservationists, 73
    professional associations' duty to
        protect, 232
    public choice theory, 73
    questions examined, 71
    requirement to consider risks
        concerning, 85
    transparency, 182
    versus self-interest, 88
Public Interest Disclosure Act, 23
*Public Interest Disclosure of Wrongdoing
Act*, 171
public morality
    versus private morality, 28, 58, 174
public office, 116
    seeking nomination to, 117
    using for partisan gain, 132
    using for personal gain, 131, 138, 253
public policy, 80–82
    accountability for, 227
    assessing risk when developing, 86
    consulting stakeholders, 94, 228
    ethical considerations, 81
    examples with ethical dimension, 80
    explaining versus defending, 108
    ideological considerations, 89
    influence of political staff on, 112
    public participation in, 107
    reasons ethics are overlooked in, 81
    reasons to consider ethics in, 82
    separate from politics, 102
    tests in the public interest

    consensualist approach, 91
    cost-benefit approach, 89
    dominant principle approach, 86
    procedural approach, 90
    synthesizing, 93
    transparency in developing, 178
public scrutiny
    case study, 264
public servants. *see also* political neutrality,
see also decision making, *see also* ethical
behaviour, *see also* personal responsibility
    "frank and fearless" advice, 20, 78
    affinity for consequentialism, 55, 255
    and political staff, 112–14
    anonymity, 106–9
    changing role of, 5, 72
    cynicism, 62, 267
    deference to superiors, 19
    defining virtuous traits by role, 61
    designated media spokespersons, 168
    determining conflicts of interest, 135
    disclosure of interests, 265
    discretion, 121-25
    dissent, 30
    drug and alcohol testing, 191
    duty and right to report, 22, 227
    duty of confidentiality, 165
    duty of loyalty, 109–12, 124
        exceptions to, 110
    duty of political neutrality, 104
    duty to advance the public interest, 71,
        75–77
    ethical "fitness", 3
    exemplary, 61, 268
    former, 152
    ideological commitments of, 89
    membership in professions, 231
    meritorious, 105–6
    non-partisan, 116–21
    obligations with respect to privacy, 189
    operational guidelines, 91
    political rights of, 114–16
    power of, 14, 72
    right to job mobility, 153
    security of tenure, 102
    self-interest, 73
        avoiding, 92
    training, 260–61
Public Servants Disclosure Protection Act,
    22, 171, 269
public service
    anonymity, 106-9

assumption of morality, 14
centralized control, 15, 221
chain of accountability, 215
changing nature of, 4, 227
consequentialism in, 58
core values, 59
destabilizing pressures on, 6
ethics program, 262
examples of unethical behaviour, 15, 17
increasing oversight of, 213, 222-27
leaving, 153, 252
morale, 78
neo-conservativism in, 6
oversight agencies, 224
partnership with private sector, 228
political neutrality, 101
proposed charter of, 253
reform, 219
relevance of virtue ethics to, 59
team culture, 20, 227
Public Service Commission, 119, 120, 262
Public Service Employment Act, 104, 118, 262
Public Service Integrity Commissioner, 171
public service motivation, 75
Public Service of Ontario Act, 119
Public Service Staff Relations Board, 121, 157
Public Service Values and Conduct Guide, 72, 218, 248, 253, 256
public trust, 156
    effect of conflict of interest on, 134, 139
    effect of deception on, 182
    effect of media on, 4
    effect of partisanship on, 106, 116
    effect of secrecy on, 179
    enhanced through codes of conduct, 250
    erosion of, 16
Public Works and Government Services Canada, 266
Public Works, Toronto, 152
Pue W., 232
PWGSC. See Public Works and Government Services Canada
Quebec, 121, 169, 187, 188
    sovereignty-association referendum, 181
Ramirez M., 180
Rathbone, Geoff, 152
Rawls J., 49, 53, 87
RCMP, 16, 226
reason
    in ethical decision making, 51

Red Cross, 146
Redford, Alberta Premier Alison, 172
Rees A., 170
reflective equilibrium, 63, 239
    example, 64
Reid J., 164
relativism, 41–44
    and cultural differences, 41
    case study, 46
    communities of belief, 45
    compared with pluralism, 46
    counter-arguments, 44
    double standards, 43
    examples of, 42
religious freedom, 43
Rennie S., 17
Reports on Plans and Priorities, 220
residential schools, 15
resignation
    as a form of dissent, 124
responsible behaviour. See ethical behaviour
retaliation
    against whistle blowers, 171
Rider D., 152
right to report, 22
rights
    of all stakeholders, 54
    of First Nations, 43, 223
    of individuals, 52, 54, 182
        to access their personal information, 187
    of liberty and equality, 89
    of minority versus majority, 58
    of politicians, 78
    of public servants, 158
        political, 114-16, 120
        to job mobility, 153
    of stakeholders, 234
    of women, 223
    political, 103
    prioritizing conflicting, 194
    to disclose information, 170
    to information, 176
    to privacy, 164, 186, 196
risk assessment, 83
    avoiding exaggeration, 93
    before whistle blowing, 171
    case study, 84
    example of, 86
    federal communications policy requirements, 85
    risk-benefit analysis, 83

Roberts A., 166, 170, 181
Robertson G., 175
Robertson R. G., 17
Robinson F., 49
Roe E. M., 19
Rohr J., 48, 49, 62
role models, 267
Romzeck B. & Ingraham P., 221
Rosenberg A., 194
Ross W. D., 50
Roy J., 172, 190, 192, 236
Roy P. et al., 15, 17
Royal Canadian Mounted Police. See RCMP
Royal Commission on Financial Management
    and Accountability, 215
Rule J., 194, 196
rule utilitarians, 55
rules. see also commandments
    absolute versus flexible, 146
    as applied to former public servants, 152
    conflict of interest, 141
    connections to values, 60
    criteria for defensibility, 51
    difficulty enforcing, 249
    duty ethics, 49
    ethical behaviour, 1
    for accepting benefits, 145
    for political staff, 112
    for post-employment, 153
    increasing volume of, 158
    integrating into codes of conduct, 248
    justifying decision making, 48
    multitude of sources for, 249
    on partisan political activities, 116
    public comment, 122
    reciprocity test, 52
    respect for individuals test, 52
    universalization test, 51
    versus value statements, 49, 254
same-sex marriage, 239
SARS, 191
Sartre, Jean-Paul, 26
Saskatchewan, 22, 133
Saskatchewan, Public Service Commission,
    134, 135
Saunders D., 80
Savage, Halifax Mayor Mike, 172
Savoie D., 19, 20, 24, 213, 214, 215
scandals. see also Commissions of Inquiry
    computer leasing, 259, 264, 269
    E-Health Ontario contracting, 16
    ethnic vote, 113

F-35 military aircraft purchase, 224
sponsorship, 217, 224, 254
tainted blood, 16
scapegoating, 218, 221, 228, 240
Schafer A., 25, 193, 195, 196, 213
Schmidt, Edgar, 21
Schreiber, Karlheinz, 151
Schubert G., 73, 90
Schubert G. A. Jr., 73
Science and Environmental Health Network,
    284
seal hunt, 121
Second World War, 4, 17, 39, 47, 139
secrecy, 165, 174–82, see also censorship
    and anonymity, 175
    and effectiveness, 175
    as an obstacle to democracy, 178
    defining levels of, 167
    military, 176
    questions examined, 163
    stressed in codes of conduct, 166
    versus transparency, 174
Security of Information Act, 164, 165, 248
security of tenure, 102, 109
Selden S., 220
self-dealing
    category of conflict of interest, 142
senior responsible owner, 231
Service Canada, 227
shared accountability. See collective
accountability
shared responsibility. See collective
responsibility
Sheedy A., 177
Sheikh, Munir, 21
Siegel D., 79, 103, 104, 106, 108, 111, 120
Sierra Systems, 228
Singer P., 58
Smiley D., 177
Snowden, Edward, 191
social contract ethical theory, 251
social media, 4, 120, 124, 168, 172, 191,
    200, 236
    case study, 178
solicitation of benefits. See influence
peddling
Solid Waste Management Services, Toronto,
    152
Solove D., 193, 195
Somerville M., 80
Sossin L., 14
speaking truth to power, 78–79

consequences of not, 78
special interests, 94
spin. See deception
sponsorship scandal, 217, 224, 226, 254
Standards of Conduct for Public Service Employees, 123
Starr M. & Sharp M., 115
Statement of Principles, IPAC, 148
Statistics Canada, 21, 124
Stevens, Honourable Sinclair M., 265
subjective accountability. See participatory accountability
subsequent employment. See post-employment
Sudan, 43
Sumner, Andy, 80
Sunahara A. G., 17
superior's hands
    case study, 31
    excuse for rejecting personal responsibility, 19
Supreme Court, 15, 50, 104, 109, 115, 118, 120, 122
supreme emergencies, 28
surveillance, 191
    case study, 201
surveys, 271
Syria, 227
Systems of Survival, 21
tainted blood scandal, 16, 25, 226
Tait Task Force on Public Service Values and Ethics, 254
Taliban, 84
Task Force on Conflict of Interest, 157, 264
Task Force on Public Service Values and Ethics, 59, 61, 62
Taylor M. H. & Filmer A. E., 149
team culture, 20
    collective responsibility, 26
    loyalty, 21
technology
    building privacy into systems, 199
    challenges for privacy protection, 191
    enabling participatory accountability, 236
    shifting the line between public and private, 194
    to enhance transparency, 172
    using to reduce training costs, 261
The Blame Game, 18
The Directive on Privacy Practices, 189
The Responsible Public Servant
    organization of, 7-10
    using this book, 11
Third World, 139

Thomas P. G., 108, 110, 164, 168, 170, 181, 219, 226
Thompson D. F., 19, 20, 24, 25, 26, 29, 72, 156, 157
Thomson J., 194
threats to information privacy, 190
Thunder Bay, City of, 120
tolerance
    as a hallmark of relativism, 42
Toronto, 152
    City of, 135, 145, 166, 252
    computer leasing scandal, 16, 132, 259, 264
    Mayor Rob Ford, 20
    Transit Commission, 20
Toronto Star, 20
traditional accountability narrative, 214-19
    features of, 216
training
    for ethical behaviour, 260-61
    approaches to, 261
transparency, 168-74
    and effectiveness, 177
    culture of, 182
    digital technologies, 172
    obstacles to, 170
    open government, 172
    questions examined, 163
    role of whistle blowers, 170, 179
    versus secrecy, 174
Transparency and Accountability Act, 217
Transparency International Canada, 270
Transport Canada, 152
Treasury Board, 262, 268
Treasury Board of Canada Secretariat, 22, 52, 59, 61, 72, 79, 83, 85, 109, 110, 124, 132, 136, 141, 145, 151, 152, 165, 167, 168, 169, 170, 171, 173, 174, 189, 190, 218, 220, 252, 267, 269, 272
Tromp S., 169, 170
Truman, President Harry, 47
Turnbull L. & Aucoin P., 173
U.S. National Security Agency, 191
Uhr J., 215
unethical behaviour. *see also* accountability, *see also*
    personal conduct, *see also* conflict of interest
    combating through codes of conduct, 250
    consequentialism, 27
    deterring through criminal sanctions

case study, 272
examples of, 15, 17
exposure of, 108
justifying, 47-62
lesser evil, 26
under the *Criminal Code*, 248
within the law, 119
United Kingdom, 1, 11, 20, 118
United Nations Universal Declaration of Human Rights, 186
United States, 186, 264
evidence of moral courage, 18
United Way, 146
universalization test, 51
Unmasking Administrative Evil, 15
using confidential information
category of conflict of interest, 147
using government property
category of conflict of interest, 146
utilitarianism
"act" and "rule" types of, 55
classic, 55
principles, 50
value statements. *see also* codes of conduct
versus rules, 49, 254
values
candour, 180
clusters, 255
competing, 61, 92, 115, 254
connections to rules, 60
conscience as an amalgam of, 238
cynicism about, 62
fundamental to public service, 253
impartiality. See political neutrality
in codes of conduct, 253-56
promoted by privacy, 196
religious, 239
statements
inclusion of accountability, 218
statements of, 248
surveying, 271
Values and Ethics Code for the Public Sector, 52, 59, 61, 72, 79, 109, 141, 218, 263, 266
Values and Ethics Code for the Public Service, 61, 173
Values and Ethics Code, Fisheries and Oceans Canada, 225
Values and Ethics, Awards and Recognition unit, 268
Van Wart M., 253
Vancouver, 172, 174

Vancouver Airport, 226
Vandenabeele W., 75
veil of ignorance, 53, 87, 141
virtue ethics, 49, 58-62
approach to conflict of interest, 141
approach to political neutrality, 126
approach to privacy protection, 197
difficulties shared with duty ethics, 60
Walkerton Public Utilities Commission, 16
Walkerton water disaster, 226
Walzer M., 28
wartime
use of propaganda and censorship, 182
Warwick D. P., 74, 94
Web 2.0, 172
Werhane P., 64
Westin A., 193, 197
Westminster model, 1, 20, 102, 103, 175, 215
Weston G., 120
whistle blower legislation, 14, 30, 170-71, 172, 217
whistle blowers, 18, 122
case study, 185
FAIR advocacy for, 270
retalition against, 171
WikiLeaks, 174, 236
Wikipedia, 174
Wilson V. S., 107
Wingspread Statement, 84
Working Group on Collaborative Regulation of the Nova Scotia Health Professionals Regulatory Network, 234
Working Group on the Disclosure of Wrongdoing, 254
World Economic Forum, 174
wrongdoing. See unethical behaviour